MICKY DOLENZ'

Rock 'n Rollin'

TRIVIA GAME

SQUAREONE
PUBLISHERS

COVER DESIGNER: Jeannie Tudor
COVER PHOTOS: Retna Ltd.
BACK COVER PHOTO: Photographer Robert Milazzo
RESEARCH EDITOR: Anthony Pomes
RESEARCH ASSISTANTS: Gene Friedman and Dennis Golin
EDITORS: Marie Caratozzolo and Joanne Abrams
TYPESETTERS: Gary A. Rosenberg

Square One Publishers
115 Herricks Road
Garden City Park, New York 11040
www.squareonepublishers.com
(516) 535-2010 • (866) 900-BOOK

ISBN 0-7570-0289-7

CONTENTS

I would like to dedicate this book to my kids, my wife, and especially all of my fans who have been so loyal and supportive through the years, and have never failed to remind me of all the things I did that I can't remember.

ACKNOWLEDGMENTS

I want to thank all of the people at Square One Publishers—especially Rudy Shur, Anthony Pomes, Marie Caratozzolo, Joanne Abrams, and Ariel Colletti—for giving me the opportunity to dredge up all of these interesting and bizarre facts!

I also want to thank all of those rock 'n rollers out there who are the real source of all this wonderful material.

Long Live Rock and Roll!

HOW TO PLAY THE GAMES

Welcome, friends. Are you ready to put your knowledge of rock 'n roll facts and details to the test? My trivia book is built to challenge, while providing endless hours of fun and enjoyment. The games in this book have been designed in a way that allows you, the reader, to play either alone or with others. In most trivia books, when looking up the answer to a question, the reader is able to see the answers to other questions at the same time. This book doesn't allow that to happen, but you must first understand how to play the games. Ready?

THE BASICS

There are eighty games in this book, each with a dozen questions. Every game is also numbered and has been given a title that reflects the basic category of its questions, such as "The Monkees," "Grunge Rock," "One-Hit Wonders," and "The MTV Generation." Throughout, you'll also find a number of games titled "Grab Bag," which include a mix and match of questions from various categories.

THE PAGE SETUP

Each page holds four frames that are situated from the top of the page to the bottom (as seen in the example on the next page). Each frame is divided in half. The left half contains a question. The right half contains the answer to the question from a previous page. (Seem a little confusing? Not to worry—it actually sounds more complicated than it really is.) Stay with me . . .

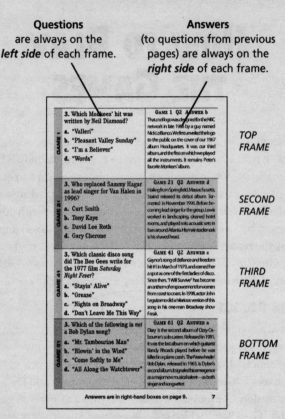

Questions are always on the **left side** of each frame.

Answers (to questions from previous pages) are always on the **right side** of each frame.

GAME 1 3. Which Monkees' hit was written by Neil Diamond? a. "Valleri" b. "Pleasant Valley Sunday" c. "I'm a Believer" d. "Words"	**GAME 1 Q2 ANSWER b** That cool logo was designed for the NBC network in late 1966 by a guy named Nick LoBianco. We first unveiled the logo to the public on the cover of our 1967 album *Headquarters*. It was our third album, and the first on which we played all the instruments. It remains Peter's favorite Monkees' album.	**TOP FRAME**
GAME 21 3. Who replaced Sammy Hagar as lead singer for Van Halen in 1996? a. Curt Smith b. Tony Kaye c. David Lee Roth d. Gary Cherone	**GAME 21 Q2 ANSWER d** Hailing from Springfield, Massachusetts, Staind released its debut album *Tormented* in November 1996. Before becoming lead singer for the group, Lewis worked in landscaping, cleaned hotel rooms, and played solo acoustic sets in bars around Atlanta. His main trademark is his shaved head.	**SECOND FRAME**
GAME 41 3. Which classic disco song did The Bee Gees write for the 1977 film *Saturday Night Fever*? a. "Stayin' Alive" b. "Grease" c. "Nights on Broadway" d. "Don't Leave Me This Way"	**GAME 41 Q2 ANSWER c** Gaynor's song of defiance and freedom hit #1 in March of 1979, and earned her a spot as one of the first ladies of disco. Since then, "I Will Survive" has become an anthem of empowerment for women from coast to coast. In 1998, actor John Leguizamo did a hilarious version of this song in his one-man Broadway show *Freak*.	**THIRD FRAME**
GAME 61 3. Which of the following is *not* a Bob Dylan song? a. "Mr. Tambourine Man" b. "Blowin' in the Wind" c. "Come Softly to Me" d. "All Along the Watchtower"	**GAME 61 Q2 ANSWER a** *Diary* is the second album of Ozzy Osbourne's solo career. Released in 1981, it was the last album on which guitarist Randy Rhoads played before he was killed in a plane crash. The *Freewheelin' Bob Dylan*, released in 1963, is Dylan's second album. It signaled his emergence as a major new musical talent—as both singer and songwriter.	**BOTTOM FRAME**

Answers are in right-hand boxes on page 9.   7

Typical Page Layout
(four frame levels on each page)

PLAYING THE GAME

The most important point to keep in mind is that the twelve questions for each game are *not* read from the top of the page to the bottom. Rather, they are found on the same frame level on succeeding pages. Let me help make this clearer with an example and some accompanying graphics.

Let's start with Game #1, which begins in the *top frame* of page 1—a *right-hand* page. Here, you will find the name and number of the game you are about to play.

Turn the page and look at the next *right-hand* page (page 3) for the game's first question, which is located on the left side of the *top frame* (see graphic below).

So where's the answer to this question? Turn the page again and continue to look at the *top frame* of the next *right-hand* page (page 5). As shown below, the answer is located on the right side of the frame. On the left side of this frame, you'll find the second question of Game #1.

Question #1 is on *left side* of top frame.

Answer to Question #1 is on next right-hand page— *right side* of top frame.

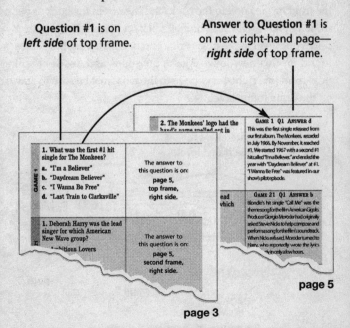

2. The Monkees' logo had the band's name spelled out in

1. What was the first #1 hit single for The Monkees?
a. "I'm a Believer"
b. "Daydream Believer"
c. "I Wanna Be Free"
d. "Last Train to Clarksville"

GAME 1

The answer to this question is on:
page 5, top frame, right side.

1. Deborah Harry was the lead singer for which American New Wave group?
Ambitious Lovers

The answer to this question is on:
page 5, second frame, right side.

GAME 1 Q1 ANSWER d
This was the first single released from our first album, The Monkees, recorded in July 1966. By November, it reached #1. We started 1967 with a second #1 hit called "I'm a Believer," and ended the year with "Daydream Believer" at #1. "I Wanna Be Free" was featured in our show's pilot episode.

GAME 21 Q1 ANSWER b
Blondie's hit single "Call Me" was the theme song for the film American Gigolo. Producer Giorgio Moroder had originally asked Stevie Nicks to help compose and perform a song for the film's soundtrack. When Nicks refused, Moroder turned to Harry, who reportedly wrote the lyrics in only a few hours.

page 5

page 3

The answer to the first question of Game #1 is on the following right-hand page—and appears on the right side of the top frame. The left side of the top frame has the game's next question.

And that's how you continue—turning the page for each new question (Q), and finding its answer (A) on the following *right-hand* page (see graphic below).

Beginning with the top frame (*and staying in that top frame*), play the games, which flow from one *right-hand* page to the next until you have reached the last page. Then simply make a U-turn and continue playing the games—still in the top frame—from the back of the book to the front. While going in this direction, however, the answers to the questions will be found on consecutive *left-hand* pages.

Once you've completed the games in the top frame from the front of the book to the back, and then from the back to the front again, you'll find yourself back on page 1. Simply drop down one level to the next frame and begin playing the games found on this new level. Again, questions and answers will flow from one right-hand page to the next. Just be sure to stay on the same frame level.

Individual games are always
played on the same frame level.

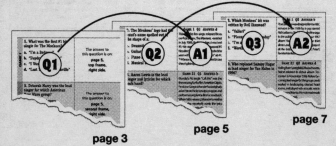

Progression of Questions and Answers

THERE'S HELP ON EVERY PAGE . . .

To be absolutely sure there's no confusion while playing the games, helpful instructions are provided on each and every page. Trust me, once you get the hang of it, you're going to love it (even a Monkee can do it!). So kick back and get ready to be entertained, amused, and enlightened by these great rock 'n roll questions and their fascinating fact-filled answers.

Have fun,

Micky Dolenz

LET'S
ROCK 'N ROLL!

GAME 1

Who Were Those Monkees, Anyway?

Turn to page 3 for the first question of Game 1.

GAME 21

Lead Vocalists

Turn to page 3 for the first question of Game 21.

GAME 41

Disco Fever

Turn to page 3 for the first question of Game 41.

GAME 61

Bob Dylan

Turn to page 3 for the first question of Game 61.

	GAME 20 Q12 ANSWER a
Game 21 begins on page 1, second frame from the top.	"Church Bells May Ring" marked the first time that chimes were used on a rock-and-roll record, care of Mr. Sedaka. At that time, Sedaka was in another doo-wop group called The Linc-Tones. After he left to go solo in 1958, the group became The Tokens, and in 1961 released their career-making hit "The Lion Sleeps Tonight."
	GAME 40 Q12 ANSWER a
Game 41 begins on page 1, third frame from the top.	Leonard Skinner was the gym teacher at Robert E. Lee High School in the band's hometown of Jacksonville, Florida. "Coach Skinner" was very strict about the school's dress code. During a gig, lead singer Ronnie Van Zant changed the group's name from One Percent to Leonard Skinner. Later, this became Lynyrd Skynyrd.
	GAME 60 Q12 ANSWER b
Game 61 begins on page 1, bottom frame.	The rock group Midnight Oil was well known for its left-wing political activism. Its song "Beds Are Burning" is featured on *Diesel and Dust*—a concept album that deals with the struggles of the Australian aborigines and environmental causes. "Beds Are Burning," which reached #17 in the US, is a plea for aboriginal land rights.
	GAME 80 Q12 ANSWER d
Well, that's all, folks! Let's play again some time . . .	That's right, Mike was born in Houston, Texas on December 30, 1942, and Davy was born in Manchester, England on the same day three years later. Peter was born in Washington, DC, on February 13, 1942, and I was born in Los Angeles on March 8, 1945.

GAME 1	**1.** What was the first #1 hit single for The Monkees? **a.** "I'm a Believer" **b.** "Daydream Believer" **c.** "I Wanna Be Free" **d.** "Last Train to Clarksville"	The answer to this question is on: **page 5, top frame, right side.**
GAME 21	**1.** Deborah Harry was the lead singer for which American New Wave group? **a.** Ambitious Lovers **b.** Blondie **c.** The Cure **d.** Meat Puppets	The answer to this question is on: **page 5, second frame, right side.**
GAME 41	**1.** Which group recorded the disco hit "Rock the Boat"? **a.** The Hues Corporation **b.** The Village People **c.** Earth, Wind and Fire **d.** Shalimar	The answer to this question is on: **page 5, third frame, right side.**
GAME 61	**1.** In what year did Bob Dylan record and release his first album? **a.** 1958 **b.** 1960 **c.** 1962 **d.** 1964	The answer to this question is on: **page 5, bottom frame, right side.**

GAME 20

12. Who played the chimes on The Willows' 1956 version of "Church Bells May Ring"?

a. Neil Sedaka
b. Lionel Hampton
c. Paul Simon
d. Neil Diamond

GAME 20 Q11 ANSWER c
Both of the B-52's most popular singles to date, "Love Shack" and "Roam," come from this album. Both songs reached #3 on the US pop charts in 1989 and 1990, respectively. In 1994, the group sang the theme song for the live-action *Flintstones* movie and even performed in the film as "The BC-52's."

GAME 40

12. What rock band based its name on the members' teacher?

a. Lynyrd Skynyrd
b. The Rivingtons
c. Jethro Tull
d. Wet Willie

GAME 40 Q11 ANSWER b
An American power band, Grand Funk Railroad was generally not received well by critics, who sometimes referred to the trio as "the loudest rock and roll band in the world." Nevertheless, in 1970, the group—which was only a year old at the time—had sold more albums than any other American band.

GAME 60

12. The Aussie band Midnight Oil had a hit in 1987 with "____ Are Burning."

a. Candles
b. Beds
c. Skies
d. Hearts

GAME 60 Q11 ANSWER d
In the 1960s, Manhattan's Brill Building housed over a hundred music businesses, including producers and their writers. Mann and Weil, Boyce and Hart, and King and Goffin all worked there, churning out hits like "On Broadway." Jeff Barry *was* a Brill Building writer, but was teamed with wife Ellie Greenwich rather than Ben Raleigh.

GAME 80

12. Which two Monkees share the same birthday?

a. Me and Peter
b. Peter and Mike
c. Me and Davy
d. Mike and Davy

GAME 80 Q11 ANSWER c
The movie ends to the Beach Boys' song "All Summer Long." Taking place during one night at the end of the summer of '62, *American Graffiti* is, in part, about the end of a cultural innocence still alive in America at that time. It was before the nation lost JFK, before The Beatles, and before Vietnam.

2. The Monkees' logo had the band's name spelled out in the shape of a:

a. Drumstick

b. Guitar

c. Piano keyboard

d. Musical note

GAME 1 Q1 ANSWER d
This was the first single released from our first album, *The Monkees*, recorded in July 1966. By November, it reached #1. We started 1967 with a second #1 hit called "I'm a Believer," and ended the year with "Daydream Believer" at #1. "I Wanna Be Free" was featured in our show's pilot episode.

---

2. Aaron Lewis is the lead singer and lyricist for which rock band?

a. Coldplay

b. Linkin Park

c. 3 Doors Down

d. Staind

GAME 21 Q1 ANSWER b
Blondie's hit single "Call Me" was the theme song for the film *American Gigolo*. Producer Giorgio Moroder had originally asked Stevie Nicks to help compose and perform a song for the film's soundtrack. When Nicks refused, Moroder turned to Harry, who reportedly wrote the lyrics and melody in only a few hours.

---

2. Which artist sang the disco version of "I Will Survive"?

a. Whitney Houston

b. Patti LaBelle

c. Gloria Gaynor

d. Donna Summer

GAME 41 Q1 ANSWER a
The trio's founder, Wally Holmes, had wanted to name the group The Children of Howard Hughes, but doing so would have caused obvious legal problems. "Rock the Boat," which reached #1 in May of 1974, was featured along with several other '70s disco hits in the Brian DePalma gangster film *Carlito's Way* (1993), starring Al Pacino.

---

2. Which of the following is *not* a Bob Dylan album?

a. *Diary of a Madman*

b. *The Freewheelin' Bob Dylan*

c. *John Wesley Harding*

d. *Nashville Skyline*

GAME 61 Q1 ANSWER c
Bob Dylan's first album, *Bob Dylan*, was recorded during two afternoon sessions in 1962. "Song for Woody," one of the album's two original songs, is dedicated to the American folk musician Woody Guthrie, a major influence on Dylan's early melodies and vocal styles. Guthrie, who wrote the song "This Land Is Your Land," died in 1967.

---

11. *Cosmic Thing* was a hit album in 1989 for which band?

a. The Rolling Stones
b. The Clash
c. The B-52's
d. The Police

GAME 20 Q10 ANSWER a
"In the Still of the Night" was recorded in 1956 in the basement of this popular quartet's local church—St. Bernadette's in New Haven, Connecticut. Although released as the B-side to the single "The Jones Girl," this was the song that ended up at #3 on the R&B charts, securing The Five Satins a place in doo-wop history.

11. For which group did the song "We're an American Band" hit #1 in 1973?

a. Steve Miller Band
b. Grand Funk Railroad
c. The Grassroots
d. Three Dog Night

GAME 40 Q10 ANSWER a
First recorded in 1956, "Louie, Louie" has had dozens of different versions recorded by different artists. The 1963 version by the Kingsmen is probably the best known and—despite the fact that the lyrics are almost completely unintelligible—rose to #2 on the Billboard Hot 100 chart, quickly becoming a teen party standard.

11. Which of the following pairs was *not* a Brill Building songwriting team?

a. Barry Mann/Cynthia Weil
b. Tommy Boyce/Bobby Hart
c. Carole King/Gerry Goffin
d. Jeff Barry/Ben Raleigh

GAME 60 Q10 ANSWER c
Released in 1975, a few months after the US had pulled out of Vietnam and a year after President Nixon had resigned the Oval Office, this song by the funk band War asked a question that so many were wondering about at the time. The song was a Top 10 hit and was nominated for a 1976 Grammy. It was re-recorded by Smash Mouth in 1997.

11. Which group sings the last song in the classic 1973 George Lucas movie *American Graffiti*?

a. The Platters
b. The Spaniels
c. The Beach Boys
d. Booker T. & The M.G.'s

GAME 80 Q10 ANSWER b
During the Beatles' 1965 concert tour of America, a meeting took place between the Fab Four and Presley at his house in Bel-Air. The Beatles had just played the biggest outdoor concert in history at New York's Shea Stadium, and Elvis had just starred in the movie *Tickle Me*. The Beatles were thrilled to finally meet "the King."

GAME 1

3. Which Monkees' hit was written by Neil Diamond?

a. "Valleri"

b. "Pleasant Valley Sunday"

c. "I'm a Believer"

d. "Words"

GAME 1 Q2 ANSWER b

That cool logo was designed for the NBC network in late 1966 by a guy named Nick LoBianco. We first unveiled the logo to the public on the cover of our 1967 album *Headquarters*. It was our third album, and the first on which we played all the instruments. It remains Peter's favorite Monkees' album.

GAME 21

3. Who replaced Sammy Hagar as lead singer for Van Halen in 1996?

a. Curt Smith

b. Tony Kaye

c. David Lee Roth

d. Gary Cherone

GAME 21 Q2 ANSWER d

Hailing from Springfield, Massachusetts, Staind released its debut album *Tormented* in November 1996. Before becoming lead singer for the group, Lewis worked in landscaping, cleaned hotel rooms, and played solo acoustic sets in bars around Atlanta. His main trademark is his shaved head.

GAME 41

3. Which classic disco song did The Bee Gees write for the 1977 film *Saturday Night Fever*?

a. "Stayin' Alive"

b. "Grease"

c. "Nights on Broadway"

d. "Don't Leave Me This Way"

GAME 41 Q2 ANSWER c

Gaynor's song of defiance and freedom hit #1 in March of 1979, and earned her a spot as one of the first ladies of disco. Since then, "I Will Survive" has become an anthem of empowerment for women from coast to coast. In 1998, actor John Leguizamo did a hilarious version of this song in his one-man Broadway show *Freak*.

GAME 61

3. Which of the following is *not* a Bob Dylan song?

a. "Mr. Tambourine Man"

b. "Blowin' in the Wind"

c. "Come Softly to Me"

d. "All Along the Watchtower"

GAME 61 Q2 ANSWER a

Diary is the second album of Ozzy Osbourne's solo career. Released in 1981, it was the last album on which guitarist Randy Rhoads played before he was killed in a plane crash. *The Freewheelin' Bob Dylan*, released in 1963, is Dylan's second album. It signaled his emergence as a major new musical talent—as both singer and songwriter.

10. "In the Still of the Night" was recorded by The Five Satins in what unusual place?

a. A church basement
b. A men's bathroom
c. An apartment house lobby
d. A subway station

GAME 20 Q9 ANSWER c
Although he normally wrote his own songs, Buddy Holly recorded this early Paul Anka tune in October 1958. He was newly married and had broken away from his group The Crickets. This song featured orchestral string arrangements. Around this time, he also featured string sections on his songs "True Love Ways" and "Raining in My Heart.".

10. Which group recorded the hit "Louie, Louie"?

a. The Kingsmen
b. Otis Day and The Knights
c. Booker T & The M.G.'s
d. Bill Haley & the Comets

GAME 40 Q9 ANSWER a
Gabriel's quirky song "Sledgehammer" reached #2 on US pop charts, and the acclaimed claymation video won numerous kudos at the MTV Music Video awards of 1987. In 1989, Gabriel made the news again with *Passion,* the 1989 soundtrack for Martin Scorsese's film *The Last Temptation of Christ.*

10. Which of these "question" songs is *not* from the '80s?

a. "Do You Really Want to Hurt Me?"
b. "Don't You Want Me?"
c. "Why Can't We Be Friends?"
d. "How Will I Know?"

GAME 60 Q9 ANSWER a
Presley won his Grammys in 1973 and 1975 for, respectively, "He Touched Me" and "How Great Thou Art." Raised in the Pentacostal Church, the artist was greatly inspired by gospel music and often said that his music came from gospel. Ironically, his own church condemned both his records and his onstage gyrations as being evil.

10. In their one and only meeting, where did Elvis Presley and The Beatles talk and jam privately?

a. Memphis
b. Los Angeles
c. London
d. New York

GAME 80 Q9 ANSWER b
The song is from Sinatra's 1993 album *Duets,* which also features Ol' Blue Eyes sharing vocals with the likes of Aretha Franklin and Carly Simon. *Duets* reached #2 on the Billboard albums chart and led to *Duets II,* which includes the rocker-meets-crooner track "Luck Be a Lady" with The Pretenders' Chrissie Hynde.

GAME 1 **4.** Which Monkee wrote the 1968 hit "Different Drum," recorded by the Stone Poneys? **a.** Peter Tork **b.** Michael Nesmith **c.** Micky Dolenz **d.** Davy Jones	**GAME 1 Q3 ANSWER c** "I'm a Believer" was the Neil Diamond song that I sung to #1, while Davy sang Diamond's other #1 Monkees' hit, "A Little Bit You, A Little Bit Me." In 1988, UB40 had a #1 hit of its own with Neil's song, "Red Red Wine." And in 2001, "I'm a Believer" was a big hit yet again for Smash Mouth in the blockbuster animated film *Shrek*.
GAME 21 **4.** Which former lead singer of Culture Club went solo in 1987 with the album *Sold*? **a.** Nick Van Eede **b.** Boy George **c.** Joe Elliot **d.** Iggy Pop	**GAME 21 Q3 ANSWER d** Gary Cherone, who had been lead singer for the hard rock band Extreme, was invited to replace Hagar after Extreme's demise. But *Van Halen III*, the single album for which Cherone produced vocals, was the worst-selling album of the group's career. Not long after the VH3 tour, Cherone left Van Halen.
GAME 41 **4.** Who recorded the disco anthem "Gloria"? **a.** Laura Branigan **b.** Alicia Bridges **c.** Donna Summer **d.** Pat Benatar	**GAME 41 Q3 ANSWER a** This movie's soundtrack remains a virtual "Best of Disco" album. The song "Stayin' Alive" and actor John Travolta (with his memorable white suit) will forever be associated with this film. Even two decades later, when Travolta hosted *Saturday Night Live*, he walked backstage during one of the skits to the tune of "Stayin' Alive."
GAME 61 **4.** Which of these songs is *not* from Dylan's classic 1966 album *Blonde on Blonde*? **a.** "Rainy Day Women #12 & 35" **b.** "Visions of Johanna" **c.** "Dear Landlord" **d.** "Pledging My Time"	**GAME 61 Q3 ANSWER c** Recorded in 1959 by a trio of high school friends called The Fleetwoods (originally Two Girls and a Guy), "Come Softly to Me" reached the #1 spot and remained there for four weeks. During that same year, Dylan (who was eighteen years old and still named Robert Zimmerman) toured briefly with singer Bobby Vee under the name "Elston Gunn."

GAME 20	**9.** Who wrote Buddy Holly's hit single "I Guess It Doesn't Matter Anymore"? **a.** Chuck Berry **b.** Buddy Holly **c.** Paul Anka **d.** Bo Diddley	**GAME 20 Q8 ANSWER b** The Velvet Underground came to chaotic life in 1965, and the group's name came from the title of a pornographic paperback. Andy Warhol was the group's manager, and he suggested that a German girl named Christa Päffgensinger (aka Nico) become the lead singer. The group's 1967 debut LP featured a peelable banana on the cover.
GAME 40	**9.** Peter Gabriel hit the charts in 1986 with a song about which of the following tools? **a.** A sledgehammer **b.** A pile driver **c.** A power drill **d.** An axe	**GAME 40 Q8 ANSWER a** The band was inspired by a club in Birmingham, England called Barbarella's, and took its name from Milo O'Shea's evil character Dr. Durand Durand. In 1982, Diana, Princess of Wales, said that Duran Duran was her favorite band, and the British press began referring to the group as "The Fab Five."
GAME 60	**9.** In which category were the only Grammys Elvis Presley ever won? **a.** Gospel **b.** Country & Western **c.** Rock **d.** Pop	**GAME 60 Q8 ANSWER b** An immediate hit in Canada, *Fumbling Towards Ecstasy* eventually became McLachlan's breakthrough album internationally. Although it never reached #1 in the States, it stayed in the middle range of the US pop charts for nearly two years, proving a consistent seller.
GAME 80	**9.** With which crooner did U2's Bono team up for the Cole Porter classic "I've Got You Under My Skin"? **a.** Tony Bennett **b.** Frank Sinatra **c.** Dean Martin **d.** Barbra Streisand	**GAME 80 Q8 ANSWER d** After having minor success in 1960 with his version of the Jerry Vale hit "You Don't Know Me," Welch sang this song and watched it rise to #5 on the pop charts. His other hit single came in 1964 with a version of "Ebb Tide," which reached #5 on the R&B charts. I'm a big Lenny Welch fan, and I often sing "Since I Fell for You" in concert.

5. Before becoming a Monkee, who earned a Tony nomination for his work on Broadway?

a. Davy Jones

b. Micky Dolenz

c. Mike Nesmith

d. Peter Tork

GAME 1 Q4 ANSWER b
Mike has always been a great song-writer, and this single featuring a young Linda Ronstadt on vocals still stands as one of his best records. When I perform concerts with my sister Coco, she always sings this classic Nesmith song while I sing another great Nez-penned tune from Monkees' days, "The Girl That I Knew Somewhere."

5. Which band's lead singer is named Stacy Ferguson, but is better known as Fergie?

a. De La Soul

b. Black Eyed Peas

c. Blink-182

d. The Fugees

GAME 21 Q4 ANSWER b
Boy George teamed up with Lamont Dozier to write many of the songs on *Sold*. More recently, Boy George wrote and starred in the original musical *Taboo*. Based on the pop icon's life, the show—which ran for over a year—was a huge success in London's East End, receiving four nominations at the 2003 Olivier Awards.

5. Which group had such '70s hits as "You Sexy Thing" and "Disco Queen"?

a. Hot Chocolate

b. Average White Band

c. The Ohio Players

d. Love Unlimited Orchestra

GAME 41 Q4 ANSWER a
Laura Branigan first achieved international stardom with this song in the early '80s. "Gloria" was even featured in the classic 1983 film *Flashdance*. Branigan's second-biggest hit single came in 1984 with "Self Control," a song that rose to #4 on the US pop charts. A four-time Grammy nominee, Branigan died in 2004.

5. The Byrds had its first hit in 1965 with which Bob Dylan song?

a. "My Back Pages"

b. "Mr. Tambourine Man"

c. "It Ain't Me, Babe"

d. "Positively 4th Street"

GAME 61 Q4 ANSWER c
"Dear Landlord" is from Dylan's 1967 album *John Wesley Harding*, which marked his change from surreal music and electric rock to plainly stated acoustic music. Dylan has implied that this shift in musical style was due to the long period of introspection following his near-fatal motorcycle accident in Woodstock, New York in 1966.

GAME 20	**8.** When Lou Reed and John Cale founded this group, they called themselves "The Primitives": **a.** The Stooges **b.** The Velvet Underground **c.** The Ramones **d.** The Violent Femmes	**GAME 20 Q7 ANSWER d** Lita Ford was sixteen years old when she joined the all-girl metal group The Runaways in 1974—Joan Jett was also a member of the group, which broke up in 1979. Sharon Osbourne was Lita Ford's manager in the '80s, and she put together this duet between Ford and Ozzy. Lita Ford had another hit in 1988 called "Kiss Me Deadly."
GAME 40	**8.** Which rock band got its name from a character in the Jane Fonda sci-fi film *Barbarella*? **a.** Duran Duran **b.** Air Supply **c.** Reo Speedwagon **d.** Iron Maiden	**GAME 40 Q7 ANSWER c** Formed in 1962, the British R&B pop band Manfred Mann had a number of hits in the UK—including Bob Dylan's "The Mighty Quinn," which was one of the few Manfred Mann songs that also did well in the US. Neveretheless, the group broke up in 1969, frustrated with its image as a singles hit band.
GAME 60	**8.** What 1993 album earned a Grammy nomination for up-and-coming singer Sarah McLachlan? **a.** *Share My World* **b.** *Fumbling Towards Ecstasy* **c.** *This Fire* **d.** *Rhythm of Love*	**GAME 60 Q7 ANSWER c** Formed in 1991, the Virginia-based Dave Matthews Band soon created a cult following through nonstop touring, including weekly performances at the Virginia clubs Trax and Floodzone. The group's debut album, *Remember Two Things,* was self-released in 1993, and reissued by RCA in 1997. Eventually, it went gold.
GAME 80	**8.** Who had a hit song in 1963 with "Since I Fell for You"? **a.** Charlie Rich **b.** Johnny Mathis **c.** Frankie Laine **d.** Lenny Welch	**GAME 80 Q7 ANSWER b** Released for The Monkees' thirtieth anniversary, *Justus* was aptly named—it was *just us.* This was the first time we played all the instruments on a Monkees album since 1967's *Headquarters.* We also wrote the album, including my song "Never Enough," Peter's "I Believe You," Mike's "Admiral Mike" (very appropriate), and Davy's "It's Not Too Late."

6. Which musician has a major role in The Monkees' movie *Head*?

a. Fats Domino

b. Frank Zappa

c. Jerry Lee Lewis

d. Captain Beefheart

GAME 1 Q5 ANSWER a
Years before I debuted on Broadway in Elton John's musical *Aida* in 2004, Davy played the role of the Artful Dodger in *Oliver!* Davy actually appeared along with the rest of the *Oliver!* cast on Ed Sullivan's TV show in February 1964— the same night that a certain "four young men from Liverpool" took America by storm.

6. What was Brian Johnson's first album as the lead singer of AC/DC?

a. *Who Made Who*

b. *Highway to Hell*

c. *Fly on the Wall*

d. *Back in Black*

GAME 21 Q5 ANSWER b
Fergie joined Black Eyed Peas in 2003, replacing Kim Hill. She recorded five songs with the group before being invited to join them permanently. Before Black Eyed Peas, Fergie sang with the all-girl band Wild Orchid, and was also a model for Bongo and Guess.

6. Which rock group had an unexpected disco hit in 1979?

a. KISS

b. AC/DC

c. Deep Purple

d. Black Sabbath

GAME 41 Q5 ANSWER a
This British band signed with The Beatles' Apple Records just as the label fell apart. The group's fate changed soon thereafter, as its 1973 song, "Brother Louie," became a hit in American record stores. "You Sexy Thing," featured in two popular 1997 films—*The Full Monty* and *Boogie Nights*—remains the group's best-known song.

6. What was the first song Bob Dylan played when he "went electric" at the 1965 Newport Folk Festival?

a. "Maggie's Farm"

b. "Like a Rolling Stone"

c. "Tombstone Blues"

d. "Blowin' in the Wind"

GAME 61 Q5 ANSWER b
The Byrds' version of "Mr. Tambourine Man," released only a few months after Bob Dylan's version was first heard in March 1965, went all the way to #1 on the pop charts that same year. The group's debut album also featured Dylan's songs "Spanish Harlem Incident," "All I Really Want to Do," and "Chimes of Freedom."

GAME 20

7. Which British rock legend sang a duet with Lita Ford on her 1988 hit "Close My Eyes Forever"?

a. Rod Stewart

b. Robert Plant

c. Roger Daltrey

d. Ozzy Osbourne

GAME 20 Q6 ANSWER b
This song's title was very similar to a lyric refrain in the 1962 hit "Make It Easy on Yourself," written by Burt Bacharach and Hal David for R&B singer Jerry Butler. In order to make his song stand out that same year, Sedaka decided to speed up its tempo. It was a good decision; the song shot to #1 in August 1962.

GAME 40

7. Who sang about the "Mighty Quinn" in a 1968 hit?

a. Ray Davies

b. Bruce Springsteen

c. Manfred Mann

d. Bob Seger

GAME 40 Q6 ANSWER a
Written by Dennis Matkosky and Michael Sembello, and performed by Sembello, "Maniac" topped the charts for two weeks. Another hit from the movie was Giorgio Moroder's "Flashdance (What a Feeling)." Sung by Irene Cara, it won the Academy Award for Best Song in 1983.

GAME 60

7. What was Dave Matthews Band's first record?

a. *Crash*

b. *Listener Supported*

c. *Remember Two Things*

d. *Everyday*

GAME 60 Q6 ANSWER c
A combination of offbeat lyrics and Brad Roberts' attention-grabbing voice quickly made Crash Test Dummies a hit in its native Canada, with its debut album *The Ghosts That Haunt Me* becoming a Canadian bestseller in 1991. The group was also featured on the soundtracks of the 1994 films *Dumb and Dumber* and *The Flintstones*.

GAME 80

7. What was the name of the Monkees' reunion album in 1996?

a. *Pool It!*

b. *Justus*

c. *Changes*

d. *Instant Replay*

GAME 80 Q6 ANSWER c
In the tradition of giving new groups a chance to break through (Lone Justice, No Doubt, and Garbage were all opening acts on previous U2 tours), U2 gave Canadian band The Arcade Fire a shot in 2005. By year's end, Arcade Fire's popularity had grown, and their debut album *Funeral* was nominated for a Best Alternative Music Grammy.

7. Which Monkee provided the voice of Skip in the Hanna-Barbera series *Funky Phantom*?

a. Michael Nesmith

b. Peter Tork

c. Davy Jones

d. Micky Dolenz

GAME 1 Q6 ANSWER b
Frank Zappa also appeared in our next-to-last TV episode as "Michael Nesmith," while Mike played "Frank Zappa" complete with fake nose and beard. In 1969, Zappa produced the first Captain Beefheart double album called *Trout Mask Replica*. Fats Domino and Jerry Lee Lewis were in our 1969 TV special, *33 1/3 Revolutions Per Monkee*.

7. Who has been the lead singer for The Spencer Davis Group, Blind Faith, and Traffic?

a. Steve Winwood

b. Robert Palmer

c. Jeff Beck

d. Roger Daltrey

GAME 21 Q6 ANSWER d
Johnson, formerly of the Newcastle rock group Geordie, replaced lead singer Bon Scott in 1980, after Scott's death. The band's first choice, Johnson is credited with pushing AC/DC in a more heavy metal direction, and *Back in Black* is regarded as a rock landmark.

7. Which disco-era group recorded "Y.M.C.A."?

a. Wings

b. Village People

c. Bee Gees

d. Emotions

GAME 41 Q6 ANSWER a
Having finished making the lamentable made-for-TV movie *KISS Meets the Phantom of the Park* a year before, KISS decided to release this disco-heavy single from their 1979 album *Dynasty*. It became their biggest worldwide hit, reaching #11 on the US pop charts but also alienating much of their die-hard KISS fan base.

7. The soundtrack of which film contains an Oscar-winning song by Bob Dylan?

a. *Wonder Boys*

b. *Hurricane*

c. *Pocahontas*

d. *The Big Chill*

GAME 61 Q6 ANSWER a
Revered as a singer-songwriter of strictly folk music, Dylan shocked the Newport audience by performing with electric instruments. After three songs, which were met with both boos and cheers, Dylan left the stage. He eventually returned and gave a brisk acoustic encore of "Mr. Tambourine Man" and "It's All Over Now, Baby Blue."

GAME 20

6. Which of these early rock-and-roll classics was written by Neil Sedaka?

a. "Splish Splash"

b. "Breaking Up Is Hard to Do"

c. "Blueberry Hill"

d. "Party Doll"

GAME 20 Q5 ANSWER a
Based out of Los Angeles, The Eagles started out in 1971 and went on to produce five #1 classic singles (including the rock staple "Hotel California"). The group won the first platinum album ever for its 1976 *Greatest Hits* (1971–1975) album, which has sold over 28 million copies to date.

GAME 40

6. What was the #1 hit song from the 1983 movie *Flashdance*?

a. "Maniac"

b. "Still the Same"

c. "Diamond Girl"

d. "Let's Dance"

GAME 40 Q5 ANSWER a
First called Roundabout when it formed in 1967, the British rock group Deep Purple rechristened itself in 1968, after its first tour. Later that year, the group enjoyed great success with Joe South's "Hush." Along with Black Sabbath and Led Zeppelin, Deep Purple has been credited with laying the groundwork for heavy metal music.

GAME 60

6. Brad Roberts' baritone can be heard on the records of which '90s group?

a. Dream Warriors

b. Korn

c. Crash Test Dummies

d. The Tragically Hip

GAME 60 Q5 ANSWER a
The Last Waltz is the name of both The Band's final concert and Martin Scorsese's 1978 documentary film about that concert. Scorsese and Band guitarist-songwriter Robbie Robertson became life-long friends and actually lived together while the film was being edited, which partly explains the movie's focus on Robertson.

GAME 80

6. Which of these bands was an opening act for U2 on the 2005 Vertigo Tour?

a. Lone Justice

b. No Doubt

c. The Arcade Fire

d. Garbage

GAME 80 Q5 ANSWER b
Written as commentary on the escalating Cold War, this video used puppet versions of the band members, Ronald Reagan, Margaret Thatcher, and Mikhail Gorbachev. "Land of Confusion" was nominated for MTV Video of the Year, but lost (ironically) to former Genesis frontman Peter Gabriel's "Sledgehammer."

GAME 1

8. Which of the following songs was *not* recorded by The Monkees?

a. "Ruby Tuesday"
b. "I'm a Believer"
c. "Pleasant Valley Sunday"
d. "Daydream Believer"

GAME 1 Q7 ANSWER d
That's right, it was me! Over the years, I have found a string of good and steady gigs from my voiceover work. In addition to *Funky Phantom*, I have also provided voices for other cartoon shows such as *Devlin* and *Those Were the Days*. And you know that sweet Snuggles the Bear in the fabric softener commercials? Yep, that's me.

GAME 21

8. In 2005, which singer won a reality TV competition to become the new lead vocalist of INXS?

a. Suzie McNeil
b. Marty Casey
c. J.D. Fortune
d. Ty Taylor

GAME 21 Q7 ANSWER a
Winwood, a member of The Spencer Davis Group since age fifteen, left to form Traffic in the late '60s. He released his first solo album in 1977. Since then, he has had great success as a solo artist with hits like "Higher Love" and "Valerie." Two of his albums were recorded at his home in Gloucestershire, with Winwood playing all the instruments.

GAME 41

8. Thelma Houston had a #1 disco hit with which song?

a. "Don't Leave Me This Way"
b. "Lady Marmalade"
c. "Love Rollercoaster"
d. "Dancing Queen"

GAME 41 Q7 ANSWER b
Known for outrageous costumes, the Village People was the brainchild of two French songwriters: Jacques Morali and Henri Belolo. Along with "Y.M.C.A.," the group's best-known songs are "Macho Man" and "In the Navy." Their 1980 movie *Can't Stop the Music* was a box office failure.

GAME 61

8. Which film heavyweight directed the 2005 Bob Dylan TV documentary *No Direction Home*?

a. Steven Spielberg
b. Cameron Crowe
c. Jesse Dylan
d. Martin Scorsese

GAME 61 Q7 ANSWER a
"Things Have Changed," written by Dylan for *Wonder Boys*, won both an Oscar and a Golden Globe in 2000. Curtis Hanson, director and producer of the movie, created and filmed this song's music video. Three other Dylan tunes are also featured in this movie, which starred Michael Douglas and Tobey Maguire.

5. Which group was awarded the first platinum album?

a. The Eagles

b. The Rolling Stones

c. Boston

d. Crosby, Stills & Nash

GAME 20 Q4 ANSWER c
Although considered mere Pearl Jam clones when they debuted in 1992, Stone Temple Pilots (aka STP) developed a large following of its own by the time the group disbanded in 2003. Since then, lead singer Scott Weiland joined forces with Guns 'N Roses lead guitarist, Slash, to start a new group called Velvet Revolver.

5. Which group recorded the 1968 hit single "Hush"?

a. Deep Purple

b. The Beach Boys

c. Peter, Paul and Mary

d. The Turtles

GAME 40 Q4 ANSWER b
The name of a song, single, and video released by The Beatles in 1995, "Free as a Bird" was originally a piece of music that John Lennon composed, but never completed. But Lennon's wife Yoko Ono gave a recording of the unfinished piece to the remaining Beatles, who then completed it.

5. Robbie Robertson is a focal point of which 1978 movie of The Band's farewell concert?

a. *The Last Waltz*

b. *Divine Madness*

c. *Gimme Shelter*

d. *Monterey Pop*

GAME 60 Q4 ANSWER c
Inspired by Anka's former babysitter Diana Ayoub, "Diana" is the song that Anka performed when he auditioned for ABC in 1957. When the single zoomed to #1 on the US charts, it gave the young Canadian-born musician instant stardom. "Diana" is also one of the best-selling 45s in music history.

5. Which Genesis video from the '80s featured a lifelike puppet of Ronald Reagan?

a. "Invisible Touch"

b. "Land of Confusion"

c. "That's All"

d. "I Can't Dance"

GAME 80 Q4 ANSWER b
Lesley Gore was only sixteen when "It's My Party" rose to #1 in 1963. Later in 1963, she had a #5 hit with a sequel to "It's My Party" called "Judy's Turn to Cry." "You Don't Own Me" hit #2 in 1964, and was heard again in the '90s film *The First Wives Club*. In 1967, Gore sang her song "California Nights" on TV's *Batman*.

Answers are in right-hand boxes on page 16.

GAME 1

9. Bob Dylan may have quit "Maggie's Farm," but Peter Tork watched out for "Your Auntie _______."

a. Mathilda

b. Grizelda

c. Mame

d. Corinna

GAME 1 Q8 ANSWER a

Released in 1967, this Rolling Stones' classic featured the multi-talented guitarist Brian Jones also playing piano and the recorder. I met Jones at the Monterey Pop Festival in San Francisco, and he seemed like a really gracious guy. We were all sad to see him go when he died in 1969 at age twenty-seven.

GAME 21

9. Bjork, whose first solo album went gold, was the lead singer of which group?

a. Shangri-Las

b. Babes in Toyland

c. Barenaked Ladies

d. Sugarcubes

GAME 21 Q8 ANSWER c

Born Jason Dean Bennison in Ontario, Canada, J.D. Fortune replaced Michael Hutchence, the band's original singer, who died in 1997. After Hutchence's death, INXS struggled with different vocalists until their discovery of Fortune through the TV show *Rock Star: INXS*.

GAME 41

9. The groove to 1979's hit "Rapper's Delight" was taken from which disco anthem?

a. "Car Wash"

b. "Jungle Boogie"

c. "Stayin' Alive"

d. "Good Times"

GAME 41 Q8 ANSWER a

This talented R&B singer never received the backing she needed for a major career. Signed first by Dunhill Records in 1969, Houston then signed with Motown in 1971. However, she didn't have a #1 hit until "Don't Leave Me This Way" in 1977. She also recorded the song "Love Masterpiece" for the 1978 film *Thank God It's Friday*.

GAME 61

9. Which introspective song is found on *The Freewheelin' Bob Dylan* album?

a. "Book of Love"

b. "Poetry in Motion"

c. "Girl From the North Country"

d. "Paperback Writer"

GAME 61 Q8 ANSWER d

The two-part documentary focuses on Dylan's life and his effect on music from 1961 to 1966. It made sense for Scorsese to create a film about Dylan—they both have had similarly iconic careers. Besides, Scorsese had already captured Dylan on film when he performed with The Band in its 1978 farewell concert film, *The Last Waltz*.

Answers are in right-hand boxes on page 21.

4. *Core* and *Purple* are the albums of which group?

a. Hole
b. Lemonheads
c. Stone Temple Pilots
d. Smashing Pumpkins

GAME 20 Q3 ANSWER b
Hailing from Gainesville, Florida, Tom Petty and his band The Heartbreakers first hit the charts in 1979 with "Refugee" from the album *Damn the Torpedoes*. In 1981, Petty received his first Grammy nomination for "Stop Draggin' My Heart Around," which he wrote with his guitarist Mike Campbell and performed with Stevie Nicks.

4. "Free as a Bird" was a 1994 single by which legendary rockers?

a. Pink Floyd
b. The Beatles
c. Simon & Garfunkel
d. The Rolling Stones

GAME 40 Q3 ANSWER b
Dion & the Belmonts recorded "I Wonder Why" for the Laurie record label in 1958. A year later, they hit it big again in 1959 with the immortal "Teenager in Love." Both of these songs are featured prominently in the 1986 Francis Coppola movie *Peggy Sue Got Married*, which involves a character's time travel back to 1960.

4. Paul Anka, high school heartthrob of the early '60s, wrote which 1957 chart topper?

a. "Joanna"
b. "Georgia on My Mind"
c. "Diana"
d. "Roseanna"

GAME 60 Q3 ANSWER d
Featuring the hits "With or Without You" and "I Still Haven't Found What I'm Looking For," 1987's *The Joshua Tree* won the Album of the Year award at the 1988 Grammys. It was also cited by *Rolling Stone* magazine as one of U2's "three masterpieces," the others being *Achtung Baby* and *All That You Can't Leave Behind*.

4. Which Lesley Gore song was her only #1 hit?

a. "Judy's Turn to Cry"
b. "It's My Party"
c. "California Nights"
d. "You Don't Own Me"

GAME 80 Q3 ANSWER c
Inspired by the true story of Jeremy Wade Delle, a Texas student who shot himself in front of his class in 1991, "Jeremy" is a tour de force by singer-lyricist Eddie Vedder. The controversial video won four MTV awards in total. Pearl Jam's next video—which used only comic book animation—came in 1998 for "Do the Evolution."

GAME 1

10. What color was the famous Monkeemobile featured on the 1960s series?

a. Lime green
b. Electric blue
c. Bright red
d. Burnt orange

GAME 1 Q9 ANSWER b
This was the first Monkees' song featuring Peter on lead vocal. It was on our second album *More of The Monkees* (aka, the "JC Penney album," because we were photographed wearing the company's clothes on the front cover).

GAME 21

10. "Stand By Me" performer Ben E. King was a lead singer of which R&B vocal act?

a. The Hollies
b. The Drifters
c. Booker T. & the M.G.'s
d. The Coasters

GAME 21 Q9 ANSWER d
Formed in 1986, the Icelandic rock band Sugarcubes enjoyed international success. But tensions mounted steadily between Bjork and band member Einar Orn, and Sugarcubes dissolved in 1992. A year later, Bjork released her solo album *Debut*.

GAME 41

10. Whose "Disco Duck" was arguably the worst record of the 1970s?

a. Rick Dees
b. Neil Diamond
c. John Davidson
d. Barry Manilow

GAME 41 Q9 ANSWER d
Using a riff from Chic's hit "Good Times," this single by The Sugarhill Gang is considered hip-hop's first mainstream hit, reaching #36 on the US pop charts. The song also gave birth to the practice of *sampling*—the borrowing of another artist's music to rap over. The success of "Rapper's Delight" led Chic to sue Sugarhill Gang.

GAME 61

10. Which Bob Dylan song did U2 perform in its concert film *Rattle & Hum*?

a. "The Times They Are A-Changin'"
b. "Masters of War"
c. "All Along the Watchtower"
d. "Desolation Row"

GAME 61 Q9 ANSWER c
This 1963 album also features "Blowin' in the Wind" and "Don't Think Twice, It's All Right." The album cover has Dylan walking down a snowy street in New York City with then-girlfriend Suze Rotolo. On his 1969 country-rock album *Nashville Skyline*, Dylan re-recorded "Girl From the North Country" as a duet with Johnny Cash.

---

3. "Here Comes My Girl," "You Got Lucky," and "Refugee" are hit songs by which musician?

a. Jackson Browne
b. Tom Petty
c. Joe Jackson
d. Don Henley

GAME 20 Q2 ANSWER a
Other hits more typical of the group include "Fight Like a Brave" and "Suck My Kiss." Although they started hitting the pop charts in the '90s, the Red Hot Chili Peppers were better known for their crazy live shows than their songs. Featuring a bassist named Flea, the group's first #1 hit was "Californication" in 2000.

3. What song by the Bronx group Dion & the Belmonts became a celebrated doo-wop anthem?

a. "Come Go With Me"
b. "I Wonder Why"
c. "Get a Job"
d. "The Book of Love"

GAME 40 Q2 ANSWER b
Steppenwolf rose to fame after their hit single "Born to Be Wild" was featured in the 1969 film *Easy Rider*. The song became an unofficial biker's anthem, and has been credited with coining the term "heavy metal." Other Steppenwolf hits include 1968's "Magic Carpet Ride" and 1969's "Rock Me."

3. Which album generated U2's first #1 hits in the United States?

a. *Rattle and Hum*
b. *War*
c. *Achtung Baby*
d. *The Joshua Tree*

GAME 60 Q2 ANSWER c
Hailing from Massachusetts, The Jamies consisted of Tom Jameson and his sister Serena, along with Jeannie Ray and Arthur Blair. This doo-wop group cracked the Top 40 twice with this one song. In 1958, "Summertime, Summertime" reached #26 on the pop charts; in 1962, it was released again and rose to #38.

3. Which Pearl Jam song won MTV's Video of the Year award in 1992?

a. "Even Flow"
b. "Alive"
c. "Jeremy"
d. "Do the Evolution"

GAME 80 Q2 ANSWER b
This song was first released in early 1964 by American singing group The Exciters under the name "Do-Wah-Diddy." A few months later, Manfred Mann added an additional "Diddy" to the song title and had a #1 hit. Later called Manfred Mann's Earth Band, the group had another #1 hit with Bruce Springsteen's "Blinded by the Light" in 1977.

11. Peter Tork did *not* play which of the following instruments?

a. Bass

b. Drums

c. Lead guitar

d. Keyboards

GAME 1 Q10 ANSWER c
Batman and Robin weren't the only '60s TV icons with a cool car. We Monkees were given a radically souped up '66 Pontiac GTO that had been redesigned by custom car design guru Dean Jefferies. Years before Bo and Luke Duke drove the General Lee all over Hazzard County, we drove around LA in search of ratings.

---

11. The lead singer for A Perfect Circle is also lead singer of what other group?

a. Tool

b. Pink Floyd

c. Nirvana

d. Metallica

GAME 21 Q10 ANSWER b
King had been singing with The Five Crowns when, in 1958, The Drifters' manager fired The Drifters and, retaining the group name, recruited The Five Crowns to replace the fired vocalists. Singing under his given name, Ben Nelson, King stayed with the group until 1960, at which time he went solo and adopted his stage name of Ben E. King.

---

11. Which disco diva turns up the heat on "Love to Love You Baby" and "On the Radio"?

a. Vicki Sue Robinson

b. Alicia Bridges

c. Donna Summer

d. Evelyn King

GAME 41 Q10 ANSWER a
Born Rigdon Osmond Dees on March 14, 1950, in Jacksonville, Florida, Rick Dees & His Cast of Idiots went to #1 in October 1976 with this silly song. Though heard briefly in *Saturday Night Fever*, "Disco Duck" was not included on the film's soundtrack album. For his DJ work, Dees was inducted into the Radio Hall of Fame in 1999.

---

11. What was the name of Bob Dylan's first wife?

a. Joanne

b. Ariel

c. Sara

d. Marie

GAME 61 Q10 ANSWER c
U2 performed this version of the song during its 1987 "Save the Yuppies" concert in San Francisco. The performance is similar to Dylan's minimalist folk version as he recorded it for his album *John Wesley Harding* (unlike the Jimi Hendrix version, which first made the song a popular chart hit).

---

2. Which group recorded the #2 hit song "Under the Bridge" in 1992?

a. Red Hot Chili Peppers
b. Nirvana
c. U2
d. Pearl Jam

GAME 20 Q1 ANSWER a
Along with the Grammy-winning song "Handy Man" on Taylor's ninth album, *JT*, "Your Smiling Face" became an audience favorite at his concerts throughout the years. Produced by Peter Asher of the '60s English duo Peter & Gordon, Taylor was the first singer-songwriter signed to The Beatles' Apple record label in 1968.

2. Which rock group took its name from the title of a novel by Hermann Hesse?

a. Aerosmith
b. Steppenwolf
c. Soul Asylum
d. Alice in Chains

GAME 40 Q1 ANSWER b
Between 1978 and 1981, Little River Band enjoyed six consecutive Top 10 US singles, including "Lonesome Loser," "Reminiscing," "Lady," "Cool Change," "The Night Owls," and "Take It Easy on Me." Broadcast Music Incorporated has recognized "Reminiscing" as one of the most frequently played songs in the history of American radio.

2. What group recorded the hit "Summertime, Summertime"?

a. The Chordettes
b. The Murmaids
c. The Jamies
d. The Chantays

GAME 60 Q1 ANSWER c
"Tangled Up in Blue" tells of a hitchhiker who feels detached from his abandoned lover and the people they knew together. Like many of the songs on the *Blood on the Tracks* album, this piece is generally viewed as reflecting Dylan's feelings of loss after his separation from first wife, Sara.

2. What British Invasion band scored a hit with "Do Wah Diddy Diddy"?

a. The Kinks
b. Manfred Mann
c. The Who
d. The Yardbirds

GAME 80 Q1 ANSWER c
Who Made Who is a 1986 album by Australian heavy metal group AC/DC. Yet another Who album with the word "Who" in the title is 1975's *The Who By Numbers*. A largely morose album that seems a frantic cry for help from Who guitarist/songwriter Pete Townshend, it does have the upbeat (and suggestive) song "Squeeze Box."

12. The mother of which Monkee actually invented liquid paper?

a. Michael Nesmith
b. Davy Jones
c. Micky Dolenz
d. Peter Tork

Of all the Monkees, Peter was the most diverse when it came to playing instruments. Although he played bass on the show, Peter actually played keyboard and banjo among other instruments on many Monkees' tracks.

12. Which rock group and its lead singer are mismatched?

a. The Union Gap/Gary Puckett
b. The Miracles/Buddy Holly
c. The Playboys/Gary Lewis
d. The Comets/Bill Haley

Ohio-born Maynard James Keenan has been a member of Tool since 1990, and a member of A Perfect Circle since 1999. A Perfect Circle was formed when the group Tool decided to take some time off, and the two bands now operate concurrently.

12. In which city did the famous "Disco Demolition Night" rally take place?

a. New York
b. Chicago
c. San Diego
d. Cincinnati

Donna "Queen of Disco" Summer also had hits in the '70s with songs like "Bad Girls," "Last Dance," "Hot Stuff," and "No More Tears (Enough Is Enough)"— her duet with Barbra Streisand. In the '80s, Summer again burned up the charts with "She Works Hard for the Money" (1983) and "This Time I Know It's for Real" (1989).

12. Bob Dylan played an unusual gig at the World _____ Conference.

a. Eucharistic
b. Jewish
c. Nudist
d. Librarian

Dylan and Sara Lownds were married in 1965. His passion for her was captured in the haunting "Sad Eyed Lady of the Lowlands" from the album *Blonde on Blonde* (1966). Their bitter split in the mid-'70s led Dylan to create the album *Blood on the Tracks* (1975), as well as the poignant song "Sara" from the album *Desire* (1976).

GAME 20	**1.** "Your Smiling Face" was released by which recording artist in the 1970s? **a.** James Taylor **b.** Kenny Rogers **c.** Leo Sayer **d.** Jimmy Buffett	The answer to this question is on: **page 24,** **top frame,** **right side.**
GAME 40	**1.** Which group sings about a "Lonesome Loser" in a golden oldie? **a.** Styx **b.** Little River Band **c.** Chicago **d.** Bad Company	The answer to this question is on: **page 24,** **second frame,** **right side.**
GAME 60	**1.** "Tangled up in Blue" is the first track on which 1975 Bob Dylan release? **a.** *Planet Waves* **b.** *New Morning* **c.** *Blood on the Tracks* **d.** *Nashville Skyline*	The answer to this question is on: **page 24,** **third frame,** **right side.**
GAME 80	**1.** Which of the following is *not* an album by The Who? **a.** *Who Are You* **b.** *Who's Next* **c.** *Who Made Who* **d.** *The Who Sell Out*	The answer to this question is on: **page 24,** **bottom frame,** **right side.**

GAME 2

Charity Songs and Concerts

Turn to page 29 for the first question.

GAME 1 Q12 ANSWER a
Mike's mother, Bette Nesmith Graham, first came up with this idea while working as a secretary in 1951. In 1956, she began the trademark and patent process for her "Liquid Paper." As a young boy, Mike and his friends would fill bottles for customers. In 1979, Bette sold Liquid Paper to the Gillette Corporation for $47.5 million.

GAME 22

Fake Bands

Turn to page 29 for the first question.

GAME 21 Q12 ANSWER b
The Miracles, an R&B group, was led by Smokey Robinson. Buddy Holly was the leader of the Crickets. Holly formed the group as a backing band for his vocals, and the Crickets' first single, "That'll Be the Day," made the singer an overnight success when it was released in 1957.

GAME 42

Rock Books

Turn to page 29 for the first question.

GAME 41 Q12 ANSWER b
In July 1979, inspired by the backlash phrase "Disco Sucks!," two Chicago radio disc jockeys organized a rally at Chicago's Comiskey Park. A huge pile of disco albums was blown up on the field during a doubleheader between the Chicago White Sox and the Detroit Tigers. After the explosion, people started destroying the stadium.

GAME 62

Doo-Wop

Turn to page 29 for the first question.

GAME 61 Q12 ANSWER a
Dylan was invited by the Pope John Paul II to perform at the annual event, which took place on September 27, 1997 in Bologna, Italy. He sang "Knockin' on Heaven's Door," "A Hard Rain's A-Gonna Fall," and "Forever Young."

GAME 20

GRAB BAG

Turn to page 26 for the first question.

GAME 19 Q12 ANSWER b
Florence Ballard was actually the founding member and original lead singer of The Primettes—signed to Motown as The Supremes in 1961. After accepting the group, Motown's Berry Gordy, Jr. decided that Diana Ross should become the lead singer. Ballard was fired from The Supremes in July 1967 and replaced with Cindy Birdsong.

GAME 40

GRAB BAG

Turn to page 26 for the first question.

GAME 39 Q12 ANSWER c
Each of Madonna's children's books attempts to deliver a moral message. For instance, *The English Roses*—the first book of the series, published in 2003—teaches readers to look beyond appearances, while the second book, *Mr. Peabody's Apples,* warns against the dangers of gossip.

GAME 60

GRAB BAG

Turn to page 26 for the first question.

GAME 59 Q12 ANSWER b
Puff Daddy's 1997 song "I'll Be Missing You" sampled the melody of The Police's Grammy-winning song "Every Breath You Take." Like the Police song, "I'll Be Missing You"—written in memory of rapper Notorious B.I.G., who was murdered in March 1997—was a smash hit, reaching #1 on the US charts.

GAME 80

GRAB BAG

Turn to page 26 for the first question.

GAME 79 Q12 ANSWER a
Born in 1961, Leif Garrett's first acting role was in the 1969 film *Bob and Carol and Ted and Alice* at age five. Following a series of TV appearances, Garrett signed a recording contract with Atlantic Records in 1976. His first album, released in 1977, was a collection of oldies, including The Beach Boys' "Surfin' USA."

GAME 2	**1.** Which 1985 concert raised money for African famine relief? **a.** Farm Aid **b.** World Aid **c.** Live Aid **d.** Band Aid	The answer to this question is on: **page 31,** **top frame,** **right side.**
GAME 22	**1.** *It's a Sunshine Day* is the soundtrack album of which popular TV show? **a.** *The Partridge Family* **b.** *The Brady Bunch* **c.** *The Andy Griffith Show* **d.** *The Flintstones*	The answer to this question is on: **page 31,** **second frame,** **right side.**
GAME 42	**1.** The Ralph J. Gleason Music Book Awards are named for the critic who co-founded which publication? **a.** *Spin* **b.** *Creem* **c.** *Entertainment Weekly* **d.** *Rolling Stone*	The answer to this question is on: **page 31,** **third frame,** **right side.**
GAME 62	**1.** Which '40s group, known for the song "If I Didn't Care," laid the groundwork for doo-wop? **a.** The Ink Spots **b.** The Pied Pipers **c.** The Ames Brothers **d.** The Four Knights	The answer to this question is on: **page 31,** **bottom frame,** **right side.**

12. Which singer was one of the original Supremes?

a. Cindy Birdsong
b. Florence Ballard
c. Lynda Lawrence
d. Scherrie Payne

Kendricks sang lead on the group's hit songs "I Can't Get Next to You" in 1969 and "Just My Imagination (Running Away With Me)," a #1 hit in 1971. This song was a return to the group's R&B sound of the mid '60s, and yet another Motown classic redone by The Rolling Stones—this time, on the group's 1978 album *Some Girls*.

12. Which 2005 book was the last in a series of five children's books written by Madonna?

a. *Ack Ick Eck*
b. *Sing on a Star*
c. *Lotsa De Casha*
d. *Mr. Tarantula's House*

"Deeper and Deeper" is a track from Madonna's 1992 release *Erotica*, an album whose sales were ultimately disappointing—possibly because it was released at about the same time as the artist's notorious book *SEX*. "Deeper and Deeper" became especially controversial when it was discovered that the song dealt with homosexuality.

12. Which Police song did Puff Daddy adapt in his hit "I'll Be Missing You"?

a. "Don't Stand So Close"
b. "Every Breath You Take"
c. "Murder By Numbers"
d. "Every Little Thing"

Andy Summers' "Mother," a short piece from 1983's *Synchronicity*, is known for its screamed vocals and its strange, Indian-like sounds. Reviewers have even been known to call the song "awful." The other three songs—"Peanuts," "Roxanne," and "Can't Stand Losing You"—are from The Police's 1978 debut album *Outlandos d'Amour*.

12. Which teen heartthrob recorded the 1979 hit "I Was Made for Dancin'"?

a. Leif Garrett
b. David Cassidy
c. Andy Gibb
d. Donny Osmond

Kirkpatrick was a member of rival boy band 'N Sync. Brian Littrell and Nick Carter are the other members of The Backstreet Boys. Formed in 1993 by Lou Pearlman (founder of Trans Continental Airlines and Art Garfunkel's cousin), the group has sold more than 87 million albums worldwide, making them the best-selling boy band to date.

GAME 2

2. Who played acoustic guitar alongside Bob Dylan during the Live Aid concerts?

a. Keith Richards
b. Bono
c. Tom Petty
d. Willie Nelson

GAME 2 Q1 ANSWER c
Two years after starring in Pink Floyd's film *The Wall* (1982), former Boomtown Rats singer Bob Geldof wrote "Do They Know It's Christmas?" for Band Aid. The UK all-star charity pop song helped raise millions to fight starvation in Ethiopia. After USA For Africa released "We Are the World," Geldof organized the Live Aid concerts.

GAME 22

2. Ron Dante and Toni Wine provided the vocals for which pop group?

a. The Partridge Family
b. The Monkees
c. The Archies
d. ABBA

GAME 22 Q1 ANSWER b
It's a Sunshine Day: The Best of the Brady Bunch was released in 1993. Included on the TV clan's album are the songs "Theme from the Brady Bunch," "Time to Change," "We Can Make the World a Whole Lot Brighter," "American Pie," and, of course, "It's a Sunshine Day."

GAME 42

2. Ken Sharp's 1993 book *Overnight Sensation* is about the rise and fall of which '70s group?

a. The Doobie Brothers
b. The Police
c. Tijuana Brass
d. The Raspberries

GAME 42 Q1 ANSWER d
The Awards committee was founded in 1989 to honor the best books on modern music. An early champion of so-called "sick" comic Lenny Bruce in the late '50s, Ralph Gleason wrote for the *San Francisco Chronicle* before he co-founded *Rolling Stone* with Jann Wenner in 1967. The magazine's first issue featured John Lennon on the cover.

GAME 62

2. Many doo-wop groups were named after what type of animal?

a. Cat
b. Bird
c. Snake
d. Fish

GAME 62 Q1 ANSWER a
Considered the first major black pop music group, The Ink Spots had a unique vocal style that led to the development of doo-wop. Their popularity, along with that of The Mills Brothers, helped black singers cross the racial barrier on radio stations. The Ink Spots' hit recordings kept them on the charts from 1939 through 1951.

Answers are in right-hand boxes on page 33.

GAME 19	**11.** Eddie Kendricks was the tenor and lead voice of which group? **a.** The O'Jays **b.** The Temptations **c.** The Four Tops **d.** Gladys Knight & the Pips	**GAME 19 Q10 ANSWER b** How could I resist making "Mickey's Monkey" one of the answer choices? It seemed a natural. "I'll Be There" was one of three #1 hits for the Jackson Five in 1970. Written by Berry Gordy, Jr., Hal Davis, Bob West, and Willie Hutch, "I'll Be There" was a #1 hit again in 1992 when Mariah Carey released a live version of the song.
GAME 39	**11.** Which Madonna song was released in the 1990s? **a.** "Live to Tell" **b.** "Deeper and Deeper" **c.** "Causing a Commotion" **d.** "La Isla Bonita"	**GAME 39 Q10 ANSWER d** This controversial film, which was largely shot in black and white, includes memorable encounters with Warren Beatty and Kevin Costner; presents conversations with friend Sandra Bernhard; features Madonna's father and brother; and highlights her relationship with the dancers and make-up artists that tour with her.
GAME 59	**11.** Which of the following songs appears on The Police's *Synchronicity* album? **a.** "Peanuts" **b.** "Mother" **c.** "Roxanne" **d.** "Can't Stand Losing You"	**GAME 59 Q10 ANSWER a** With words and music by Stewart Copeland, "On Any Other Day," from the 1979 album *Reggatta de Blanc,* is a hilarious view of a man who's suffering through a mid-life crisis. Another humorous song on this album is Copeland's "Does Everyone Stare," which tells of a man's bumbling attempts to woo the girl he loves.
GAME 79	**11.** Which of these singers was *not* a member of The Backstreet Boys? **a.** Kevin Richardson **b.** Chris Kirkpatrick **c.** A.J. McLean **d.** Howie Dorough	**GAME 79 Q10 ANSWER b** Airing on ABC from 1964 to 1966, *Shindig!* was where America first saw Sherman. In 1967, he appeared on *The Monkees* as "Frankie Catalina," and from 1968 to 1970, he was "Jeremy Bolt" in the TV series *Here Come the Brides.* Sherman then went on to have his first chart hits—"Little Woman" in 1969 and "Easy Come, Easy Go" in 1970.

3. Who organized The Concert for New York City after the September 11 attacks?

a. Rudy Giuliani

b. Bob Geldof

c. Paul McCartney

d. Billy Joel

GAME 2 Q2 ANSWER a

Keith Richards and fellow Rolling Stones' guitarist Ron Wood helped Dylan close the American wing of the Live Aid concerts by playing "Blowin' in the Wind" at JFK Stadium in Philadelphia. Meanwhile, Stones' frontman, Mick Jagger, sang "It's Only Rock and Roll" along with Tina Turner at the Wembley Stadium concert in the UK.

3. *Up to Date* is a gold album by which fabricated music group?

a. The Chipmunks

b. The Monkees

c. Spinal Tap

d. The Partridge Family

GAME 22 Q2 ANSWER c

The Archies appeared on *The Archie Show*, and were a group of fictional characters including Archie Andrews, Reggie Mantle, Jughead Jones, Betty Cooper, and Veronica Lodge. Their most famous song was Jeff Barry and Andy Kim's "Sugar, Sugar," which rose to #1 on the pop chart in 1969.

3. Who wrote the 1994 book *Dancing in the Street: Confessions of a Motown Diva*?

a. Martha Reeves

b. Diana Ross

c. Mary Wells

d. Mary Wilson

GAME 42 Q2 ANSWER d

Reared on the sounds of the British Invasion, The Raspberries started their brief but memorable time in the limelight in 1972 with "Go All the Way," which went to #5 on the charts. The Raspberries broke up in 1974, but the group's singer-guitarist Eric Carmen had two hits in the '80s with "Hungry Eyes" and "Make Me Lose Control."

3. Doo-wop groups were so called because of the many _____ in their songs.

a. Sexual references

b. Nonsense words

c. Rhymed phrases

d. Incomplete sentences

GAME 62 Q2 ANSWER b

The '50s sounds of doo-wop began with small groups of kids singing a cappella on inner-city street corners. Many of these groups named themselves after birds, such as The Orioles, The Crows, The Penguins, The Ravens, The Flamingos, and The Larks. Some doo-wop groups are still together, and appear on PBS fundraising specials.

10. Which of these songs was *not* a hit for Smokey Robinson and the Miracles?

a. "Mickey's Monkey"
b. "I'll Be There"
c. "Going to a Go-Go"
d. "Tracks of My Tears"

GAME 19 Q9 ANSWER a
Before starting the Motown label, Berry Gordy, Jr. was a songwriter and producer. He met Jackie Wilson in 1957, and wrote a number of Wilson's best R&B singles. Later that same year, he became producer to Smokey Robinson and the Miracles. After creating Tamla Records in January 1959, Gordy founded Motown on December 14, 1959.

---

10. During which tour was the Madonna documentary *Truth or Dare* filmed?

a. Virgin
b. True Blue
c. Breathless
d. Blonde Ambition

GAME 39 Q9 ANSWER a
Madonna's seventh studio album, *Ray of Light* shows the influence of a number of Eastern philosophies, including Hinduism and the Kabbalah, and incorporates Eastern instruments such as the sitar. (Original titles for the 1998 album included "Mantra.") Both a critical and a commercial success, the album earned five Grammys.

---

10. "On Any Other Day" is unique in The Police's work because it is:

a. Sung by Stewart Copeland
b. A long Sting bass solo
c. Featured on a Cher album
d. Based on a Weill song

GAME 59 Q9 ANSWER b
The instrumental "Behind My Camel" was guitarist Andy Summers' first solo composition, and was not popular with the other Police members. Sting supposedly refused to play, making it necessary for Summers to overdub the bass line himself. Later, when the piece won a Grammy, Sting received an award for a recording he hadn't made.

---

10. On what '60s musical variety show did teen idol Bobby Sherman frequently appear?

a. *Dinner Party*
b. *Shindig!*
c. *Get Together*
d. *Square Dance*

GAME 79 Q9 ANSWER b
"Lost in Your Eyes," "Only in My Dreams," and "Shake Your Love" were all pop hit songs performed by Debbie Gibson. "I Think We're Alone Now," which was originally a hit for Tommy James & the Shondells, became the first of Tiffany's two #1 chart hits in 1987. The other song to reach #1 was "Could've Been."

GAME 2	**4.** Which musician created Farm Aid with Willie Nelson and Neil Young? **a.** John Mellencamp **b.** Bruce Springsteen **c.** Johnny Cash **d.** Eric Clapton	**GAME 2 Q3 ANSWER c** McCartney was actually in New York City on September 11, 2001. He worked fast to put together a concert that went on to raise over $30 million to benefit victims of the World Trade Center attacks. Highlights of the show included Billy Joel's poignant performance of "New York State of Mind" and a blistering set by The Who.
GAME 22	**4.** Who was the manager of those singing chipmunks, Simon, Theodore, and Alvin? **a.** Darren Raymond **b.** Will Moses **c.** David Seville **d.** Mark Johnson	**GAME 22 Q3 ANSWER d** *Up to Date* is one of the ten albums bearing the name of this popular TV family. Capitalizing on the sitcom's success, The Partridge Family was a phenomenon—even though the only actors who actually sang were Shirley Jones and real-life stepson, David Cassidy, and none of the television characters really played their instruments.
GAME 42	**4.** The 1994 book *Dream Lovers* was written by the son of which singer? **a.** Roy Orbison **b.** Bobby Darin **c.** Don Everly **d.** Dean Torrence	**GAME 42 Q3 ANSWER a** The lead singer of Martha and the Vandellas, whose hits included "Heat Wave" and "Dancing in the Street," Martha Reeves pulled no punches in her "bare-all" book. She was honored by Black Women in Publishing for both her book and her contributions to *Soul* magazine. In 2005, she also won a seat to the Detroit City Council.
GAME 62	**4.** What was the orignal name of the doo-wop group The Coasters? **a.** The Robins **b.** The Seagulls **c.** The Wrens **d.** The Finches	**GAME 62 Q3 ANSWER b** Some credit Gus Gosset, a New York City DJ, with coining the term "doo-wop." It refers to the repeated nonsense sounds in the lyrics, such as those in the songs "Yakety Yak" and "Shimmy, Shimmy, Ko-Ko-Bop." Other components of doo-wop music include a wide range of vocal parts, group harmony, and simple beat, music, and lyrics.

9. Berry Gordy's "That's Why I Love You So" and "Reet Petite" were hits for which R&B great?

a. Jackie Wilson
b. Little Richard
c. Marvin Gaye
d. James Brown

GAME 19 Q8 ANSWER a
"What's Goin' On?" was the title track of Marvin Gaye's groundbreaking 1971 album, and it reached #2 on the US pop charts. Martha and the Vandellas' "Dancin' in the Streets" also went to #2 on the charts in 1964, and was remade twice in the '80s—first by Van Halen in 1982, and then as a duet by Mick Jagger and David Bowie in 1985.

9. On which Maverick Records album does "Frozen" appear?

a. *Ray of Light*
b. *Bedtime Stories*
c. *American Life*
d. *Music*

GAME 39 Q8 ANSWER c
Many people gave higher marks to the sexy wedding dress than to the album itself, and some guys supposedly bought the CD just for the cover. But despite the less-than-stellar reactions from critics, *Like a Virgin* was a huge success on the charts, becoming Madonna's first multiplatinum hit album.

9. What instrumental piece from *Zenyatta Mondatta* was a Grammy winner?

a. "Roxanne"
b. "Behind My Camel"
c. "Peanuts"
d. "Born in the 50's"

GAME 59 Q8 ANSWER c
In 1984's *"Weird Al" Yankovic in 3-D*, the song parodist's "King of Suede" is a take on The Police's 1983 release "King of Pain." Unlike the tormented King of Pain, the King of Suede's biggest problems appear to be that he never made it past the second grade and has tough competition from Willy's Fun Arcade.

9. Which of these songs was recorded by '80s pop star Tiffany?

a. "Lost in Your Eyes"
b. "I Think We're Alone Now"
c. "Only in My Dreams"
d. "Shake Your Love"

GAME 79 Q8 ANSWER b
Hailing from Fargo, North Dakota, Bobby Vee—born Robert Velline—had his first big hit single in 1961 with "Take Good Care of My Baby," which rose to #1 in both the US and the UK. Other hits included 1963's "The Night Has a Thousand Eyes" and 1967's "Come Back When You Grow Up."

5. Which 1985 heavy metal charity project was organized to help wipe out starvation in Africa?

a. Metal Aid

b. Hear'n Aid

c. Armband Aid

d. Scream'n Aid

GAME 2 Q4 ANSWER a

Bob Dylan got the ball rolling during the US Live Aid concert, when he suggested that someone organize a charity concert to help America's farmers. Then Mellencamp, Nelson, and Young took over, and the first Farm Aid concert was staged on September 22, 1985 in Champaign, Illinois.

5. Which fictional rock group included Dirk McQuickly?

a. The Monkees

b. The Rutles

c. Eddie & The Cruisers

d. The Commitments

GAME 22 Q4 ANSWER c

Ross Bagdasarian—whose stage name was David Seville—brought the group to life in the 1950s under the name David Seville and the Chipmunks. All of the voices were performed by Bagdasarian, who sped up the playback to create the distinctive high-pitched vocals of the chipmunks.

5. Which musician's 1978 book, *The Basketball Diaries*, was made into a well-received film in 1995?

a. Henry Rollins

b. Jim Carroll

c. Lou Reed

d. Kurt Cobain

GAME 42 Q4 ANSWER b

Dodd Darin is the son of Bobby Darin and Sandra Dee. Protective of his father's legacy, Dodd had insisted that Kevin Spacey use Bobby Darin's recordings in the 2004 biopic *Beyond the Sea*. In the end, though, Dodd couldn't tell the difference between Spacey's version of "Mack the Knife" and that of his father.

5. Which of these doo-wop songs was a big hit for The Chords?

a. "Sh-Boom"

b. "Earth Angel"

c. "Sincerely"

d. "My Prayer"

GAME 62 Q4 ANSWER a

As The Robins, this LA-based group had a hit with "Smokey Joe's Café." It then broke up and re-formed as The Coasters. Recording the songs of music writers Lieber & Stoller gave the group such hits as "Searchin'," "Charlie Brown," and "Poison Ivy." The Coasters were inducted into the Rock and Rock Hall of Fame in 1987.

GAME 19

8. Which of these songs was *not* a hit for Martha and the Vandellas?

a. "What's Goin' On?"

b. "Heat Wave"

c. "Dancin' in the Streets"

d. "Nowhere to Run"

GAME 19 Q7 ANSWER d
Gaye wanted to record with his fellow Detroit native, but it never happened. He did, however, record "Once Upon a Time" with Mary Wells in 1964 and "It Takes Two" with Kim Weston in 1967, before pairing with Tammi Terrell on the classic duets "Ain't No Mountain High Enough" in 1967 and "Nothing Like the Real Thing" in 1968.

GAME 39

8. On which CD cover is Madonna wearing a frothy white wedding dress?

a. *True Blue*

b. *Ray of Light*

c. *Like a Virgin*

d. *Immaculate Collection*

GAME 39 Q7 ANSWER b
"Lucky Star"—which is the first song that Madonna wrote after signing with Warner Bros.—is a track from the debut album *Madonna,* and also the singer's fifth single. The 1984 song has the distinction of being Madonna's first Top 5 hit on the Billboard Hot 100—the first, in fact, of the artist's *sixteen* consecutive Top 5 hits.

GAME 59

8. Which of the following is an actual "Weird Al" Yankovic parody of a Police hit?

a. "Message in a Potty"

b. "Every Cake You Bake"

c. "King of Suede"

d. "Doo Doo Doo Doo Doo Doo"

GAME 59 Q7 ANSWER b
"Invisible Sun," which deals with the problems in Northern Ireland, was released as a single before the release of *Ghost in the Machine,* and rose to #2 in the UK—even though the BBC banned the video for its images of Northern Ireland. Later, another single from the album, "Every Little Thing She Does Is Magic," hit #3 in the US.

GAME 79

8. Which teen idol had hits with "Devil or Angel," "Rubber Ball," and "Take Good Care of My Baby"?

a. Frankie Lyman

b. Bobby Vee

c. John Travolta

d. Ricky Nelson

GAME 79 Q7 ANSWER d
Considered by many to be the original boy band, this Scottish group was so popular in the mid-'70s that comparisons to "Beatlemania" were made for a time. The group even had its own BBC TV show called *Shang-a-Lang,* named after its hit song. Yet The Bay City Rollers had only one #1 hit in the US—1976's "Saturday Night."

---

6. Which John Lennon song did Madonna perform on NBC's 2005 tsunami relief concert?

a. "Power to the People"

b. "Starting Over"

c. "Imagine"

d. "Give Peace a Chance"

In May 1985, legendary heavy metal singer Ronnie James Dio gathered together Hear'n Aid to write and record a charity song called "Stars." The recording featured over forty metal icons, including members of Judas Priest, Mötley Crüe, Quiet Riot, Twisted Sister, Iron Maiden, and even the parody group Spinal Tap.

---

6. Whose shock was evident as he accepted a Grammy for the title song from the film *A Mighty Wind*?

a. Albert Brooks

b. Adam Sandler

c. Eugene Levy

d. Dan Aykroyd

Eric Idle played the McCartney-like musician McQuickly in this group, which parodied The Beatles. The Rutles are best known for *All You Need Is Cash*, Idle's 1978 "mockumentary" film that showed the rise and fall of the group, paralleling much of the history of the Beatles. George Harrison makes a cameo appearance in the film.

---

6. *Songs in the Rough: Rock's Greatest Hits in Rough-Draft Form* is a book compiled by:

a. Paul Williams

b. Stephen Bishop

c. John Sebastian

d. Barry Manilow

Best-known for his hard-edged '80s punk song "People Who Died," Jim Carroll was both a promising New York City basketball prodigy and a desperate heroin addict in the mid-'60s. By 1973, he was publishing his own troubled poetry and working for Pop Art legend Andy Warhol. Leonardo DiCaprio portrayed Carroll in the film.

---

6. The Cleftones are best remembered for its rendition of which oldie?

a. "I'll Never Smile Again"

b. "Seems Like Old Times"

c. "Heart and Soul"

d. "Glow-Worm"

Also known as "Life Could be a Dream," "Sh-Boom," was first recorded by The Chords in 1954, and reached #2 on the R&B charts. It was, however, The Crew-Cuts' version that made it to #1 on the pop charts a year later. "Earth Angel" was a hit for The Penguins; The Moonglows sang "Sincerely;" and "My Prayer" was a hit for The Platters.

---

7. Marvin Gaye recorded Top 20 hits with all of these vocalists except:

a. Mary Wells

b. Kim Weston

c. Tammi Terrell

d. Aretha Franklin

GAME 19 Q6 ANSWER d
"Respect" was written by Southern soul man Otis Redding, whose version of the song was released in the summer of 1965 and crossed over from the R&B charts to ultimately peak at #35 on the pop single charts. Of course, the song became an instant #1 hit when Aretha Franklin recorded her career-defining version in 1967.

7. Which of the following Madonna singles is *not* also the title of the album that features it?

a. "Ray of Light"

b. "Lucky Star"

c. "American Life"

d. "Like a Prayer"

GAME 39 Q6 ANSWER c
In this 1986 song, a pregnant teenager tells her father that she plans to keep and raise her child. While conservatives applauded Madonna's apparent stand against abortion, others attacked it. But Madonna maintains that the song is not really about abortion, but about courage and taking responsibility.

7. The Police hit "Invisible ____" is from the 1981 album *Ghost in the Machine.*

a. World

b. Sun

c. Man

d. Eye

GAME 59 Q6 ANSWER a
In the 1970s, before his work as guitarist for The Police, Summers did prolific session work with a variety of artists, including Neil Sedaka, Kevin Ayers, Joan Armatrading, Kevin Coyne, and Tim Rose. Summers' extensive musical credits also include the score for the 1986 film *Down and Out in Beverly Hills.*

7. What group appealed to teen girls with hits like "Bye Bye Baby" and "Shang-a-Lang"?

a. The Styx

b. The Boomtown Rats

c. The Romantics

d. The Bay City Rollers

GAME 79 Q6 ANSWER c
In both 1977 and 1989, updated versions of the 1950s' *Mickey Mouse Club* were presented on TV. The 1989 incarnation, available on the Disney Channel, showcased a number of young talents, including not only Britney Spears, Justin Timberlake, and J.C. Chasez, but also Keri Russell, Ryan Gosling, and Christina Aguilera.

7. Which Live Aid performer also took the stage at Live 8 in 2005?

a. David Bowie

b. Bryan Adams

c. Elton John

d. Bob Dylan

GAME 2 Q6 ANSWER c
As a result of this televised benefit concert, Americans pledged an estimated $18.3 million to the American Red Cross International Response Fund to help with tsunami relief in Asia. Lennon's song "Imagine" remains a beacon of hope in times of sorrow—Neil Young also performed the song during the 9/11 benefit concert in 2001.

7. The cartoon group Gorillaz is a project from Damon Albarn of which UK band?

a. Placebo

b. Cast

c. Blur

d. Oasis

GAME 22 Q6 ANSWER c
"The songs aren't real," Levy noted, while claiming the award for Best Song Written for a Movie on the behalf of himself, Michael McKean, and Christopher Guest. But critics and fans disagreed and applauded the title song, which, in the 2003 film, is performed in a rousing star-studded jamboree.

7. Which singing star published a 1998 book of poetry titled *A Night Without Armor*?

a. Usher

b. Sting

c. Jewel

d. Brandy

GAME 42 Q6 ANSWER b
Published in 1996, Bishop's book includes such pop-song first-draft lyrics as Bob Dylan's "Blowin' in the Wind," The Beatles' "Sergeant Pepper's Lonely Hearts Club Band," and the Elvis Presley classic "Heartbreak Hotel." It even includes the photo of an airline ticket with the lyrics to The Bee Gees' "Stayin' Alive."

7. The Platters are featured in which 1956 rock movie?

a. *Rock Pretty Baby*

b. *Rock Around the World*

c. *Rock You Sinners*

d. *Rock Around the Clock*

GAME 62 Q6 ANSWER c
Written by Hoagy Carmichael and Frank Lesser in 1939, "Heart and Soul" had been charted six times before The Cleftones' 1961 hit version. It was a hit for Eddy Duchin in 1939, and for The Four Aces in 1952. In a classic scene from the 1988 movie *Big*, Tom Hanks and Robert Loggia played "Heart and Soul" on a giant foot piano.

GAME 19	**6.** Which of the following pop classics was *not* written (or co-written) by Smokey Robinson? **a.** "Shop Around" **b.** "My Guy" **c.** "My Girl" **d.** "Respect"	**GAME 19 Q5 ANSWER d** Written by Ronald Miller and Orlando Murden, this song was also recorded by Motown groups Gladys Knight and the Pips and The Temptations, but it was Wonder's spirited version that hit #2 on the charts in 1968.
GAME 39	**6.** Which Madonna song was attacked by feminists for its apparent anti-abortion stance? **a.** "Live to Tell" **b.** "One More Chance" **c.** "Papa Don't Preach" **d.** "I'll Remember"	**GAME 39 Q5 ANSWER d** Released in 1982, this song originally appeared on a four-track demo tape that Madonna would bring to clubs, hoping that they would be played. When "Everybody" was finally played at the nightclub Danceteria, it received a great response, and club DJ Mark Kamis decided to produce it.
GAME 59	**6.** Which member of The Police once played with Neil Sedaka? **a.** Andy Summers **b.** Sting **c.** Stewart Copeland **d.** Simon Le Bon	**GAME 59 Q5 ANSWER b** Formed in 1989, Animal Logic also featured renowned jazz bassist Stanley Clarke and singer-songwriter Deborah Holland. Although the trio enjoyed success with their first album, Animal Logic disbanded after a disappointing followup. Copeland then went on to write movie soundtracks, including those for *Talk Radio* and *Wall Street*.
GAME 79	**6.** Which of these pop idols did *not* appear on TV's *Mickey Mouse Club*? **a.** Britney Spears **b.** Justin Timberlake **c.** Nick Carter **d.** J.C. Chasez	**GAME 79 Q5 ANSWER d** Born Fabiano Anthony Bonaparte, Philadelphia-born Fabian was only sixteen years old when this song reached #3 on the pop charts in the summer of 1959. His other hit singles included "Hound Dog Man," "I'm a Man," and "Turn Me Loose." In addition to pop success, the singer appeared in more than thirty films.

8. Who headlined the "Molson Canadian Rocks for Toronto" concert in 2003?

a. Santana

b. The Rolling Stones

c. The Who

d. Crosby, Stills, Nash & Young

GAME 2 Q7 ANSWER b
Canadian singer and songwriter Bryan Adams was one of the first big '80s music video stars. His video for "Cuts Like a Knife" ran constantly on MTV throughout most of 1983. At Live Aid, he sang "It's Only Love" with Tina Turner. At Live 8, he played at the Barrie, Ontario show in the midst of a US tour with '80s group Def Leppard.

---

8. On *The Simpsons*, the Be Sharps staged a reunion on the rooftop of which place?

a. Moe's Tavern

b. Kwik-E-Mart

c. Krusty Burger

d. Simpson Home

GAME 22 Q7 ANSWER c
Fronted by Blur leader Albarn, Gorillaz—a "virtual hip-hop group"—uses cartoon characters from animator Jamie Hewlett. The virtual band's 2005 album *Demon Days* sold over 4 million copies, producing the hit singles "Dirty Harry," "Feel Good Inc.," and "Dare."

---

8. What "Luka" songstress published a 1999 book titled *The Passionate Eye*?

a. Susanna Hoffs

b. Rickie Lee Jones

c. Tracy Chapman

d. Suzanne Vega

GAME 42 Q7 ANSWER c
Raised on an eighty-acre farm in Homer, Alaska, Jewel Kilcher based this first collection of 109 poems on her diaries. The book followed on the heels of her mega-successful 1994 debut album, *Pieces of You*, which yielded the Top 10 hits "You Were Meant for Me," "Who Will Save Your Soul?," and the #1 hit "Foolish Games."

---

8. Before achieving success as a solo artist, Dion had a string of doo-wop hits with which group?

a. The Stardusters

b. The Belmonts

c. The Sensations

d. The Wings

GAME 62 Q7 ANSWER d
This 1956 "B-movie" also featured performances by early rock 'n rollers Bill Haley & the Comets and Freddie Bell and the Bellboys. In the movie, The Platters sing "Only You (and You Alone)" and "The Great Pretender." *Rock Around the Clock* was the year's surprise box-office hit. The sequel, *Don't Knock the Rock*, didn't do as well.

---

5. Which song was *not* written by Stevie Wonder?

a. "Sir Duke"

b. "Living for the City"

c. "Jungle Fever"

d. "For Once in My Life"

GAME 19 Q4 ANSWER a
Together with Louis Armstrong's recording of "Hello, Dolly," this single broke The Beatles' three-month run of consecutive #1 songs in the spring of 1964. The Beatles, however, were big fans of Wells, and they invited her to tour with them in England. By way of thanks, she later recorded an album called *Love Songs to The Beatles.*

5. Which of the following songs was Madonna's first single?

a. "Lucky Star"

b. "Holiday"

c. "Papa Don't Preach"

d. "Everybody"

GAME 39 Q4 ANSWER b
Madonna's second studio album, *Like a Virgin* was somewhat controversial because of both its title track and "Material Girl." Nevertheless, these hits helped the album top Billboard's pop album chart, and became two of the artist's best-known and most enduring songs.

5. Which band did Stewart Copeland found after the breakup of The Police?

a. Weather Report

b. Animal Logic

c. XTC

d. Acoustic Alchemy

GAME 59 Q4 ANSWER a
This song, which describes a castaway lost on an island, is one of many that Sting wrote about isolation and loneliness. "Message in the Bottle" and "Walking on the Moon"—the other single from the 1979 Police album *Reggatta de Blanc*—both rose to #1 in the UK.

5. With what song did teen idol Fabian have a hit song in 1959?

a. "Hungry Like the Wolf"

b. "Alley Cat"

c. "The Lion Sleeps Tonight"

d. "Tiger"

GAME 79 Q4 ANSWER a
Heart Break is a 1988 album by New Edition, a popular African-American singing group created in 1980 by producer Maurice Starr. After the band and producer split in 1984, Starr immediately created New Kids on the Block as the "white" equivalent of New Edition.

Answers are in right-hand boxes on page 42.

9. At the Live 8 concert in London, U2 and Paul McCartney teamed up to perform:

a. "Sgt. Pepper's Lonely Hearts Club Band"

b. "Let It Be"

c. "Ticket to Ride"

d. "Drive My Car"

GAME 2 Q8 ANSWER b
Held to revive Toronto's economy after the SARS outbreak in 2003, this show was attended by about 450,000 people and was quickly nicknamed "Canada's Woodstock." While Santana, The Who, and Crosby, Stills, Nash & Young all played at the original Woodstock festival in Bethel, New York in 1969, The Rolling Stones did not.

---

9. In 1990, which group became the first ever to have its Grammy award taken back?

a. Tears for Fears

b. Color Me Badd

c. Wilson Phillips

d. Milli Vanilli

GAME 22 Q8 ANSWER a
The 1993 episode spoofing the Fab Four's famed rooftop concert features an animated appearance by George Harrison. Homer's fellow barbershop quartet members include Principal Skinner; Apu, the convenience store proprietor; and Barney, a regular of Moe's Tavern.

---

9. Which of the following bands called its 2002 autobiography *The Dirt*?

a. Aerosmith

b. Mötley Crüe

c. The Nitty Gritty Dirt Band

d. Pearl Jam

GAME 42 Q8 ANSWER d
The book is a collection of Vega's writings, including lyrics, poetry, and prose. An especially fascinating part of the book features an interview between Vega and Canadian songwriter Leonard Cohen. It's no surprise that Vega became a published author—she majored in English literature at Columbia University's Barnard College.

---

9. The Marcels hit it big in 1961 with a doo-wop version of which Rodgers and Hart love song?

a. "My Funny Valentine"

b. "Blue Moon"

c. "This Can't Be Love"

d. "Bewitched"

GAME 62 Q8 ANSWER b
Dion & the Belmonts had a number of hits, including "I Wonder Why," "Teenager in Love," and "Where or When." In 1960, Dion DiMucci went out on his own. Backed by The Del-Satins, he recorded such hits as "Runaround Sue," "Lovers Who Wander," and "Ruby Baby." In 1968, he had a hit with the protest song "Abraham, Martin, and John."

GAME 19

4. The only song by R&B singer Mary Wells to reach #1 was:

a. "My Guy"
b. "Love Hangover"
c. "Upside Down"
d. "Endless Love"

GAME 19 Q3 ANSWER a
Many Motown artists looked to the supreme songwriting team of Holland-Dozier-Holland. Lamont Dozier, together with brothers Brian Holland and Edward Holland, Jr., were responsible for twenty-five Top 10 hit singles, including "Where Did Our Love Go."

GAME 39

4. Which of these songs came from the 1984 Madonna album *Like a Virgin*?

a. "Live to Tell"
b. "Material Girl"
c. "Lucky Star"
d. "Express Yourself"

GAME 39 Q3 ANSWER c
Although 1990's "Justify My Love" was written by Lenny Kravitz and Ingrid Chavez, Chavez was not initially credited—supposedly, to prevent rumors that she was seeing Kravitz. This #1 hit was unique at the time of its release because Madonna actually sings very little, mostly whispering and speaking suggestively throughout the song.

GAME 59

4. Which Police song promises to send out an SOS?

a. "Message in a Bottle"
b. "Walking on the Moon"
c. "So Lonely"
d. "King of Pain"

GAME 59 Q3 ANSWER d
The title of this fifth album of The Police was inspired by one of Sting's favorite authors, Arthur Koestler, whose book *The Roots of Coincidence* mentions Carl Jung's theory of Synchronicity. Another of Koestler's works, *The Ghost in the Machine*, lent its title to The Police's fourth album.

GAME 79

4. Which of these albums was *not* recorded by New Kids on the Block?

a. *Heart Break*
b. *Step By Step*
c. *Hangin' Tough*
d. *Face the Music*

GAME 79 Q3 ANSWER d
Managed by her mother Susan Duff, fourteen-year-old Hilary first found fame in 2001 on the Disney Channel's comedy show *Lizzie McGuire*. Movies soon followed, with *The Lizzie McGuire Movie* in 2003 and a supporting role in that year's remake of *Cheaper By the Dozen*. Between 2002 and 2005, Duff also released four hit music albums.

10. Who was the only performer to play at both Live Aid concerts in 1985?

a. Mick Jagger
b. David Bowie
c. Phil Collins
d. Madonna

This concert marked the first time this song was performed live by a Beatle. The first time it was *ever* performed live was in 1967 by Jimi Hendrix. Of course, this was *not* the first time U2 had performed a Beatles' song live—their version of "Helter Skelter" is on the movie soundtrack of *Rattle and Hum* (1988).

---

10. Alexander Cabot III is the manager of which cartoon band?

a. Josie and The Pussycats
b. The Archies
c. Barbie and The Rockers
d. Jem and The Holograms

In November 1990, after the record *Girl You Know It's True* skipped during a live performance, Frank Farian—creator of the Milli Vanilli sound—revealed that the duo composed of Fabrice Morvan and Rob Pilatus did not actually make Milli Vanilli's recordings. The Grammy was rescinded four days later.

---

10. Published in 1999, *Real Love* is a book of drawings for children by which of the following musicians?

a. John Lennon
b. Mel Torme
c. Frank Sinatra
d. Bob Marley

Written by all four group members along with writer Neil Strauss, the story of this hell-raising metal quartet from LA makes The Rolling Stones look like the Mormon Tabernacle Choir by comparison. In 2004, with the help of rock writer Anthony Bozza, Crüe drummer, Tommy Lee, published his own personal memoir, *Tommyland*.

---

10. Who mentioned The Penguins, The Moonglows, The Orioles, and The Five Satins in a 1983 song?

a. James Taylor
b. Paul Simon
c. Bob Dylan
d. Sting

Written by Richard Rodgers and Lorenzo Hart in 1934, "Blue Moon" has been recorded by the likes of Billie Holiday, Frank Sinatra, Tony Bennett, Ella Fitzgerald, Louis Armstrong, Elvis Presley, and Rod Stewart. It was, however, The Marcels who had the hit. Although it was the group's only hit, it sold over 1 million records.

GAME 19	**3.** What was the first US #1 hit for The Supremes? **a.** "Where Did Our Love Go" **b.** "Baby Love" **c.** "Come See About Me" **d.** "You Can't Hurry Love"	**GAME 19 Q2 ANSWER b** Written by Smokey Robinson, "Going to a Go-Go" was a hit for The Miracles in 1965. Always inspired by American soul and R&B, the song was covered by The Rolling Stones during the early '80s. It became a Top 30 hit and a popular video, as featured on the Stones' 1982 live album, *Still Life* (*American Concert 1981*).
GAME 39	**3.** Who shared songwriting credit with Madonna on "Justify My Love"? **a.** Sean Penn **b.** David Bowie **c.** Lenny Kravitz **d.** Sandra Bernhard	**GAME 39 Q2 ANSWER d** "You Must Love Me," written especially for the film version of *Evita*, won the Academy Award for Best Song. But although Madonna won a Golden Globe for her performance in the film, she missed out on an Oscar nomination. Her performance at the Academy Awards ceremony was condemned by some as being mechanical.
GAME 59	**3.** "Wrapped Around Your _____" is one of many hits from The Police's album *Synchronicity*. **a.** Heart **b.** Mind **c.** Body **d.** Finger	**GAME 59 Q2 ANSWER c** This 1980 hit touches on the girl's obsession with her teacher, the teacher's own nervousness about the situation, and the reactions of others in the school. Although Sting, who wrote the song, once worked as an English teacher, he has denied that the song is in any way autobiographical.
GAME 79	**3.** What pop princess topped the album charts in the summer of 2005 with *Most Wanted*? **a.** Lindsay Lohan **b.** Kelly Clarkson **c.** Britney Spears **d.** Hilary Duff	**GAME 79 Q2 ANSWER c** Shaun (David's half-brother) reached #1 with this song in 1977. An instant teen idol, he went on to record cover versions of Eric Carmen's songs "Hey Deanie" and "That's Rock 'N' Roll"—each of which became a Top 10 hit. In 1978, he starred with Parker Stevenson on TV's *Hardy Boys Mysteries*.

11. Neil Young and his wife hold an annual concert benefiting:

a. The Bridge School
b. World AIDS Foundation
c. American Cancer Society
d. Save the Music

In a wonderful publicity stunt, Genesis singer/drummer and solo artist Phil Collins performed first in Live Aid at Wembley Stadium in the UK. He then hopped aboard a Concorde jet and zoomed off to play drums with the reunited Led Zeppelin at JFK Stadium in Philadelphia.

---

11. On the TV series *Lost*, which character was a member of the fictional UK band Drive Shaft?

a. John
b. Charlie
c. Kate
d. Hurley

Alexander is the conniving, extremely wealthy manager of Pussycats Josie, Melody, and Valerie. In the TV series *Josie and the Pussycats,* the manager's voice is supplied by Casey Kasem, who also provides the voice for Scooby-Doo's Shaggy.

---

11. Which musician wrote *Tarantula,* a book of Beat poetry and introspection?

a. Joan Baez
b. Pete Seeger
c. Bob Dylan
d. Joni Mitchell

Just as first son Julian's school drawing inspired John Lennon to write "Lucy in the Sky With Diamonds," the cheerful and witty drawings in this children's book were originally created by John to delight and inspire his second son, Sean. *Real Love* features a heartfelt introduction by John's widow, Yoko Ono.

---

11. The 1998 movie *Why Do Fools Fall in Love* told the story of which doo-wop singer?

a. Otis Williams
b. Frankie Lymon
c. Johnny Maestro
d. Bobby Day

Paul Simon pays homage to the surreal artist Rene Magritte in his song "Rene and Georgette Magritte with Their Dog After the War." Found on the *Hearts and Bones* album, the song implies that the artist and his wife were secret admirers of doo-wop music. Its title came from the caption of an actual photo of the two and their dog.

2. Which of these dance songs was recorded by Smokey Robinson and the Miracles?

a. "'E' Street Shuffle"

b. "Going to a Go-Go"

c. "Macarena"

d. "Twist and Shout"

GAME 19 Q1 ANSWER a
This song was a #1 hit for the Four Tops in October 1966—just three weeks before The Monkees first went to the top of the singles chart with "Last Train to Clarksville." Based out of Detroit, Michigan, the original members of this Motown quartet were together for over forty years when group member Lawrence Payton died in 1997.

2. At the 1996 Oscars, Madonna sang a song from which of the following movies?

a. *Dick Tracy*

b. *A League of Their Own*

c. *Truth or Dare*

d. *Evita*

GAME 39 Q1 ANSWER d
Madonna's 1984 debut album—called *The First Album* in Europe—yielded the hit single "Borderline." Both composed and produced by Reggie Lucas, "Borderline" was Madonna's first Top 10 hit on the Billboard Hot 100, and also made it onto several other charts, including the UK singles chart.

2. Which Police song concerns a young girl's crush on her teacher?

a. "Every Breath You Take"

b. "So Lonely"

c. "Don't Stand So Close to Me"

d. "Next to You"

GAME 59 Q1 ANSWER d
Released in 1978, The Police's debut album *Outlandos d'Amour* first did poorly. This was largely due to the BBC's banning of the singles "Roxanne," which deals with prostitution, and "Can't Stand Losing You," which deals with suicide. Eventually, though, the songs got more airplay and did well, and the album itself peaked at #6.

2. Which teen idol's career began with a cover of The Crystals' hit "Da Doo Ron Ron"?

a. Frankie Avalon

b. Pat Boone

c. Shaun Cassidy

d. Donny Osmond

GAME 79 Q1 ANSWER c
Before winning the hearts of American girls as Dr. Noah Drake on the ABC soap opera *General Hospital,* Springfield was a member of Zoot—a popular late '60s rock band from his native Australia. Released in 1981, "Jessie's Girl" won Springfield a Grammy for Best Male Rock Vocal. He went on to record a total of seventeen Top 40 hits.

GAME 2

12. The 1971 recording of which charity concert was Bob Dylan's first official live release?

a. Concert for Bangladesh

b. Live Aid

c. Live 8

d. Concert for New York

GAME 2 Q11 ANSWER a
The Bridge School is an educational program that helps handicapped children communicate. Inspired by their own son's special needs, Neil Young and wife, Pegi, organized the first Bridge School benefit concert in 1986. The annual concerts have featured great performers like Metallica, Dave Matthews Band, and Alanis Morrisette.

GAME 22

12. Which band's name was originally a fictional band in a Monty Python sketch?

a. Hootie and the Blowfish

b. Toad the Wet Sprocket

c. New Kids on the Block

d. Temple of the Dog

GAME 22 Q11 ANSWER b
Drive Shaft formed in Manchester, and enjoyed explosive worldwide success. The group's biggest (and perhaps only) hit was a song called "You All Everybody." Charlie, played by Dominic Monaghan, was bass guitarist in the group.

GAME 42

12. What is the title of the "Micky Dolenz" autobiography?

a. *That Was Then, This Is Now*

b. *Words*

c. *I'm a Believer*

d. *Steppin' Stone*

GAME 42 Q11 ANSWER c
In 1966, around the time of the motorcycle accident that sent him into seclusion for nearly eight years, Dylan wrote this book of scattered verse and vision in a style of writing that Beat poet Allen Ginsberg often called "spontaneous Bop prosody." The book was first formally published as a hardcover in 1971.

GAME 62

12. Which song was a big hit for The Penguins in 1954?

a. "Earth Angel"

b. "Only You"

c. "The Great Pretender"

d. "Smoke Gets in Your Eyes"

GAME 62 Q11 ANSWER b
With the 1955 hit "Why Do Fools Fall In Love," Frankie Lymon (lead singer of The Teenagers and credited writer of the song) became a singing sensation at thirteen. He went solo in 1957, but was unsuccessful. In 1968, Lymon died from a drug overdose. The movie is about the battle of his three ex-wives over royalties from the hit song.

GAME 19	**1.** Which song was *not* a #1 hit for The Temptations? **a.** "Reach Out I'll Be There" **b.** "My Girl" **c.** "I Can't Get Next to You" **d.** "Just My Imagination (Running Away With Me)"	The answer to this question is on: **page 50,** **top frame,** **right side.**
GAME 39	**1.** What was the name of Madonna's debut album? **a.** *True Blue* **b.** *Like a Prayer* **c.** *Like a Virgin* **d.** *Madonna*	The answer to this question is on: **page 50,** **second frame,** **right side.**
GAME 59	**1.** What album from The Police contains the hit single "Roxanne"? **a.** *Reggatta de Blanc* **b.** *Ghost in the Machine* **c.** *Zenyatta Mondatta* **d.** *Outlandos d'Amour*	The answer to this question is on: **page 50,** **third frame,** **right side.**
GAME 79	**1.** In this #1 hit song, whose girl does Rick Springfield wish he had? **a.** Johnny's girl **b.** Jimmy's girl **c.** Jessie's girl **d.** Jamie's girl	The answer to this question is on: **page 50,** **bottom frame,** **right side.**

The Harry Ride

My first encounter with Harry Nilsson came in 1967. He was working the night shift at a bank and writing songs during the day when our producer, Chip Douglas, brought him into the studio to play one of his songs for Davy to record—"Cuddly Toy." Years later, Harry told me that when Davy agreed to record that tune, the music publisher took him out into the hallway and told him, "Harry, you can quit the bank."

In two short years, Harry Nilsson went from working at a bank to being called "my favorite group" by John Lennon during a 1968 press conference announcing Apple Records in New York City. By 1969, he was a Grammy winner for his classic version of Fred Neil's song "Everybody's Talkin'" for the film *Midnight Cowboy*. That same year, he gave Three Dog Night their first Top 40 hit with "One" and wrote the theme song for TV's *The Courtship of Eddie's Father*. Harry's second Grammy arrived in 1971 for his wonderful recording of Badfinger's song "Without You." And he did all this without ever having to perform live, give interviews, or do TV and radio appearances. But it wasn't because he couldn't. Harry once told me that he just didn't want to have to be "on" at 8:00 one night. "What if I don't feel like it?" he would say.

Harry and I soon became good friends and began hanging out in Los Angeles. It was the early seventies and LA was a pretty wild place to be—even by LA's standards. My favorite quote about that period of time is, "I've heard it all, seen it all and done it all. I just can't remember it all."

For a few years, I was a regular passenger on what came to be known affectionately as "the Harry Ride." And it was a wild ride, indeed. John Lennon spent most of his legendary "Lost Weekend" in Los Angeles on the Harry Ride (although John had a pretty wild ride of his own), including the infamous incident at the West Hollywood nightclub The Troubadour, where Harry and John got thrown out for heckling the Smothers Brothers.

By the mid-seventies, I was looking to move further into film directing and producing. Harry unwittingly provided the catalyst by inviting me over to England to appear in the London production of his musical *The Point!* The show did fairly well, and I decided to stay on in the UK for a while. That "a while" ended up being nearly twelve years, during which time I honed my craft as a filmmaker and built a solid reputation for myself as director "Michael Dolenz."

And what about my friend Harry Nilsson? While not as popular as he had been in the '60s and '70s, Harry continued to create music while also making a family with his lovely wife, Una, and fighting for gun control after his friend John Lennon was killed. I maintained my friendship with Harry throughout this time, and was thrilled when he asked me to be godfather to one of his children.

Harry died of heart failure the night of January 15, 1994. True to his musical spirit, he finished recording vocals for his final album earlier that same day. People often ask me what I remember best about Harry Nilsson. It's impossible to say. There were so many good songs, good memories, good mornings, and good nights that he gave to us all—fans and friends alike. I suppose for me, it always goes back to hearing that first song of his in 1967. And the memory of that quiet young man working at the bank . . . and writing his dreams. ■

GAME 3

Grunge Rock

*Turn to page 57
for the first question.*

GAME 2 Q12 ANSWER a
Organized by "quiet Beatle" George Harrison, the Concert for Bangladesh was truly the first rock-star benefit concert. It also signaled Dylan's first moments on-stage after a 1966 motorcycle accident sent him into self-imposed exile from live performance that lasted five years. In 1974, he started touring again with The Band.

GAME 23

One-Hit Wonders

*Turn to page 57
for the first question.*

GAME 22 Q12 ANSWER b
Eric Idle thought the name was so absurd that no real band would ever use it. He was wrong. The American folk pop band Toad the Wet Sprocket formed in 1986 at San Marcos High School just outside Santa Barbara, California, and released several albums before its formal breakup in 1988.

GAME 43

Hair Metal

*Turn to page 57
for the first question.*

GAME 42 Q12 ANSWER c
I wrote my show-biz memoir with veteran rock writer Mark Bego in 1993. It had been nearly thirty years since I first got in the Monkees cage, and I wanted to set down my thoughts on the whole shebang. The Monkees experience has been a big chapter (or two) in my life—but only chapters, after all . . .

GAME 63

Canada Rocks

*Turn to page 57
for the first question.*

GAME 62 Q12 ANSWER a
One of the first R&B hit records to cross over to the pop charts, "Earth Angel" was the only hit for this LA-based group, but it became an instant classic. Although the song was originally released as the B-side of the song "Hey Senorita," DJs liked playing it better. The other song choices on the list were hits for The Platters.

GAME 19

The Motown Sound

Turn to page 52
for the first question.

GAME 18 Q12 ANSWER b
Booker T. and the M.G.'s backed Otis Redding at the Monterey Pop Festival. On records, they were the back-up band for such R&B artists as Sam & Dave, The Staple Singers, and Wilson Pickett. Their best-known song is the 1962 hit "Green Onions," which was used by George Lucas in the racing scene of his film *American Graffiti* (1973).

GAME 39

Madonna

Turn to page 52
for the first question.

GAME 38 Q12 ANSWER d
In 1953, Presley paid Sun Studios $4 to record a double-sided demo of the songs "My Happiness" and "That's When Your Heartaches Begin"—and reportedly gave the demo to his mother as a gift. Other recordings followed. Presley's association with Sun records ended in 1955, when Colonel Tom Parker negotiated a deal with RCA.

GAME 59

The Police

Turn to page 52
for the first question.

GAME 58 Q12 ANSWER c
Born Brandy Rayana Norwood in 1979, Brandy first became known for her TV work on the '90s sitcom *Moesha*. She had her first #1 pop chart hit and Grammy win for "The Boy Is Mine," her 1998 duet with fellow one-name R&B singer Monica. The song was inspired by the Michael Jackson and Paul McCartney duet of 1982, "The Girl Is Mine."

GAME 79

Teen Idols

Turn to page 52
for the first question.

GAME 78 Q12 ANSWER c
To promote her 2003 debut album, Lisa Marie appeared in concert in the UK—something that father Elvis never did. Her second album, *Now What*, was released in 2005, and rose to #9 on the Billboard 200. Lisa Marie's singles have included 2003's "Lights Out" and "Sinking In," and 2005's "Dirty Laundry" and "Idiot."

GAME 3

1. Which Soundgarden album has the hits "Fell on Black Days" and "Black Hole Sun"?

a. *Down on the Upside*
b. *Superunknown*
c. *Badmotorfinger*
d. *Louder Than Love*

The answer to this question is on:

page 59, top frame, right side.

GAME 23

1. "Hey Mickey" was the only pop hit for which artist?

a. Samantha Fox
b. Toni Basil
c. Martika
d. Kiki Dee

The answer to this question is on:

page 59, second frame, right side.

GAME 43

1. Sebastian Bach was the frontman for which heavy metal group?

a. Skid Row
b. Nine Inch Nails
c. Metallica
d. Anthrax

The answer to this question is on:

page 59, third frame, right side.

GAME 63

1. Which singer-songwriter was a noted poet and novelist before recording his first album?

a. David Clayton-Thomas
b. Leonard Cohen
c. Rene Simard
d. Robbie Robertson

The answer to this question is on:

page 59, bottom frame, right side.

12. Booker T. Jones of Stax Records fame played which instrument in the label's house band?

a. Flute

b. Organ

c. Viola

d. Sitar

GAME 18 Q11 ANSWER b
Laura Nyro was a great singer-songwriter whose songs were often bigger hits when recorded by other groups. Blood, Sweat & Tears had a Top 10 hit in 1969 with "And When I Die;" The 5th Dimension's "Stoned Soul Picnic" went to #3 in 1968; and in 1969, "Eli's Coming" reached #10 for Three Dog Night.

---

12. Which of the following songs did Presley record at Sun Studios?

a. "Suspicious Minds"

b. "Poor Boy"

c. "Love Me Tender"

d. "That's When Your Heartaches Begin"

GAME 38 Q11 ANSWER b
The 1953 recording of Leiber and Stoller's "Hound Dog" was Big Mama Thornton's one major hit. Presley recorded a different version of the song in 1956—with lyrics he had heard sung by Freddie Bell and the Bellboys—and it became the most successful single of his career, selling over 5 million copies in the United States.

---

12. Whose 2005 *Best of . . .* album includes the hits "Full Moon" and "Brokenhearted"?

a. Monica

b. Toni Braxton

c. Brandy

d. Whitney Houston

GAME 58 Q11 ANSWER c
"Let's Get It On" was a #1 hit for Marvin Gaye in 1973. "Here I Am," "Let's Stay Together," and "Livin' for You" were all Al Green hits in the early '70's, before he became an ordained pastor in 1976.

---

12. What album by Lisa Marie Presley went to #5 on the charts in 2003?

a. *Systems Layers*

b. *Doll Revolution*

c. *To Whom It May Concern*

d. *0304*

GAME 78 Q11 ANSWER d
Randy Bachman was lead guitarist and songwriter for the '70s rock band The Guess Who until differences led him to leave the group. In 1970, Bachman formed Brave Belt, which eventually became the hit band Bachman-Turner Overdrive. The latter group's biggest hit was "Takin' Care of Business," which was written by Bachman.

GAME 3

2. Members of Soundgarden and Pearl Jam recorded *Temple of the Dog* as a memorial to:

a. Andrew Wood

b. Keith Moon

c. Kristen Pfaff

d. Hillel Slovak

GAME 3 Q1 ANSWER b
Featuring the powerhouse vocals of band leader Chris Cornell, Seattle-grown grunge band Soundgarden really hit their stride when their fifth album *Superunknown* hit the album charts in 1994. "Black Hole Sun" won a MTV Best Music Video Award that same year, and can now be heard big-band style on Paul Anka's *Rock Swings* album.

GAME 23

2. Which 1997 song was the only major hit for The Verve?

a. "Sex and Candy"

b. "Meet Virginia"

c. "The Remedy"

d. "Bittersweet Symphony"

GAME 23 Q1 ANSWER b
Basil had a considerable career as an actress and choreographer before her 1982 hit. I enjoyed meeting her on the set of The Monkees' 1968 movie *Head*, in which she choreographed a dance number that she performed alongside Davy Jones to the tune of Harry Nilsson's "Daddy's Song."

GAME 43

2. Which group had a hit in 1988 with "Seventeen"?

a. Scorpions

b. Winger

c. Dio

d. Warrant

GAME 43 Q1 ANSWER a
One of the last big-selling '80s metal bands before the Seattle grunge of the'90s, Skid Row was not the first group to use the name—there was a '70s group called Skid Row led by blues guitarist Gary Moore. Lead singer Bach spent three years on probation for throwing a bottle back into an unruly crowd during a concert in 1989.

GAME 63

2. Which of the following artists was one of the first to be signed by Madonna's "Maverick" label?

a. Shania Twain

b. k.d. lang

c. Jane Siberry

d. Alanis Morissette

GAME 63 Q1 ANSWER b
Prior to a music career, Cohen had published three books of poetry and won Canada's Governor General's Award for his book *Selected Poems: 1956–1968*. His song "Suzanne" was a 1967 hit for Judy Collins. Over the years, Cohen's music has been covered by over 1,000 artists, including Johnny Cash, Bob Dylan, Suzanne Vega, and Tori Amos.

11. Which Laura Nyro hit did Blood, Sweat & Tears sing at Monterey Pop?

a. "Stoned Soul Picnic"

b. "And When I Die"

c. "Eli's Coming"

d. "Save the Country"

GAME 18 Q10 ANSWER d
Janis Joplin came to San Francisco in 1966 from Port Arthur, Texas, and began singing with Big Brother and the Holding Company. After her inspired performance at Monterey, Joplin became a star. She had two more groups, Kozmic Blues Band and Full Tilt Boogie Band, before she died in 1970 at age twenty-seven.

11. Which Presley hit was first recorded by Big Mama Thornton?

a. "Heartbreak Hotel"

b. "Hound Dog"

c. "Little Sister"

d. "Hunk of Burning Love"

GAME 38 Q10 ANSWER c
Having been raised in the Pentecostal church—and despite the fact that his own church viewed Presley's on-stage gyrations as an affront—Elvis was greatly affected by southern gospel music and recorded several albums of gospel tunes. He often said that he "knew every gospel song there is."

11. Which of these songs was *not* a hit song for Al Green?

a. "Here I Am"

b. "Let's Stay Together"

c. "Let's Get It On"

d. "Livin' for You"

GAME 58 Q10 ANSWER a
D'Angelo is considered one of the first of the "nu soul" singers, who began to blend R&B with soul and hip-hop in the '90s. D'Angelo released his second album, *Voodoo*, five years after *Brown Sugar*. It won a Grammy for Best R&B Album, while the single "Untitled (How Does It Feel)," earned a Best Male R&B Vocal Grammy.

11. What group did singer Tal Bachman's father formerly belong to?

a. Deep Purple

b. Bad Company

c. Led Zeppelin

d. The Guess Who

GAME 78 Q10 ANSWER c
Born David Marley in Kingston, Jamaica, Ziggy learned how to play guitar and drums from musician father Bob Marley, and—along with his siblings—made his record debut in 1985 as a member of the group The Melody Makers. The reggae album *Dragonfly* was Ziggy's first solo attempt.

3. With whom did Kurt Cobain form Nirvana in 1987?

a. Dave Grohl
b. Sean Miller
c. Krist Novoselic
d. Chris Barron

GAME 3 Q2 ANSWER a
Singer Andrew Wood's 1990 death from an overdose came just a month before Mother Love Bone's only album, *Apple,* was released. The group's guitarist, Stone Gossard, and bassist, Jeff Ament, picked up the pieces, found a new front-man vocalist named Eddie Vedder, and started another group called . . . Pearl Jam.

3. In the 1980s, in whose hit song did we learn that "Jenny" could be reached at 867–5309?

a. The Tubes
b. Modern English
c. Flock of Seagulls
d. Tommy Tutone

GAME 23 Q2 ANSWER d
Appearing on the British band's album *Urban Hymns,* "Bittersweet Symphony" was released as a single in 1997—prior to the album's release—and reached #2 on the UK singles chart. Against the band's will, the song was later used in a Nike shoe commercial.

3. "Metal Health (Bang Your Head)" is a song from which group?

a. Whitesnake
b. Ratt
c. Quiet Riot
d. Beastie Boys

GAME 43 Q2 ANSWER b
The group was founded in 1986 by ballet-trained singer/bassist Kip Winger. After "Seventeen" climbed to #26 in the charts, Winger cracked the Top 10 in 1990 with "Miles Away." But in the mid-'90s, MTV's *Beavis and Butt-head* featured next-door geek, Stewart, wearing a Winger t-shirt—the group's been considered lame ever since . . .

3. Canadian power trio Rush wrote a song named after which Mark Twain character?

a. Huckleberry Finn
b. Tom Sawyer
c. Pudd'nhead Wilson
d. Captain Stormfield

GAME 63 Q2 ANSWER d
Morissette's collaboration with song-writer-producer Glen Ballard resulted in *Jagged Little Pill*—her 1995 debut album with Maverick Records. A phenomenal success, the album has sold over 30 million copies and includes such hits as "You Oughta Know" and "Ironic." At the 1996 Grammys, it won Album of the Year and Best Rock Album.

<table>
<tr>
<td>GAME 18</td>
<td>

10. What was the name of Janis Joplin's band at Monterey Pop?

a. Band of Gypsys

b. Kozmic Blues Band

c. Full Tilt Boogie Band

d. Big Brother and the Holding Company

</td>
<td>

GAME 18 Q9 ANSWER b
Although he later had his only Top 40 hit with a cover of Dylan's "All Along the Watchtower" in 1968, Hendrix played "Like a Rolling Stone" at Monterey. During the song's intro, he gave everyone a laugh when he referred to his bassist, Noel Redding, as Bob Dylan's "grandmother." Dylan himself was not at the festival.

</td>
</tr>
<tr>
<td>GAME 38</td>
<td>

10. Which of the following is one of Elvis Presley's gospel albums?

a. *Elvis for Everyone*

b. *That's the Way It Is*

c. *His Hand in Mine*

d. *Long Lonely Highway*

</td>
<td>

GAME 38 Q9 ANSWER a
First performed on Broadway in 1960, *Bye Bye Birdie* tells the story of hip-thrusting rock-and-roll idol Conrad Birdie, who is drafted into the army—to the displeasure of countless teenage girls, as well as Birdie's agent. The agent then comes up with a last-ditch publicity stunt to be played out on *The Ed Sullivan Show*.

</td>
</tr>
<tr>
<td>GAME 58</td>
<td>

10. Which male R&B singer released the debut album *Brown Sugar* in 1995?

a. D'Angelo

b. Maxwell

c. R. Kelly

d. Joe

</td>
<td>

GAME 58 Q9 ANSWER b
Hailing from Atlanta, Georgia, this popular R&B quartet was signed to Puff Daddy's Bad Boy Records in the mid-'90s (before the P. Diddy period . . . and then, y'know, just Diddy). 112 was the opening act for Janet Jackson's All for You Tour in 2001. In 2003, 112 split from Bad Boy Records and signed with Def Jam Records.

</td>
</tr>
<tr>
<td>GAME 78</td>
<td>

10. What 2003 album was released by Bob Marley's son Ziggy?

a. *Boombastic*

b. *Ziggworld*

c. *Dragonfly*

d. *Legalize*

</td>
<td>

GAME 78 Q9 ANSWER d
Born Liv Rundgren, Liv Tyler grew up believing that rock star Todd Rundgren was her biologic father. Then at the age of eleven, when Liv noticed that Mia Tyler, the daughter of Aerosmith's Steven Tyler, looked like her twin, mother Bebe Buell told Liv that Tyler is her real father. The actress then changed her surname.

</td>
</tr>
</table>

GAME 3	**4. What was Pearl Jam's original name?** **a.** Mookie Blaylock **b.** Babe Ruth **c.** Yogi Berra **d.** Micky Dolenz	**GAME 3 Q3 ANSWER c** Lanky long-haired bassist Krist Novoselic was already in place alongside Kurt Cobain when Nirvana recorded its first album, *Bleach* (1989), with Chad Channing on drums. Dave Grohl joined as Nirvana's drummer in 1990, only to become lead singer and guitarist of Foo Fighters shortly after Cobain's untimely death in 1994.
GAME 23	**4. Lou Bega's Latin dance hit is titled "____ No. 5."** **a.** Mambo **b.** Tango **c.** Cha Cha **d.** Salsa	**GAME 23 Q3 ANSWER d** The 1981 song, which was both-written and performed by Tutone, implied that the phone number was real, and had been acquired from a bathroom wall. Unbelievably, this caused many fans to call the number—valid in many area codes—asking for Jenny.
GAME 43	**4. Which metal band recorded the 1989 album *Dirty Rotten Filthy Stinking Rich*?** **a.** Warrant **b.** Poison **c.** Van Halen **d.** Bon Jovi	**GAME 43 Q3 ANSWER c** Lead singer Kevin DuBrow formed Quiet Riot in 1975 with guitar-god-in-waiting Randy Rhoads. When Rhoads left to become Ozzy Osbourne's guitarist in 1979, the group replaced him with Carlos Cavazo. In 1982, Rhoads was killed in a plane crash. Devastated by his death, Quiet Riot dedicated its 1984 song "Thunderbird" to him.
GAME 63	**4. What is the only Neil Young tune to reach #1 on the charts?** **a.** "Heart of Gold" **b.** "Helpless" **c.** "Sugar Mountain" **d.** "Old Man"	**GAME 63 Q3 ANSWER b** Rush opened its 1981 quadruple-platinum album *Moving Pictures* with this brash and energetic song named after one of Twain's best-known characters. Literary references are nothing new for Rush—its drummer and song lyricist Neil Peart is a voracious reader who has referenced everything from Ayn Rand to Shakespeare over the years.

9. Which Bob Dylan song did Jimi Hendrix perform at the Monterey Pop Festival?

a. "All Along the Watchtower"

b. "Like a Rolling Stone"

c. "Mr. Tambourine Man"

d. "My Back Pages"

GAME 18 Q8 ANSWER c
This American folk song was the group's #1 hit in 1964. By 1967, however, the original line-up of The Animals had already broken up. Lead vocalist Eric Burdon had the New Animals perform his song "San Franciscan Nights" at Monterey Pop. Bassist Bryan "Chas" Chandler had been Jimi Hendrix's manager since 1966.

9. What musical was supposedly based on Elvis Presley's experience with the draft?

a. *Bye Bye Birdie*

b. *Soldier in the Rain*

c. *Singing in the Rain*

d. *Flaming Star*

GAME 38 Q8 ANSWER a
In the 1957 film *Loving You*—the one in which Presley received his very first screen kiss—Presley plays rock singer Deke Rivers, who falls for a girl in the band. The song "Teddy Bear," featured in the film, quickly rose to #1 on the pop, country, and R&B charts.

9. Which R&B group had a 2001 hit with "Peaches and Cream"?

a. K-Ci and JoJo

b. 112

c. Bone Thugs-n-Harmony

d. Jagged Edge

GAME 58 Q8 ANSWER d
"Superfly," "People Get Ready," and "Gypsy Woman" are all by R&B legend Curtis Mayfield. "Shaft" was written and performed by Hayes for the 1971 film of the same name. The song won an Academy Award that year for Best Original Song. A new *Shaft* movie was made in 2000 starring Samuel L. Jackson. It features Hayes in a small cameo.

9. Which Liv Tyler movie soundtrack featured the Aerosmith song "I Don't Want to Miss a Thing"?

a. *Heavy*

b. *That Thing You Do!*

c. *Stealing Beauty*

d. *Armageddon*

GAME 78 Q8 ANSWER d
In the early '90s, Gilliam Chynna Phillips was a singer in the all-girl band Wilson Phillips along with Carnie and Wendy Wilson—the daughters of Beach Boy Brian Wilson. Chynna has also acted in films such as 1988's *Caddyshack II* and 1997's *The Invisible Kid*.

GAME 3

5. Which member of Alice in Chains had a cameo in the film *Jerry Maguire*?

a. Layne Staley
b. Sean Kinney
c. Mike Inez
d. Jerry Cantrell

GAME 3 Q4 ANSWER a
Nope, not Micky Dolenz! Actually, Mookie Blaylock was a popular NBA basketball player. The band was forced to change its name to Pearl Jam in honor of Eddie Vedder's great grandmother Pearl's allegedly hallucinogenic homemade jam. *Ten,* the group's first album title, is said to be a reference to Mookie Blaylock's jersey number.

GAME 23

5. "Hey! Baby" hit #1 in 1962 for which one-hit wonder?

a. The Buckinghams
b. Bruce Channel
c. Gene Pitney
d. Jimmy Gilmer

GAME 23 Q4 ANSWER a
This famous mambo dance song was originally composed and recorded by Perez Prado in 1952. Bega's 1999 version, which included added lyrics, was a hit in over a dozen countries. Since then, many variations of the song have been performed.

GAME 43

5. "Wait" was one offering of which late '80s metal band?

a. White Lion
b. Yellow Lion
c. Tawny Lion
d. Black Lion

GAME 43 Q4 ANSWER a
On the eve of hair metal's demise, Warrant appeared in 1989 with a decidedly cheerful sound that was like Van Halen's early days with David Lee Roth in the late '70s. Even though their second album, *Cherry Pie,* spawned a Top 10 hit in 1990 with the title track, it wasn't long before bands like Nirvana and Pearl Jam changed things.

GAME 63

5. In which film does Alanis Morissette appear as the "Almighty"?

a. *Mallrats*
b. *Chasing Amy*
c. *Clerks*
d. *Dogma*

GAME 63 Q4 ANSWER a
After having numerous hits with Buffalo Springfield and then Crosby, Stills, Nash & Young, Neil Young recorded "Heart of Gold," which jettisoned both his solo career and the 1972 album *Harvest* to the top. In the 1984 film *Iceman,* Timothy Hutton plays an anthropologist who sings "Heart of Gold" with a prehistoric caveman.

---

8. According to The Animals, what had "been the ruin of many a poor boy" in New Orleans?

a. "Mardi Gras"

b. "The French Quarter"

c. "House of the Rising Sun"

d. "Dixieland Jazz"

GAME 18 Q7 ANSWER c
The Association kicked off the Monterey Pop Festival with this song. Reaching #7 on the charts a year earlier in 1966, this jaunty tune faced some resistance from radio programmers who believed it was about marijuana. Any worries about the group soon disappeared when its next single, "Cherish," went to #1 later that year.

---

8. Which was Presley's first color film, and the one to feature "Teddy Bear"?

a. *Loving You*

b. *Speedway*

c. *Blue Hawaii*

d. *Viva Las Vegas*

GAME 38 Q7 ANSWER d
Written by George Weiss, Hugo Peretti, and Luigi Creatore, "Can't Help Falling in Love" peaked at #2 on the Billboard charts when it was released in 1961. Since then, numerous artists—from Perry Como to Al Martino to UB40—have recorded their own version of this classic ballad.

---

8. Which of the following songs was written by Isaac Hayes?

a. "Superfly"

b. "People Get Ready"

c. "Gypsy Woman"

d. "Shaft"

GAME 58 Q7 ANSWER b
"My Boo" also won a Grammy in 2005 for Best R&B Performance by a Duo. On her own, Keys is no stranger to Grammys. She won Album of the Year Grammys for her first two albums—*Songs in A Minor* (2002) and *The Diary of Alicia Keys* (2005). She also wrote a best-selling book of poems and lyrics in 2004 called *Tears for Water*.

---

8. What is the name of John and Michelle Phillips' singing daughter?

a. Shelby

b. Gabrielle

c. Skyler

d. Chynna

GAME 78 Q7 ANSWER a
Lil' Romeo records teen-friendly hip-hop music on father Master P's No Limit record label. He had a #1 hit in 2001 with the song "My Baby"; had a small role in the 2001 movie *Max Keeble's Big Move* and the 2004 movie *Honey*; and starred in his own Nickelodeon television show, *Romeo!*

---

6. Which song by Screaming Trees is on the *Singles* soundtrack?

a. "Seasons"
b. "Dyslexic Heart"
c. "Birth Ritual"
d. "Nearly Lost You"

GAME 3 Q5 ANSWER d
Appearing briefly as a Kinko's employee, AIC lead guitarist, Jerry Cantrell, also showed up with his fellow bandmates in *Singles*, a film that stands as Cameron Crowe's valentine to the Seattle grunge movement. The group's lead singer Layne Staley died from an alleged drug overdose in April 2002.

6. One-hit wonder Meredith Brooks of "Bitch" fame was formerly a member of which group?

a. Garbage
b. The Graces
c. The Waitresses
d. The Breeders

GAME 23 Q5 ANSWER b
Bruce Channel had been performing "Hey! Baby" for two years before he recorded the hit with harmonica player Delbert McClinton. The harmonica break in the song is said to have inspired John Lennon's harmonica playing on "Love Me Do" and later recordings. Channel's only other Top 20 recording was 1968's "Keep On."

6. Which band's only #1 single to date is "Love Bites" from the 1987 album *Hysteria*?

a. Cinderella
b. Def Leppard
c. J. Geils Band
d. Aerosmith

GAME 43 Q5 ANSWER a
White Lion was formed in 1983 in New York City. Reaching #8 on the pop charts, "Wait" was the first single from the group's second album, *Pride* (1987). As the opening act for KISS that year, White Lion also scored big with "When the Children Cry," which reached #3 on the charts and epitomized the late '80s "power ballad."

6. The Barenaked Ladies sing about which TV series in the #1 hit "One Week"?

a. *The X-Files*
b. *Scooby Doo*
c. *The Blair Witch Project*
d. *When Animals Attack*

GAME 63 Q5 ANSWER d
All of these movies were directed by Kevin Smith, but it was *Dogma* (1999) that had Morissette cast in the role of God. Although best known as a singer, Morissette is no stranger to acting—she was a child actor on Canadian TV, and has appeared in many music videos and TV shows, including *Sex and the City* and *Curb Your Enthusiasm*.

7. What was The Association's first hit?

a. "Get Off of My Cloud"
b. "Mr. Tambourine Man"
c. "Along Comes Mary"
d. "Monday, Monday"

GAME 18 Q6 ANSWER a
None other than jazz great Miles Davis recommended this folk-rock group to Columbia Records, who signed them in 1964. Though the group made great music, there was a lot of tension between Byrds guitarists Roger McGuire and David Crosby. Not long after the Monterey show, Crosby left the group and was replaced by Gram Parsons.

7. In which movie did Elvis Presley sing "Can't Help Falling in Love"?

a. *Clambake*
b. *Jailhouse Rock*
c. *Double Trouble*
d. *Blue Hawaii*

GAME 38 Q6 ANSWER b
"Jailhouse Rock," a Leiber and Stoller song, is featured in the 1957 movie of the same name—a movie that is widely regarded as being one of Presley's best films. When the single of "Jailhouse Rock/Treat Me Nice" was released in September 1957, it skyrocketed to #1 on the Billboard charts.

7. In 2004, whose duet with Usher, "My Boo," hit #1 on the US singles chart?

a. Macy Gray
b. Alicia Keys
c. Beyonce
d. Lil' Mo

GAME 58 Q6 ANSWER c
In that episode, Charlie sits at a piano with Davy and shows him the difference between "Motown soul" and "white soul." Charlie Smalls went on to write the '70s soul musical *The Wiz*, portions of which I heard Smalls play in Davy's living room back in the day.

7. Who is the famous father of rapper Lil' Romeo?

a. Master P
b. DMX
c. Jay-Z
d. Mike Jones

GAME 78 Q6 ANSWER c
After Julian's debut album *Valotte* was released, he made his first-ever tour in 1985. The tour was documented as part of *Stand By Me: A Portrait of Julian Lennon*—a film begun by director Sam Peckinpah and, after Peckinpah's death, directed by producer Martin Lewis.

Answers are in right-hand boxes on page 66.

7. Which Stone Temple Pilots' (STP) song is *not* from the band's first album?

a. "Vasoline"

b. "Creep"

c. "Plush"

d. "Dead & Bloated"

GAME 3 Q6 ANSWER d
Screaming Trees was a Seattle-based group known for infighting back when it was formed in 1983. Although it played a big role in shaping grunge music, the group spent much of the early '90s on hiatus. Drummer Barrett Martin played with Alice in Chains' Layne Staley and Pearl Jam's Mike McCready in the side project *Mad Season*.

---

7. What was the only Top 10 hit for rapper Young MC?

a. "Rump Shaker"

b. "Around the Way Girl"

c. "Just a Friend"

d. "Bust a Move"

GAME 23 Q6 ANSWER b
"Bitch" was Meredith Brooks' first single, and not only became a hit, reaching #2 in May 1997, but also garnered the singer-songwriter a Grammy nomination for Best Female Rock Vocal Performance. In the song, Brooks lists "bitch" as being only one of many aspects of herself.

---

7. Robbin Crosby was a guitarist with which band?

a. Hole

b. Ratt

c. Scorpions

d. Black Sabbath

GAME 43 Q6 ANSWER b
Though this ballad went to #1 on the pop charts, most metal fans prefer other hits from *Hysteria,* like "Pour Some Sugar on Me" (reached #2) and "Armageddon It" (went to #3). Meanwhile, the J. Geils Band had a hit single in 1980 called "Love Stinks." Adam Sandler did a hilarious version of it in the 1998 film *The Wedding Singer*.

---

7. Record producer Robert John "Mutt" Lange is married to which Canadian chanteuse?

a. Shania Twain

b. k.d. lang

c. Celine Dion

d. Holly Cole

GAME 63 Q6 ANSWER a
This super-hyper hit, which made the group famous outside Canada, contains numerous lyrical references, including: Aquaman, wasabe, Leann Rhimes, Bert Kaempfert, Chinese chicken, Harrison Ford, Sting, Snickers, Kurasawa, samurai, anime, and Birchmount Stadium. "One Week" is featured in the 1999 comedy *American Pie*.

---

6. What was The Byrds' final album with David Crosby?

a. *Younger Than Yesterday*

b. *Turn! Turn! Turn!*

c. *Fifth Dimension*

d. *Mr. Tambourine Man*

GAME 18 Q5 ANSWER c
With thirty-two acts in place, Monterey was the first big music festival of the late '60s. It promoted a new openness in music, as groups like The Association and The Grateful Dead performed on the same bill as R&B singer Lou Rawls and India's Ravi Shankar. By 1970, the Isle of Wight Festival featured forty-nine different groups.

6. Which of these songs was first recorded by Elvis Presley?

a. "Folsom Prison Blues"

b. "Jailhouse Rock"

c. "Chain Gang"

d. "Ladies Love Outlaws"

GAME 38 Q5 ANSWER d
Written by Jerry Leiber and Mike Stoller, "Bossa Nova Baby" is featured in the King's 1963 movie *Fun in Acapulco*, which also boasts Ursula Andress. Although the plot of the movie is far-fetched, the song made it to #8 on the US Top 40 singles chart.

6. Which R&B songwriter taught Davy Jones about soul music in an episode of the Monkees' TV show?

a. Marvin Gaye

b. Aretha Franklin

c. Charlie Smalls

d. Billy Preston

GAME 58 Q5 ANSWER d
Born as Samuel Cook in 1931 in Mississippi, Cooke did much more in his career than add a letter to his last name. In 1959, he started his own record label (SAR Records), and then his own music publishing and management companies. In circumstances that remain unclear, Cooke was shot and died in 1964 at age thirty-three.

6. For what son of a famous father was "Too Late for Goodbyes" a Top 20 hit?

a. Frank Sinatra, Jr.

b. Gary Lewis

c. Julian Lennon

d. Hank Williams, Jr.

GAME 78 Q5 ANSWER a
The daughter of Ozzy and Sharon Osbourne, singer Kelly Lee Osbourne first came to public attention in the 2002—2005 reality TV series *The Osbournes*. Kelly's 2002 debut album was released to only moderate sales, but a later single—a father-daughter duet of the Black Sabbath song "Changes"—hit #1 on the UK charts.

8. What is the Foo Fighters second album?

a. *There Is Nothing Left to Lose*

b. *Monkey Wrench*

c. *The Colour and the Shape*

d. *One by One*

GAME 3 Q7 ANSWER a
First playing together in 1990 under the name Mighty Joe Young, STP found great success in the fall of 1992 when its first album, *Core*, was released and its first video for the song "Plush" scored big with MTV viewers. The group's second album, *Purple* (1994), produced the hit song "Vasoline." STP stayed together until 2003.

8. Which 1980s New Wave band is best known for its only Top 20 hit, "True"?

a. OMD

b. Spandau Ballet

c. a-ha

d. Simple Minds

GAME 23 Q7 ANSWER d
The 1989 hit "Bust a Move" won a Grammy Award for best Rap Record. Not long afterwards, Young MC's career took a dive. Yet the rapper—whose real name is Marvin Young—did collaborate with Tone-Loc on the hits "Wild Thing" and "Funky Cold Medina."

8. Which heavy metal band had its only hit with "Turn Up the Radio" in 1985?

a. Autograph

b. Mr. Big

c. Danzig

d. Accept

GAME 43 Q7 ANSWER b
Six and a half feet tall, Crosby was a founding member of this '80s glam-metal band, whose first big hit was "Round and Round" from the 1984 album *Out of the Cellar*. (The MTV video of the song featured comic legend Milton Berle dressed in drag.) An admitted heroin addict, Crosby died at forty-two after a long battle with AIDS.

8. Which of the following Canadian actors has recorded two albums?

a. Jim Carrey

b. William Shatner

c. Donald Sutherland

d. Mike Myers

GAME 63 Q7 ANSWER a
Lange started out as a successful music producer of heavy metal bands, including AC/DC and Def Leppard. Later, he produced albums with Foreigner, The Cars, and Bryan Adams. Shortly after marrying Twain in 1993, he produced her second album, *The Woman in Me*. It won the 1995 Grammy for Best Country Album and brought Shania fame.

5. How many different musical groups performed at Monterey Pop?

a. 49
b. 31
c. 32
d. 67

GAME 18 Q4 ANSWER b
This folky foursome started out in New York, but soon moved to California and became known officially as The Mamas and the Papas in 1965. Group leader John Phillips co-financed the Monterey Pop Festival with record producer Lou Adler.

---

5. In 1963, which of the following dance tunes gave Elvis Presley a Top 10 hit?

a. "Mashed Potato Time"
b. "Do the Clam"
c. "The Locomotion"
d. "Bossa Nova Baby"

GAME 38 Q4 ANSWER c
"Burning Love" was released as a single on August 1, 1972, and on October 21 of that year, it was the #2 song on the singles chart. The recording has the distinction of being Presley's last Top 10 hit on the Billboard Hot 100 chart, and one of the last real rock songs that Presley released.

---

5. In 1957, Sam Cooke hit #1 on the charts with his second single:

a. "People Get Ready"
b. "The Masquerade Is Over"
c. "Chances Are"
d. "You Send Me"

GAME 58 Q4 ANSWER b
Along with songs like "I Gotta Be Me" and "Mr. Bojangles," "The Candy Man" is a song that is nearly always associated with Sammy Davis, Jr. "The Candy Man" was written by Leslie Bricusse and Anthony Newley for the popular 1971 film *Willy Wonka & the Chocolate Factory*. Sammy Davis, Jr.'s version was a #1 pop hit in June 1972.

---

5. What is the name of Kelly Osbourne's 2002 debut album?

a. *Shut Up*
b. *Buzz Off*
c. *Whatever*
d. *Get Lost*

GAME 78 Q4 ANSWER c
By age thirteen, Rufus was touring with his mother, folk-music legend Kate McGarrigle; sister Martha; and aunt Anna, as the McGarrigle Sisters and Family. Although he has released several solo albums—including 2001's *Poses*—the singer-songwriter still often performs with his sister on backup vocals.

9. Bassist Matt Lukin was a founding member of which grunge group?

a. Mudhoney

b. Green River

c. Mol Triffid

d. Screaming Trees

GAME 3 Q8 ANSWER c
Formed by ex-Nirvana drummer Dave Grohl, Foo Fighters became one of the most successful groups of the '90s. This 1997 album featured the tracks "My Hero" (inspired by Grohl's friendship with Nirvana frontman Kurt Cobain), "Monkey Wrench," and "Everlong," which Grohl performed live on Howard Stern's radio show in 2000.

9. Rockwell, whose single hit was "Somebody's Watching Me," is the son of which famous man?

a. Clive Davis

b. John Hammond

c. Jerry Wexler

d. Berry Gordy

GAME 23 Q8 ANSWER b
A popular British band in the 1980s, Spandau Ballet was originally called The Makers. Its 1983 album *True* topped the charts on both sides of the Atlantic and launched the hit single of the same name. But the group's followup album *Parade* was panned when it was released in 1984.

9. Which of the following '80s hair metal bands was Japanese?

a. Loudness

b. Armored Saint

c. Venom

d. Blue Oyster Cult

GAME 43 Q8 ANSWER a
After winning fans as the opening band during Van Halen's 1984 tour, Autograph signed a record deal with RCA Records and released its first album, *Sign In, Please,* in 1984. "Turn Up the Radio" was a chart hit and became an MTV video favorite, featuring the incredible guitar playing of Steve Lynch. Autograph broke up in 1987.

9. Which 1970 hit lifted Anne Murray from relative obscurity to international stardom?

a. "Walk Right Back"

b. "He Thinks I Still Care"

c. "Son of a Rotten Gambler"

d. "Snowbird"

GAME 63 Q8 ANSWER b
Thirty-six years after releasing *The Transformed Man* (his "so-bad-it's-good" album), Shatner decided to give music another shot. Filled with Shatner's introspective talk-sing vocals, and arranged and produced by singer-songwriter Ben Folds, *Has Been* was released in 2004 to largely positive reviews.

4. John and Michelle Phillips, Cass Elliot, and _____ were The Mamas and the Papas.

a. Barry McGuire
b. Denny Doherty
c. Felix Cavaliere
d. Eric Carmen

GAME 18 Q3 ANSWER d
This 1965 UK hit with the classic line "Hope I die before I get old" established The Who as a rock band with a harder and more aggressive attitude than The Beatles and The Rolling Stones combined. After the group's explosive show at Monterey, its classic song "I Can See for Miles" reached #9 in the US in October 1967.

4. Which of these Elvis Presley songs was a 1970s hit?

a. "A Big Hunk O' Love"
b. "Love Me Tender"
c. "Burning Love"
d. "I Need Your Love Tonight"

GAME 38 Q3 ANSWER c
Presley was born in a two-room house in East Tupelo on January 8, 1935. When he was thirteen, his family moved to Memphis, Tennessee, eventually living in a public housing development. There, Presley took up the guitar, practicing in the basement laundry room and playing with the other musicians who lived there.

4. Which of the following songs is *not* associated with Ray Charles?

a. "Georgia on My Mind"
b. "The Candy Man"
c. "Hit the Road, Jack"
d. "I Got a Woman"

GAME 58 Q3 ANSWER c
Released in 1996, *Secrets* is Toni Braxton's second album and features the #1 hit pop songs "You're Makin' Me High" and "Un-Break My Heart." *The Velvet Rope* is Janet Jackson's 1997 album. *Fear of Flying*, released in 2000, is Mya's second album. And the 1994 *CrazySexyCool* is girl-group trio TLC's second album.

4. Singer Rufus Wainwright is the son of which famous folk legend?

a. Charles Wainwright
b. Bailey Wainwright Jr.
c. Loudon Wainwright III
d. Paris Wainwright IV

GAME 78 Q3 ANSWER a
Although Natalie enjoyed several hits in the '70s and '80s, she achieved her greatest success with the 1991 album *Unforgettable . . . with Love*, which features new arrangements of father Nat King Cole's greatest hits. Included on the album is a duet with her father, created by splicing a recording of his vocals onto the track.

10. Which of the following grunge albums was *not* released in 1993?

a. *In Utero*

b. *Superunknown*

c. *Vs.*

d. *Siamese Dream*

GAME 3 Q9 ANSWER a
Mudhoney stands as some kind of Seattle grunge matrix point—Pearl Jam members Jeff Ament and Stone Gossard played in an early version of the group called Green River during the mid-'80s. When bassist Matt Lukin quit Mudhoney in 1999, Pearl Jam had already immortalized him with the song "Lukin" from their third album, *No Code*.

---

10. The disco number "Turn the Beat Around" was recorded by which one-hit wonder?

a. Alicia Bridges

b. Vicki Sue Robinson

c. Anita Ward

d. Loleatta Holloway

GAME 23 Q9 ANSWER d
Born Kennedy Gordy, Rockwell secured a contract with the Motown label without the knowledge of his father, Motown founder Berry Gordy. His single featured vocals by Michael and Germaine Jackson, and was a Top 10 pop hit in the US. But when later singles performed poorly, Rockwell's career with Motown ended.

---

10. Richie Sambora is the guitarist for which band?

a. Van Halen

b. Whitesnake

c. Bon Jovi

d. Red Hot Chili Peppers

GAME 43 Q9 ANSWER a
Formed in 1981 by virtuoso guitarist Akira Takasaki, Loudness was first introduced to America after signing with Atlantic Records in 1985. The group's first album released here, *Thunder in the East*, is really the fifth album of its career. While Blue Oyster Cult is not Japanese, the band did record a song in 1977 called "Godzilla."

---

10. k.d. lang sang with which fellow Canadian singer-songwriter on the 1993 hit "Calling All Angels"?

a. Jane Siberry

b. Gordon Lightfoot

c. Celine Dion

d. Bryan Adams

GAME 63 Q9 ANSWER d
"Snowbird" hit the US Top 10 pop charts and crossed over to become a country hit as well. Since then, Anne Murray has had eleven #1 country hits. I first saw her perform in 1973 at the Troubadour in LA. After that show, a photo was taken of Anne with Harry Nilsson, John Lennon, Alice Cooper, and me. It's one I've always treasured.

---

3. The Who recorded this song with a stuttering vocal that became a youth anthem:

a. "Won't Get Fooled Again"
b. "I'm the Face"
c. "Substitute"
d. "My Generation"

GAME 18 Q2 ANSWER d
Rumor has it that Jimi Hendrix and The Who guitarist Pete Townshend tossed a coin backstage to see who would play first. The Who went first and smashed all their equipment. When Jimi came on-stage, we heard the most amazing guitar playing ever—he even set his guitar on fire as a sacrifice!

---

3. Elvis Presley lived and died in Tennessee, but he was born in:

a. Louisiana
b. Kentucky
c. Mississippi
d. Arkansas

GAME 38 Q2 ANSWER b
Presley appeared six times on the *Dorsey Brothers Stage Show*. But perhaps his most famous television appearance occurred his third time on *The Ed Sullivan Show*, when host Sullivan, in response to controversy over the singer's trademark hip gyrations, showed Presley only from the waist up.

---

3. Which of the following albums is by Toni Braxton?

a. *The Velvet Rope*
b. *Fear of Flying*
c. *Secrets*
d. *CrazySexyCool*

GAME 58 Q2 ANSWER b
Since first reaching the top of the charts in 1990 with "Vision of Love," Mariah Carey has recorded sixteen more #1 songs in her career to date. "We Belong Together" was the second single from her fourteenth album, *The Emancipation of Mimi*, and it represents a comeback of sorts from the failure of *Glitter*, her 2001 album.

---

3. Which singer won six Grammys for an album featuring a duet with his or her parent?

a. Natalie Cole
b. Lisa Marie Presley
c. Arlo Guthrie
d. Wynonna Judd

GAME 78 Q2 ANSWER c
The daughter of Paul and Linda McCartney, Stella had already worked with designer Christian Lacroix by the time of her 1995 graduation from London's Central Saint Martins College of Art & Design. She now produces her own line of clothing in association with Gucci.

GAME 3

11. Which grunge band and album is mismatched?

a. Pearl Jam/*Yield*

b. Nirvana/*Incesticide*

c. Soundgarden/*Kerplunk*

d. Smashing Pumpkins/*Gish*

GAME 3 Q10 ANSWER b
Soundgarden was the only hold-out, waiting until 1994 to release its album *Superunknown*. But the height of grunge was definitely in 1993, and it took Kurt Cobain's death in 1994 to bring the fun and excitement of the grunge scene to a sudden and gloomy halt. Before too long, *NSYNC and the Backstreet Boys were topping the charts.

GAME 23

11. "Eve of Destruction" singer Barry McGuire once sang for which of the following groups?

a. The Grass Roots

b. The New Christy Minstrels

c. The Weavers

d. Brothers Four

GAME 23 Q10 ANSWER b
Vicki Sue Robinson was born to professional singers who encouraged her to pursue a career in the entertainment industry. Prior to her 1977 hit, she joined the Broadway casts of both *Hair* and *Jesus Christ Superstar*. Although subsequent singles were less successful than "Turn the Beat Around," Robinson remained a performer for many years.

GAME 43

11. Which metal band had a chart hit in 1985 with "Summertime Girls"?

a. Mötley Crüe

b. Van Halen

c. Whitesnake

d. Y&T

GAME 43 Q10 ANSWER c
Although first labeled a hair metal band, Bon Jovi has survived better than most groups of that era. Except for bassist Alec John Such, who left the band in 1994, all the original band members are still in place. A talented singer himself, Richie Sambora released his first solo album, *Stranger in This Town*, in 1991.

GAME 63

11. Which Canadian musician appeared in the 1984 film *This Is Spinal Tap*?

a. Geddy Lee

b. Robbie Robertson

c. Bruce Cockburn

d. Paul Shaffer

GAME 63 Q10 ANSWER a
Jane Siberry first achieved popularity during the New Wave years of the early '80s with such hits as "Mimi on the Beach" and "One More Colour." The "Calling All Angels" duet appeared on Siberry's own 1993 album, *When I Was a Boy*, and re-recorded in 2000 for the soundtrack of the film *Pay It Forward*.

GAME 18

2. Which left-handed guitar player stole the show at the Monterey Pop?

a. Paul McCartney

b. Bob Dylan

c. B.B. King

d. Jimi Hendrix

GAME 18 Q1 ANSWER d
Peter Tork and I were both at the festival. Otis Redding, along with newcomers Janis Joplin and Jimi Hendrix, was fantastic. His version of "Try a Little Tenderness" is as powerful today as it was then. He recorded his big hit, "(Sitting on) the Dock of the Bay," right before his fatal plane crash in December 1967.

GAME 38

2. Which song did Elvis Presley sing in his 1956 TV debut?

a. "Jailhouse Rock"

b. "Heartbreak Hotel"

c. "In the Ghetto"

d. "Hunk of Burning Love"

GAME 38 Q1 ANSWER a
When master promoter Colonel Tom Parker took control of Presley's career, one of his first acts was to negotiate the now-famous deal with RCA. Less than a year later, Elvis Presley reached stardom when his double-sided "Don't Be Cruel/Hound Dog" spent eleven weeks at the top of the charts.

GAME 58

2. Which singer's "We Belong Together" was a #1 hit in 2005?

a. Tyrese

b. Mariah Carey

c. Usher

d. Faith Evans

GAME 58 Q1 ANSWER d
Both "Superstition" (1972) and "I Wish" (1977) hit #1 for Stevie Wonder, while "My Cherie Amour" went to #4 in 1969. Meanwhile, Lionel Richie's band, The Commodores, enjoyed success with the 1977 ballad "Easy" before achieving its first #1 pop hit with "Three Times a Lady" in 1978.

GAME 78

2. Paul McCartney's daughter _____ has a flourishing career as a fashion designer.

a. Janet

b. Natasha

c. Stella

d. Mia

GAME 78 Q1 ANSWER c
Jakob Dylan, son of Bob Dylan, plays guitar and is lead vocalist for The Wallflowers. The group's second album, 1996's *Bringing Down the Horse*, yielded its sole #1 hit single—"One Headlight." Other hits featured on the album include "6th Avenue Heartache" and "Difference."

12. Which instrument did Jimmy Chamberlin play for The Smashing Pumpkins?

a. Keyboard

b. Cello

c. Drums

d. Bass guitar

GAME 3 Q11 ANSWER c
Kerplunk (1991) is the second album recorded by proto-punk group Green Day before its third album *Dookie* was released to major breakout success in 1994. Ten years after winning its first Grammy for Best Alternative Music Performance in 1995, Green Day won a Best Rock Album Grammy for its ninth album *American Idiot*.

---

12. "Exordium and Terminus" is the subtitle of which dark one-hit wonder tune?

a. "Eve of Destruction"

b. "In the Year 2525"

c. "Sound of Silence"

d. "Wild in the Streets"

GAME 23 Q11 ANSWER b
Oklahoma-born singer-songwriter Barry McGuire joined The New Christy Minstrels in 1962, and wrote the group's greatest hit single, "Green, Green." His single "Eve of Destruction," written by P.F. Sloan, hit #1 on The Billboard Top 40 in 1965.

---

12. What hard-rocking band had minor hits in 1988 with "Edge of a Broken Heart" and "Cryin'"?

a. Vixen

b. Bon Jovi

c. Poison

d. Guns N' Roses

GAME 43 Q11 ANSWER d
While Van Halen sang about "Beautiful Girls" in 1979 and Mötley Crüe celebrated "Girls, Girls, Girls" in 1987, Y&T rocked with this song (and video) hit. This was the only studio-recorded song on the group's live album, *Open Fire*. Y&T, which stands for "Yesterday and Today," is still led by lead guitarist/singer Dave Meniketti.

---

12. Whose 2004 album *Hymns of the 49th Parallel* is a tribute to her fellow Canadian artists?

a. k.d. lang

b. Joni Mitchell

c. Anne Murray

d. Sarah McLachlan

GAME 63 Q11 ANSWER d
Playing Artie Fufkin, hapless promo man for Polymer Records, Shaffer's performance is a highlight of this film. Over the years, Shaffer's career has included acting, comedy, singing, and music. Before joining *The Late Show with David Letterman* as music director in 1983, Shaffer played piano in the *Saturday Night Live* band from 1975 to 1980.

---

1. Which soul man performed at the 1967 Monterey Pop Festival?

a. Smokey Robinson

b. Isaac Hayes

c. Marvin Gaye

d. Otis Redding

The answer to this question is on:

page 78, top frame, right side.

1. What company purchased Elvis Presley's contract for $40,000 from Sun Records in 1955?

a. RCA

b. Capitol

c. Warner Bros.

d. Decca

The answer to this question is on:

page 78, second frame, right side.

1. All of these songs were Top 10 pop hits for Stevie Wonder except:

a. "I Wish"

b. "My Cherie Amour"

c. "Superstition"

d. "Three Times a Lady"

The answer to this question is on:

page 78, third frame, right side.

1. Which rock offspring is the lead singer of The Wallflowers?

a. Elijah Allman

b. Frank Sinatra, Jr.

c. Jakob Dylan

d. Ben Taylor

The answer to this question is on:

page 78, bottom frame, right side.

GAME 4

GRAB BAG

Turn to page 83 for the first question.

GAME 3 Q12 ANSWER c

For a time, Chamberlin's role as the group's drummer was threatened by his struggles with heroin. Fired in 1996 by Pumpkins' leader Billy Corgan, Chamberlin was brought back into the group for its final album, *Machina: The Machines of God* (2000). In 2003, Chamberlin played drums again for Corgan in his next band, Zwan.

GAME 24

GRAB BAG

Turn to page 83 for the first question.

GAME 23 Q12 ANSWER b

Produced by Denny Zager and Richard Evans in 1964, this hit was originally released on a small local record label. After being popularized by a Texas radio station, it was picked up by RCA Records. The apocalyptic tune remained at #1 on the Billboard Charts for six weeks in 1969.

GAME 44

GRAB BAG

Turn to page 83 for the first question.

GAME 43 Q12 ANSWER a

First formed in Minnesota in 1980 by guitarist Jan Kuehnemund, Vixen finally started to make the scene after moving to Los Angeles in 1985. The all-female group also had a hit with "How Much Love" from its 1990 album *Rev It Up*. The group split up in 1991, but reunited in 1997, and again in 2001.

GAME 64

GRAB BAG

Turn to page 83 for the first question.

GAME 63 Q12 ANSWER a

The album is k.d. lang's sixth. In it, she performs songs by Neil Young, Joni Mitchell, Leonard Cohen, and others. She says, "These songs are part of my cultural fabric, my Canadian soundtrack." *Hymns of the 49th Parallel* reached the #2 spot on the Canadian Billboard chart. In addition to singing, lang is a talented guitarist and pianist.

GAME 18

Monterey International Pop Festival

*Turn to page 80
for the first question.*

Turn to page 80
for the first question.

GAME 17 Q12 ANSWER d
Famous for its sing-along lyric that questions "What are we fighting for?" this song quickly became the anthem to a profoundly anti-war sentiment that was alive and growing as the Vietnam "conflict" continued to escalate. Country Joe McDonald also played at Woodstock '99.

GAME 38

Elvis Is in the House!

*Turn to page 80
for the first question.*

Turn to page 80
for the first question.

GAME 37 Q12 ANSWER a
Consisting of Lamont Dozier and brothers Brian Holland and Edward Holland, Jr., this team was responsible for much of the Motown sound of the '60s. Before leaving Motown in 1968, Holland-Dozier-Holland produced twenty-five Top 10 hit singles, from "Stop! In the Name of Love" to "It's the Same Old Song."

GAME 58

R&B

*Turn to page 80
for the first question.*

Turn to page 80
for the first question.

GAME 57 Q12 ANSWER c
Soul singer, Flack recorded "The First Time Ever I Saw Your Face" in 1969, but it didn't hit #1 on the pop charts until it was featured in Clint Eastwood's 1971 directorial debut film *Play Misty for Me*. After winning a Record of the Year Grammy for this song in 1972, she won again in 1973 for "Killing Me Softly With His Song"—a tribute to singer Don McLean.

GAME 78

Rock Offspring

*Turn to page 80
for the first question.*

Turn to page 80
for the first question.

GAME 77 Q12 ANSWER a
After radio stations began getting requests for the original recording of the song, from the 1964 album *Wednesday Morning, 3 A.M.*, Wilson dubbed an electric guitar and drums into the track and released it as a single, backed with "We've Got a Groovy Thing Goin'." This turned the folk tune into folk-rock, and the single hit #1 in 1965.

GAME 4	**1.** What song was Janet Jackson singing during the 2004 Super Bowl incident? **a.** "Nasty" **b.** "Rhythm Nation" **c.** "Bye Bye Bye" **d.** "Rock Your Body"	The answer to this question is on: **page 85,** **top frame,** **right side.**
GAME 24	**1.** In what state did Buddy Holly's plane crash occur? **a.** Ohio **b.** Iowa **c.** Illinois **d.** Minnesota	The answer to this question is on: **page 85,** **second frame,** **right side.**
GAME 44	**1.** New Wave group Landscape had an MTV video hit with a song about which movie-screen killer? **a.** Michael Myers **b.** Freddy Krueger **c.** Jason Voorhees **d.** Norman Bates	The answer to this question is on: **page 85,** **third frame,** **right side.**
GAME 64	**1.** Which song is *not* included on the Tears for Fears album *Songs from the Big Chair*? **a.** "Shout" **b.** "Everybody Wants to Rule the World" **c.** "Sowing the Seeds of Love" **d.** "Head Over Heels"	The answer to this question is on: **page 85,** **bottom frame,** **right side.**

GAME 17

12. Who entertained fans at Woodstock with "I-Feel-Like-I'm-Fixin'-to-Die-Rag"?

a. John Sebastian
b. Gordon Lightfoot
c. Arlo Guthrie
d. Country Joe and the Fish

GAME 17 Q11 ANSWER d
The Who played an incredible twenty-four songs, including "Pinball Wizard," "See Me, Feel Me," and an over-the-top version of Eddie Cochran's '50s hit "Summertime Blues." As expected, Pete Townshend smashed his Gibson SG electric guitar during the set, and then casually tossed it into the audience.

GAME 37

12. Which songwriting team wrote the Motown classics "Baby Love" and "Jimmy Mack"?

a. Holland-Dozier-Holland
b. Leiber and Stoller
c. Rodgers and Hart
d. Lennon and McCartney

GAME 37 Q11 ANSWER d
King and Goffin were a young couple when friend Neil Sedaka introduced them to music producer Don Kirshner in 1960. "Will You Love Me Tomorrow" was the first hit they wrote for Kirshner's Aldon Music. Before their breakup, the team produced many more hits, including "Up on the Roof."

GAME 57

12. Which singer won the Grammy for Record of the Year in 1972 and 1973?

a. Carly Simon
b. James Taylor
c. Roberta Flack
d. Carole King

GAME 57 Q11 ANSWER b
"Michelle" is from *Rubber Soul* (1965) and features Paul McCartney on lead vocals. It's also the Beatles' only song to feature French lyrics—although some Italian words found their way into "Sun King" from *Abbey Road* (1969). In 1964, the Fab Four recorded German-language versions of "She Loves You" and "I Want to Hold Your Hand."

GAME 77

12. Who produced Simon & Garfunkel's "The Sound of Silence"?

a. Tom Wilson
b. Phil Ramone
c. Nick Lowe
d. Clive Langer

GAME 77 Q11 ANSWER b
Dr. Dre began producing as a member of the World Class Wreckin' Cru. In 1986, he helped establish the gangsta rap group N.W.A., but left in 1991 to form Death Row Records. Since then, he has produced not only his own albums, but also the work of Snoop Dogg, Eminem, and 50 Cent, and is one of the best-known figures in hip-hop.

GAME 4

2. Alien Ant Farm had a big hit in 2001 with a cover of what 1987 Michael Jackson song?

a. "Bad"

b. "Billie Jean"

c. "Thriller"

d. "Smooth Criminal"

GAME 4 Q1 ANSWER d
Making the phrase "wardrobe malfunction" a permanent part of pop culture, Jackson's performance with Justin Timberlake spurred debates about levels of decency on television. The NFL took no chances in 2005, and hired legendary Beatle Paul McCartney to help America "get back" to where it once belonged.

GAME 24

2. Which band hit its stride at *14:59*?

a. Matchbox Twenty

b. Smash Mouth

c. Limp Bizkit

d. Sugar Ray

GAME 24 Q1 ANSWER b
Ritchie Valens, The Big Bopper, and Buddy Holly played their last concert together on February 2, 1959. Early the next morning, they took off from Mason City, Iowa in a small four-passenger plane and crashed several minutes later. As a result, February 3, 1959 is remembered as "the day the music died."

GAME 44

2. At the 1998 Grammys, a man with the words _____ on his chest interrupted Bob Dylan's set.

a. You Da Man

b. Shag-a-delic

c. Free Tibet

d. Soy Bomb

GAME 44 Q1 ANSWER d
This British synthesizer pop quintet was one of the first groups to have a music video aired on MTV. The black-and-white video featured an eerie man who was dressed as an old woman, just like Anthony Perkins in the Alfred Hitchcock film *Psycho* (1960). "Norman Bates" and "Einstein A Go-Go" were both 1981 UK chart hits for Landscape.

GAME 64

2. Which of the following Tom Petty songs was nominated for a Grammy?

a. "Refugee"

b. "Square One"

c. "You Got Lucky"

d. "The Waiting"

GAME 64 Q1 ANSWER c
Climbing to #2 on the US pop charts, "Sowing the Seeds of Love" was on the group's 1989 album *The Seeds of Love*. Tears for Fears were one of the biggest bands of the '80s, with "Shout" and "Everybody Wants to Rule the World" both going to #1 in the US in 1985. The group is based around founding members Roland Orzabal and Curt Smith.

Answers are in right-hand boxes on page 87.

11. Which group played the most songs in its set at Woodstock?

a. Sly & the Family Stone
b. Ten Years After
c. Mountain
d. The Who

GAME 17 Q10 ANSWER a
Arriving at the local airport, Iron Butterfly demanded that a helicopter be sent for them so they didn't have to battle traffic. The festival organizers said "No, thanks"—but not in those words. The Jeff Beck Group, featuring a young Rod Stewart on vocals, was also set to play Woodstock, but broke up a month before the festival.

11. Who was Carole King's husband and co-writer in the early 1960s?

a. Burt Bacharach
b. Neil Sedaka
c. Phil Spector
d. Gerry Goffin

GAME 37 Q10 ANSWER c
Tommy Boyce and Bobby Hart, who began their collaboration in the early 1960s, also wrote such beloved Monkees tunes as "I Wanna Be Free," "She," and "Valleri." Nearly every original Monkees album includes songs by Boyce and Hart. In 1976, Davy Jones and I teamed up with this prolific duo for a successful album and tour.

11. Which Beatles' tune was the only one to win a Best Song Grammy?

a. "Something"
b. "Michelle"
c. "Yesterday"
d. "The Long and Winding Road"

GAME 57 Q10 ANSWER d
"American Woman" was a #1 hit for The Guess Who in 1970. Nearly thirty years later, Kravitz recorded it especially for the Mike Myers' "Austin Powers" sequel, *The Spy Who Shagged Me*. From 1999 to 2002, Kravitz won four consecutive Best Male Rock Vocal Grammys for the songs "Fly Away," "American Woman," "Again," and "Dig In."

11. Which former member of the rap group N.W.A. produced his own debut solo album *The Chronic*?

a. Yella
b. Dr. Dre
c. Eazy E
d. Ice Cube

GAME 77 Q10 ANSWER c
Rodgers began his career as a sessions guitarist, and then played in the bands The Boys and Chic. When Chic's sound became popular, he began producing records—first for Sister Sledge, and then for Diana Ross, David Bowie, Madonna, and many others. In 1996, Rodgers was named the "Top Producer in the World" by *Billboard Magazine*.

3. John Mayer won a 2004 Grammy for Song of the Year with a tune entitled:

a. "Brothers"

b. "Fathers"

c. "Daughters"

d. "Mothers"

GAME 4 Q2 ANSWER d
Alt-metal favorite Alien Ant Farm hit the charts by turning Jackson's popular dance track from his album *Dangerous* into a song much harder and louder than the original. This song was featured on the group's 2001 album *ANThology*, while its own song "Bug Bites" was featured a year later in the first new Spider-Man film.

3. Which No Doubt song is found on *Rock Steady*?

a. "Hella Good"

b. "Excuse Me Mr."

c. "Don't Speak"

d. "Sunday Morning"

GAME 24 Q2 ANSWER d
After the popularity of their song "Fly" in 1997, critics called Sugar Ray a one-hit wonder. The band's successful third album *14:59*—whose title implied that the group's fifteen minutes of fame were not yet up—was a response to these accusations, and produced the pop hits "Someday" and "Every Morning."

3. Along with The Who and The Beatles, which of the following groups was part of the British invasion of the mid-'60s?

a. Van Halen

b. Bad Company

c. The O'Jays

d. The Yardbirds

GAME 44 Q2 ANSWER d
As he performed his Grammy-nominated song "Love Sick," Dylan was only briefly distracted as a background dancer named Michael Portnoy stood next to him and started to dance and contort wildly before being escorted off the stage. "Love Sick" was next heard on TV in a Victoria's Secret ad—along with a brief cameo by Dylan himself!

3. Brothers Ray and Dave Davies belonged to which British Invasion band?

a. The Smiths

b. The Who

c. The Kinks

d. The Animals

GAME 64 Q2 ANSWER b
Released the very same year that British group Coldplay also put out a song called "Square One," Petty's song was featured in Cameron Crowe's 2005 film *Elizabethtown*. It was nominated for a Grammy in the category of Best Song Written for a Motion Picture. Petty received the Best Male Rock Vocal in 1994 for "You Don't Know How It Feels."

10. Which of the following acts was cancelled from playing at Woodstock ?

a. Iron Butterfly
b. Cream
c. The Doobie Brothers
d. Three Dog Night

GAME 17 Q9 ANSWER b
Yasgur, a dairy farmer, charged admission for the event. Of course, his farm might never have been selected as the location for the concert had it not been for a man named Elliot Tiber, who granted concert organizers the crucial permit needed to put on the public concert.

10. What duo wrote the hits "(I'm Not Your) Stepping Stone" and "Last Train to Clarksville"?

a. Wilson and Phillips
b. Mann and Weil
c. Boyce and Hart
d. Jagger and Richards

GAME 37 Q9 ANSWER d
Pitney began his career writing songs for other artists. But in 1961, longing for a hit of his own, he recorded "(I Wanna) Love My Life Away," which rose to #39. This attracted the attention of songwriters Burt Bacharach and Hal David, who worked with Pitney to produce such hit recordings as "(The Man Who Shot) Liberty Valence."

10. Lenny Kravitz won a 1999 Grammy for his cover of which 1970 rock song?

a. "Smoke on the Water"
b. "Born to Be Wild"
c. "Time Is on My Side"
d. "American Woman"

GAME 57 Q9 ANSWER d
Out of Time gave R.E.M. the Grammy for Best Alternative Album in 1992—it was also the first year an award was given in that category. That year, the group also won the Best Pop Performance Grammy for the #1 single "Losing My Religion." The video for this song also won six MTV Video Music Awards in 1991, including Best Video of the Year.

10. Who produced *Like a Virgin* for Madonna and *Let's Dance* for David Bowie?

a. Don Was
b. Phil Ramone
c. Nile Rodgers
d. Jimmy Jam & Terry Lewis

GAME 77 Q9 ANSWER c
In 1977, Templeman, along with colleague Mo Ostin, convinced Warner Brothers to sign on the then-unknown group Van Halen. Templeman went on to produce the group's albums, establishing them as a best-selling act. Then in 1985, Roth quit Van Halen and persuaded Templeman to produce his first solo project—1986's *Eat 'em and Smile*.

4. Which OutKast song offers an apology for making someone's daughter cry?

a. "Mrs. Robinson"

b. "Ms. Jackson"

c. "Me and Mrs. Jones"

d. "Mr. Tambourine Man"

GAME 4 Q3 ANSWER c
Mayer also won a Grammy that year for Best Male Pop Vocal Performance. Often compared to fellow singer-songwriter Dave Matthews, Mayer went to Berklee School of Music in Boston for a brief time before heading to Atlanta, Georgia, in 1998. In 2005, he toured with bassist Pino Palladino and drummer Steve Jordan as the John Mayer Trio.

4. Which of the following doo-wop groups was racially integrated?

a. The Del-Vikings

b. The Clovers

c. The Moonglows

d. The El Dorados

GAME 24 Q3 ANSWER a
The other songs listed are from the No Doubt 1995 album *Tragic Kingdom,* which allowed the band to achieve mainstream success. In fact, the single "Don't Speak" was the year's most popular radio hit. *Rock Steady* was a later album, appearing in 2001, and produced two Grammy Award-winning singles, including "Hey Baby."

4. Beyoncé Knowles gained fame as the lead singer of which pop music group?

a. The Donnas

b. TLC

c. Destiny's Child

d. The Spice Girls

GAME 44 Q3 ANSWER d
Guitar gods Eric Clapton, Jeff Beck, and Jimmy Page all started with The Yardbirds. Their move towards pop success with "For Your Love" in 1965 drove bluesman Clapton from the band. Beck joined next, and used heavy distortion and feedback in his virtuoso guitar solos. After Page joined in 1966, he and Beck were soon trading leads.

4. Who wrote "Miss Misery," a 1998 Oscar-nominated song from the movie *Good Will Hunting*?

a. Jeff Buckley

b. Mark Mothersbaugh

c. Elliott Smith

d. Bob Dylan

GAME 64 Q3 ANSWER c
Before the '90s gave us the feuding Gallagher brothers of Oasis, the '60s gave us the Davies brothers. Ray and Dave Davies drove The Kinks to rock music excellence despite more than thirty years of fights with promoters, record companies, and each other. Best known for the 1964 hit "You Really Got Me," The Kinks broke up in 1996.

Answers are in right-hand boxes on page 91.

9. Who allowed the use of his property for the '69 Woodstock festival?

a. David Goldbeck

b. Max Yasgur

c. John Sebastian

d. Bob Dylan

GAME 17 Q8 ANSWER d
With arms flailing and face twitching, English blues singer Joe Cocker became famous for his performance of this Beatles' song at Woodstock. He later recorded a cover of "She Came in Through the Bathroom Window," while Aerosmith had a hit in 1978 with "Come Together."

9. Which songwriter wrote "Hello Mary Lou" for Rick Nelson and "He's a Rebel" for The Crystals?

a. Carole King

b. Roy Orbison

c. Phil Spector

d. Gene Pitney

GAME 37 Q8 ANSWER b
Although a singer in his own right, with well over a dozen albums to his credit, for many years, Canadian-born Gordon Lightfoot was best known as a songwriter. Cover versions of his tunes have been recorded by artists such as Bob Dylan, Elvis Presley, Barbra Streisand, and Johnny Cash.

9. Which album earned R.E.M. its first Grammy victory?

a. *Automatic for the People*

b. *Green*

c. *Murmur*

d. *Out of Time*

GAME 57 Q8 ANSWER b
This group's fifth album, *Blood Sugar Sex Magik*, brought it mainstream success. In addition to "Give It Away," the album also made hits of "Under the Bridge," "Breaking the Girl," and "Suck My Kiss." At the 1992 Grammys, the band was given its award in the category of Best Hard Rock Performance With Vocal.

9. Who produced David Lee Roth's first post-Van Halen album?

a. Mo Ostin

b. David Geffen

c. Ted Templeman

d. Norman Whitfield

GAME 77 Q8 ANSWER b
Wilson and Parks first worked together in 1966, when Parks was commissioned by Wilson to write the lyrics for the album *Smile*. In 1995, the two teamed up again for *Orange Crate Art*, with Parks writing the songs and producing, and Wilson providing the vocals. Unfortunately, the album received mixed reviews and failed to chart.

GAME 4

5. Which 1970s group recorded "(Don't Fear) the Reaper"?

a. Blue Oyster Cult
b. Thin Lizzy
c. Ten Years After
d. Foghat

GAME 4 Q4 ANSWER b
Hailing from the Atlanta hip-hop scene, OutKast has sold well over 20 million copies of its albums to date. Comprised only of André "André 3000" Benjamin and Antwan "Big Boi" Patton, the group had its first big crossover success from the 2003 song "Hey Ya!" off the duo's Grammy-winning double album *Speaker-boxxx/The Love Below*.

GAME 24

5. On the cover of *King of America,* Elvis Costello is depicted:

a. Seated on a throne
b. Wearing a crown
c. In front of a castle
d. Riding in a carriage

GAME 24 Q4 ANSWER a
The Del-Vikings formed in 1955 at a Pittsburgh Air Force base. Baritone David Lerchey was white, while the other four group members were black. Their first and biggest hit, "Come Go With Me," was released in 1956 and quickly rose to the Top 10 position. Although the group never had another big hit, this song remains well-known.

GAME 44

5. Which song was the only Top 40 hit by Right Said Fred?

a. "Ice Ice Baby"
b. "Hot Pants"
c. "I'm Too Sexy"
d. "Rapture"

GAME 44 Q4 ANSWER c
Michelle Williams and Kelly Rowland are the other two members of the popular girl group. Destiny's Child had its first Top 10 hit with "No, No, No" in 1998. A multiple Grammy-award winner, Beyoncé released her first solo album, *Dangerously in Love,* in 2003. Her first single, "Crazy in Love," was #1 for two months straight.

GAME 64

5. Greg Graffin is lead singer for which band?

a. Smashing Pumpkins
b. Sonic Youth
c. Bad Religion
d. Collective Soul

GAME 64 Q4 ANSWER c
Elliott Smith's dark, introspective songs (often of troubled relationships and loneliness) earned him a strong underground following. His music reached the mainstream only after several of his songs, including "Miss Misery," were used in the hit movie *Good Will Hunting.* In 2003, Smith died of an apparent suicide at age thirty-four.

Answers are in right-hand boxes on page 93.

8. Which Beatles' song did Joe Cocker perform at Woodstock?

a. "She Came in Through the Bathroom Window"
b. "Help"
c. "Come Together"
d. "With a Little Help From My Friends"

GAME 17 Q7 ANSWER b
Known as The Hawks when touring with Bob Dylan as his back-up band during the "electric" tour of 1966, The Band lived in Woodstock. They used to rehearse there in a house they called Big Pink. Bob Dylan also lived in Woodstock, where he had a near-fatal motorcycle accident that led to his years-long period of seclusion.

---

8. Who wrote the song "Early Morning Rain" for Peter, Paul and Mary?

a. John Denver
b. Gordon Lightfoot
c. Randy Newman
d. Bob Dylan

GAME 37 Q7 ANSWER c
While Barry Manilow's classic performance of the song rose to #1 in 1976, "I Write the Songs" was actually written by Bruce Johnston. Back in 1965, Johnston became a member of The Beach Boys, replacing future "Rhinestone Cowboy" star Glen Campbell on bass. This soft-rock classic won Johnston a Grammy in 1977 for Song of the Year.

---

8. Which group won a Grammy for the song "Give it Away"?

a. Van Halen
b. Red Hot Chili Peppers
c. Aerosmith
d. Traveling Wilburys

GAME 57 Q7 ANSWER a
Come Dance With Me (1959) featured the big band arrangements of Billy May. *September of My Years* was released in 1965 on the eve of Sinatra's fiftieth birthday. Music arranger Gordon Jenkins won a 1966 Grammy for his work on the album, while Sinatra won a Best Male Vocal Grammy for the album's song "It Was a Very Good Year."

---

8. Who produced the 1995 Brian Wilson and Van Dyke Parks album *Orange Crate Art*?

a. Brian Wilson
b. Van Dyke Parks
c. John Fogerty
d. Joe Cocker

GAME 77 Q7 ANSWER a
In addition to producing *Boy*, Lillywhite also produced the group's next two releases, 1981's *October* and 1983's *War*, the latter of which was the band's breakthrough album. Throughout his career, Lillywhite collected Grammys, including the 2006 Producer of the Year award for U2's *How to Dismantle an Atomic Bomb*.

GAME 4

6. What's the name of Kanye West's 2005 Grammy-winning album?

a. *A Good Ass Job*
b. *Late Registration*
c. *Graduation*
d. *The College Dropout*

GAME 4 Q5 ANSWER a
This marginal hit by Blue Oyster Cult was featured playing on a car radio in the John Carpenter horror classic Halloween (1978). In April 2000, the song was forever immortalized in a *Saturday Night Live* skit about a band in which Christopher Walken repeatedly asks SNL alum Will Ferrell for "more cowbell."

GAME 24

6. "Little Miss Can't Be Wrong"' was a hit single from an album by which group?

a. Blues Traveler
b. Spin Doctors
c. Big Head Todd & Monsters
d. Gin Blossoms

GAME 24 Q5 ANSWER b
Costello returns to his folk-rock and pub rock roots in this 1986 album. At the time of this release, the British singer legally changed his name back to Declan Patrick Aloysius MacManus, making this the first of several albums in which the songs are credited to MacManus, but the album itself is credited to Costello.

GAME 44

6. What musician's album *Civilization Phaze III* was released after his death?

a. Frank Zappa
b. Jimi Hendrix
c. Harry Nilsson
d. John Denver

GAME 44 Q5 ANSWER c
The group consisted of Richard and Fred Fairbrass, two bald brothers from England who claimed in the song that they were too sexy for anything. "I'm Too Sexy" was released in 1991 and shot to #1 on the charts. The song entered the pop culture, and was featured in the Jack Lemmon /Walter Matthau comedy *Grumpy Old Men* (1993).

GAME 64

6. In 1995, Neil Young teamed up with which grunge band to record the album *Mirror Ball*?

a. Nirvana
b. Stone Temple Pilots
c. Pearl Jam
d. Metallica

GAME 64 Q5 ANSWER c
Formed in LA in 1980, this hardcore punk band released ten albums and sold almost a million records on its own label, Epitaph, before signing with Atlantic Records in 1993. Though many considered the move to Atlantic a sell-out, the 1994 album *Stranger Than Fiction* gave the group three singles on Billboard's Modern Rock charts.

7. Which of the following groups played at Woodstock in '69?

a. The Doors
b. The Band
c. Black Sabbath
d. Cream

GAME 17 Q6 ANSWER d
Joan Baez first sang this song at Martin Luther King's march on Washington in 1963. When she sang it at Woodstock in 1969, her then-husband, David Harris, was being imprisoned for draft resistance. Although they later divorced in 1973, Baez recorded an album of country music in 1969 for her husband called *David's Album*.

---

7. Who wrote the song "I Write the Songs"?

a. Barry Manilow
b. Randy Newman
c. Bruce Johnston
d. Paul Williams

GAME 37 Q6 ANSWER a
While Paul dealt with Lennon's death by writing the emotional song "Here Today" in 1981, Harrison expressed similar feelings of remembrance in this song from his *Somewhere in England* album. George was joined on the song by Paul and Ringo, marking the first time all three had recorded together since The Beatles breakup in 1970.

---

7. Which artist won Album of the Year Grammys for *Come Dance With Me* and *September of My Years*?

a. Frank Sinatra
b. Pat Boone
c. Tony Bennett
d. Paul Anka

GAME 57 Q6 ANSWER d
Riding a nine-week ride at the top of the pop charts in 2003 with the single "Hey Ya!," OutKast's double-album *Speakerboxxx/The Love Below* won this Grammy in 2004. Jay-Z won the 1999 Best Rap Album Grammy for *Vol. 2: Hard Knock Life*, while Puff Daddy (before he became P. Diddy . . . then Diddy) won for *No Way Out* the year before.

---

7. Who signed on U2 and produced the group's 1980 album *Boy*?

a. Steve Lillywhite
b. Daniel Lanois
c. Brian Eno
d. Mark Ellis

GAME 77 Q6 ANSWER d
Mardin began as an assistant to Nesuhi Ertegun, Atlantic's co-founder, but he rose through the ranks quickly, eventually assuming the role of senior vice president. The countless artists he produced include Diana Ross, Patti LaBelle, The Bee Gees, Carly Simon, Phil Collins, Roberta Flack, Manhattan Transfer, and Willie Nelson.

GAME 4

7. Which London landmark was the subject of a #1 song in 1966?

a. Buckingham Palace

b. The Tower of London

c. Westminster Abbey

d. Winchester Cathedral

GAME 4 Q6 ANSWER d
A college dropout himself, West was a noted music industry producer for such major hip-hop/R&B artists as Ludacris and Alicia Keys. Although he didn't have the typical rapper image, West still found immediate success with his first solo album, *The College Dropout*, which includes such hits as "Through the Wire" and "Jesus Walks."

GAME 24

7. What was the name of Radiohead's 1997 album?

a. *OK Computer*

b. *The Bends*

c. *My Iron Lung*

d. *Pablo Honey*

GAME 24 Q6 ANSWER b
"Little Miss Can't Be Wrong" is from the *Pocket Full of Kryptonite* album. Released in 1991, the album first sold poorly. But sales picked up when radio stations and MTV began playing the songs, and eventually, the album went gold, selling 5 million copies in the United States.

GAME 44

7. What instrumentalist recorded the hit songs "Forty Miles of Bad Road" and "Rebel Rouser"?

a. Duane Eddy

b. Acker Bilk

c. Les Paul

d. Chet Atkins

GAME 44 Q6 ANSWER a
After Zappa's death in 2003, his two-CD epic was released on his Barking Pumpkin label. Although he had organized some of the best backup bands a musician could hope for, Zappa spent most of the late '80s and early '90s writing and recording scores of orchestral pieces with a Synclavier digital synthesizer.

GAME 64

7. In 1968, where did The Amboy Dukes take us on a "Journey"?

a. Center of the Mind

b. Scarborough Fair

c. Far Side of the Moon

d. Inside Daisy Clover

GAME 64 Q6 ANSWER c
Young's influence on Pearl Jam is evident from its concert versions of his songs, such as "Keep on Rockin' in the Free World." On *Mirror Ball*, the band humbly chose to perform just as Neil Young's back-up band. In 1994, Pearl Jam frontman Eddie Vedder presented Young with his induction into the Rock and Roll Hall of Fame.

Answers are in right-hand boxes on page 97.

6. Who sang "We Shall Overcome" at the '69 Woodstock festival?

a. Melanie

b. Janis Joplin

c. Joe Cocker

d. Joan Baez

GAME 17 Q5 ANSWER c
Tom Fogerty died in 1990 from complications of tuberculosis. Joplin died in October 1970 at age twenty-seven. Tim Hardin, whose song "If I Were a Carpenter" was a Top 10 hit for Bobby Darin in 1966, died in December 1980, while Canned Heat's Alan Wilson died in September 1970.

6. Who wrote the song "All Those Years Ago" as a tribute to John Lennon?

a. George Harrison

b. Paul McCartney

c. Elton John

d. Yoko Ono

GAME 37 Q5 ANSWER c
"Here Comes the Sun" is one of many Beatles classics composed by George Harrison, who generally wrote and sang lead on one or two songs per album. Other Harrison-penned Beatles tunes include "If I Needed Someone," "Taxman," and "Something," the last of which is the second most covered Beatles song. (The first is "Yesterday.")

6. Which hip-hop act/artist was the first to win a Grammy for Album of the Year?

a. Jay-Z

b. Puff Daddy

c. TLC

d. OutKast

GAME 57 Q5 ANSWER b
Titelman won his first Grammy in 1987 as a producer for Steve Winwood's #1 hit "Higher Love." Both Clapton and Winwood played together in the early '70s group Blind Faith. Actually, one of Titelman's first songs was written for The Monkees—he and Gerry Goffin penned "I'll Be True to You" for Davy to sing on our 1966 debut album.

6. Which celebrated producer began his career with Atlantic Records in 1963?

a. Brian Holland

b. Harold Beatty

c. Lamont Dozier

d. Arif Mardin

GAME 77 Q5 ANSWER c
Rubin first signed and worked with Slayer in 1986, when he and Russell Simmons produced records for Def Jam. After the two producers parted ways, Rubin established Def American Records, where he signed on a number of heavy rock acts, including Slayer. Rubin's trademark is a "stripped-down" sound of naked vocals and bare instrumentation.

GAME 4

8. Who teams up with the Foo Fighters on the acclaimed single "Virginia Moon"?

a. Mick Jagger
b. Alicia Keys
c. Brad Paisley
d. Norah Jones

GAME 4 Q7 ANSWER d
The New Vaudeville Band, brainchild of British composer and producer Geoff Stephens, sang this hit song. It's a pleasure for me to tell you who knocked this song from the top slot on the US pop charts in December 1966—that's right, it was The Monkees with our recording of Neil Diamond's song "I'm a Believer." Hooray for us!

GAME 24

8. U2's "Angel of Harlem" is a tribute to which of the following women?

a. Billie Holliday
b. Aretha Franklin
c. Dorothy Dandridge
d. Rosa Parks

GAME 24 Q7 ANSWER a
OK Computer, Radiohead's third album, was recorded at Saint Catherine's Court, a sixteenth-century mansion owned by actress Jane Seymour. The album met with both commercial and critical success on both sides of the Atlantic, winning a Grammy Award in 1998.

GAME 44

8. Which of the following singers did *not* become an American Idol?

a. Ruben Studdard
b. Bo Bice
c. Kelly Clarkson
d. Fantasia Barrino

GAME 44 Q7 ANSWER a
Known for his "twangy" guitar style, Duane Eddy scored fifteen Top 40 instrumental hits between 1958 and 1963. On the strength of his first single, "Movin' and Groovin'," in 1957, he was invited to perform on Dick Clark's *American Bandstand* TV show. Eddy was inducted into the Rock and Roll Hall of Fame in 1994.

GAME 64

8. What was Elvis Presley's longest chart-topping song?

a. "Hound Dog"
b. "Love Me Tender"
c. "Don't Be Cruel"
d. "Suspicious Minds"

GAME 64 Q7 ANSWER a
Founded in Detroit by legendary guitarist Ted Nugent, The Amboy Dukes had a Top 20 hit with "Journey to the Center of the Mind." Nugent, known as the "Motor City Madman," had a more successful solo career in the '70s with rock anthems like "Cat Scratch Fever" and "Wango Tango." In the '90s, he played in the group Damn Yankees.

---

5. All of these original Woodstock performers died of a drug overdose except:

a. Janis Joplin
b. Tim Hardin
c. Tom Fogerty
d. Alan Wilson

Although not shown in the film, Yippie protester Abbie Hoffman leapt up on-stage during The Who's set to condemn the fact that John Sinclair of the Black Panthers was still in prison. On The Who's CD box set *30 Years of Maximum R&B*, you can hear Townshend tell Hoffman in no uncertain terms to get off his stage! Peace and love?

5. Which of the following songs is *not* credited to Paul McCartney and John Lennon?

a. "A Day in the Life"
b. "Michelle"
c. "Here Comes the Sun"
d. "Please Please Me"

Elvis Costello began a long-running collaboration with Paul McCartney in 1987, and McCartney's 1989 comeback album *Flowers in the Dirt* features quite a number of McCartney-Costello songs, including the hit "My Brave Face." According to McCartney, Costello mirrors some personality aspects of longtime collaborator John Lennon.

5. Besides Eric Clapton's "Tears in Heaven," Russ Titelman also produced which Grammy-winning song?

a. "Don't Worry, Be Happy"
b. "Higher Love"
c. "Rosanna"
d. "We Are the World"

Starting as a writer of commercial jingles and then as Bette Midler's musical arranger, Manilow hit his stride as a chart-topping solo artist in the mid-'70s. His Top 10 hit "Copacabana" earned him a Grammy for Best Male Pop Vocal in 1979. That song, along with "Ready to Take a Chance Again," is heard in the 1978 film *Foul Play*.

5. What was the first group Rick Rubin signed to Def American after leaving Def Jam Records?

a. Geto Boys
b. Black Crowes
c. Slayer
d. Danzig

Although Spector was the mastermind behind The Crystals' biggest hits, there was often tension between him and the group—especially when he began recording singer Darlene Love under their name. When Spector began focusing his time on The Ronettes in the mid-'60s, The Crystals' career suffered, and the group disbanded in 1966.

Answers are in right-hand boxes on page 96.

9. Which baby boomer act appreciates "The Finer Things" in a 1986 hit?

a. Steve Winwood

b. Bryan Adams

c. Don Henley

d. John Fogerty

GAME 4 Q8 ANSWER d
Grammy-winning sensation Norah Jones sings guest vocals on this ballad from the group's fifth album, *In Your Honor* (2005). The group has compared this double-disc formatted album to Led Zeppelin's 1975 masterpiece *Physical Graffiti*. The album features a cameo from Zeppelin's own John Paul Jones on piano.

9. Which MTV hit was the biggest splash for the '80s band Modern English?

a. "I Melt With You"

b. "Don't You Want Me, Baby?"

c. "Tainted Love"

d. "East End Girls"

GAME 24 Q8 ANSWER a
Found on the band's 1988 album *Rattle and Hum*, the horn-driven song refers to "Lady Day" and "Birdland." "Angel of Harlem" was created during U2's 1987 Joshua Tree Tour. The album on which it appears—an homage to American music—was loved by fans, but received mixed-to-negative reviews from critics.

9. The U2 hit "New Year's Day" appears on which 1983 release?

a. *The Unforgettable Fire*

b. *Joshua Tree*

c. *War*

d. *Zooropa*

GAME 44 Q8 ANSWER b
Although he landed in second place, much of America tends to remember Bo Bice and his fellow Idol-finalist "rocker" Constantine Maroulis as the stand-outs of the 2004–2005 season. The winner that year was, in fact, Carrie Underwood.

9. Johnny Rotten was the lead singer of which band?

a. The Clash

b. Black Flag

c. The Sex Pistols

d. The Buzzcocks

GAME 64 Q8 ANSWER c
In 1956, Elvis had nine Top 20 hits on Billboard's pop charts; five of them, including "Don't Be Cruel," went to #1. "Don't Be Cruel" stayed at #1 for eleven weeks-the longest period of time a song was in the #1 slot. This record remained unbroken until 1992, when Boyz II Men's "End of the Road" stayed at #1 for thirteen weeks.

4. Who did Pete Townshend bash in the head with his electric guitar while onstage during Woodstock?

a. Janis Joplin

b. Martin Scorsese

c. Carlos Santana

d. Abbie Hoffman

GAME 17 Q3 ANSWER c
Legend has it that Crosby, Stills, and Nash officially began during a jam session held at Joni Mitchell's California apartment after a 1968 concert. Woodstock was the group's second live performance. Mitchell's fellow Canadian Neil Young performed with the others at Woodstock, but didn't want to be shown in the movie.

4. British songwriter Elvis Costello co-wrote many of the songs on this Paul McCartney album:

a. *Pipes of Peace*

b. *Ram*

c. *All the Best*

d. *Flowers in the Dirt*

GAME 37 Q3 ANSWER d
Jerry Leiber and Mike Stoller met while attending Los Angeles City College. Their first big song was "Hard Times," a 1952 R&B hit. In addition to writing for Elvis Presley, Leiber and Stoller created tunes for Big Mama Thornton, The Drifters, The Coasters, and many other artists of the '50s and '60s.

4. Which song earned Barry Manilow his only Grammy to date?

a. "Copacabana"

b. "Mandy"

c. "I Write the Songs"

d. "Could It Be Magic"

GAME 57 Q3 ANSWER d
This song from the 1979 album *Slow Train Coming* marked the beginning of Dylan's conversion to Christianity. His religious zeal didn't serve everyone—John Lennon even made a parody of this song called "Serve Yourself." After receiving a Lifetime Achievement Grammy in 1991, Dylan won three Grammys for his 1997 album *Time Out of Mind*.

4. As Phil Spector's first band, which singers recorded hits such as "Da Doo Ron Ron"?

a. The Crystals

b. Rosie & The Originals

c. The Shirelles

d. The Chantels

GAME 77 Q3 ANSWER b
As a boy growing up in Bremerton, Washington, trumpeter Quincy Jones teamed with friend Ray Charles to play local weddings and jazz clubs. He later played with bandleaders Lionel Hampton and Dizzy Gillespie, as well as with his own band, before starting a highly successful career as a record producer.

10. Which flowery song from 1988 was Poison's only #1 hit?

a. "Every Rose Has Its Thorn"
b. "When You Wore a Tulip"
c. "An Orchid to You"
d. "Mum's the Word"

GAME 4 Q9 ANSWER a
Before joining the group Traffic or jamming electric organ on "Voodoo Chile" from the 1968 Jimi Hendrix album *Electric Ladyland*, "Stevie" Winwood was lead singer for The Spencer Davis Group. Their hit song "Gimme Some Lovin'" remains one of my all-time favorites. It's the song I most like to play when I get up in a club and jam.

10. What was the name of Led Zeppelin's custom record label?

a. Swan Song
b. Rocket
c. Tuff Gong
d. Grunt

GAME 24 Q9 ANSWER a
Like many one-hit wonders, "I Melt With You" sounds nothing like the rest of this New Wave band's music. In the late 1990s, the song was used in a Burger King commercial, prompting Modern English, which had disbanded in 1991, to return to the recording studio.

10. Elvis Presley was drafted into what branch of the military?

a. Army
b. Navy
c. Coast Guard
d. Air Force

GAME 44 Q9 ANSWER c
Although U2 had released two albums (*Boy* and *October*), it was *War* that first put the group (and especially frontman Bono) on the map. "New Year's Day" was the band's first international hit, but "Sunday Bloody Sunday" really won the attention of critics and concertgoers and has remained the group's best-known anthem.

10. Which of the following is *not* a Steely Dan album?

a. *Pretzel Logic*
b. *Two Against Nature*
c. *The Nightfly*
d. *Aja*

GAME 64 Q9 ANSWER c
Mostly the brainchild of British music impresario Malcolm McLaren, The Sex Pistols was an attempt at manufactured chaos. At his audition, Johnny Rotten became the singer mainly because of his "I Hate Pink Floyd" t-shirt. After Glen Matlock quit the band in 1977, Rotten's friend Sid Vicious joined—even though he couldn't play bass.

3. Whose song "Woodstock" was a major hit for Crosby, Stills, Nash, & Young?

a. Joan Baez
b. Carole King
c. Joni Mitchell
d. Judy Collins

GAME 17 Q2 ANSWER a
The emblem was created for the 1969 concert by the artist Arnold Skolnik, and it has been used for other Woodstock revival shows to date. Although the original festival was associated with peace and love, the 1999 event suffered negative press because of an unusually high level of violent outbreaks among the concertgoers.

3. Who wrote the Elvis hits "Loving You," "Hound Dog," and "Jailhouse Rock"?

a. Goffin and King
b. Carl Perkins
c. Big Mama Thornton
d. Leiber and Stoller

GAME 37 Q2 ANSWER a
Sedaka's lengthy career began in the 1950s with "Oh! Carol" and "The Diary." Years later, after a lean period and a split with his longtime collaborator Howard Greenfield, Sedaka got back on the US charts with the help of Elton John. The 1975 recording of "Bad Blood" features John on the backing vocals.

3. Who won a Grammy for Best Male Rock Vocal with "Gotta Serve Somebody"?

a. John Lennon
b. Bruce Springsteen
c. Paul Simon
d. Bob Dylan

GAME 57 Q2 ANSWER b
"Here We Go Again" came from the eight-time Grammy-winning album *Genius Loves Company,* Ray Charles' last album before he died in 2004. The 2005 Grammy Awards presentation was dedicated to "brother Ray," and he was also posthumously awarded the 2005 Grammy Hall of Fame Award for his 1972 recording of "America the Beautiful."

3. Which record producer began his career as a jazz trumpeter?

a. Jerry Wexler
b. Quincy Jones
c. Phil Spector
d. Burt Bacharach

GAME 77 Q2 ANSWER c
Sometimes called "the fifth Beatle," Martin signed the group on in 1962, after they had been turned down by most major British record labels—and even though he thought they sounded "pretty awful." Then, using his musical expertise, he proceeded to fill the gap between The Beatles' raw talent and the sound they wanted to create.

GAME 4

11. Who had an early hit with the double-sided "I Walk the Line/Get Rhythm"?

a. Porter Wagoner

b. Hank Williams

c. Lefty Frizzell

d. Johnny Cash

GAME 4 Q10 ANSWER a
This glam metal quartet from Harrisburg, Pennsylvania, first hit the charts in 1986 with "Talk Dirty to Me," which also became a popular video on MTV. "Every Rose Has Its Thorn" was a pop-chart "power ballad" that led to glam metal's demise by 1991. In 2001, Poison singer Bret Michaels did a cameo on the CBS sitcom *Yes, Dear*.

GAME 24

11. Which of the follow groups sang the 1960s hit "Turn, Turn, Turn"?

a. The Beatles

b. The Byrds

c. The Animals

d. The Turtles

GAME 24 Q10 ANSWER a
Launched in 1974, the label was named after a song that Led Zeppelin had never recorded for commercial release. Bad Company, Dave Edmunds, Pretty Things, Maggie Bell, Detective, Midnight Flyer, and Wildlife are among the other artists who recorded for the group's label.

GAME 44

11. Which of the following Monkees' songs features a Moog synthesizer?

a. "Daily Nightly"

b. "Cuddly Toy"

c. "The Door Into Summer"

d. "Hard to Believe"

GAME 44 Q10 ANSWER a
Elvis was served with draft papers on December 20, 1957. He served in the Army, and was stationed in Germany for the duration of his two-year service. While in Germany, he met future wife Priscilla Beaulieu. Elvis received an honorable discharge on March 5, 1960, and quickly recorded his first #1 hit in stereo, "Stuck on You."

GAME 64

11. Which British Invasion group had a hit single in 1964 with "Hippy Hippy Shake?"

a. The Swinging Blue Jeans

b. The Animals

c. Herman's Hermits

d. Gerry and the Pacemakers

GAME 64 Q10 ANSWER c
Steely Dan showcases the songwriting partnership of Walter Becker and Donald Fagen. After *Gaucho* (the seventh Steely Dan album) was released in 1980, Becker and Fagen parted ways. Donald Fagen put out his first solo album, *The Nightfly*, in 1982. The next Steely Dan album was the 2000 Grammy-winner *Two Against Nature*.

---

2. A _____ perched on a guitar is the official Woodstock emblem.

a. White bird
b. Dancing hippie chick
c. Peace sign
d. Red heart

GAME 17 Q1 ANSWER a

The Who, Janis Joplin, Joe Cocker, and Santana appeared along with several other musical acts at this historic three-day concert. While they didn't play at Woodstock, The Doors did play the popular Isle of Wight Festival in 1970 along with The Who and Jimi Hendrix. It was Jimi's last performance—he died only a few weeks later.

---

2. Elton John collaborated with Neil Sedaka on which #1 hit song?

a. "Bad Blood"
b. "Tower of Babel"
c. "Bennie and the Jets"
d. "Philadelphia Freedom"

GAME 37 Q1 ANSWER a

"Both Sides Now" is one of Mitchell's best-known songs, but Mitchell didn't release it on one of her own albums until 1969's *Clouds*. That LP—which won the 1969 Grammy for best folk album—also features "Chelsea Morning," the song after which Bill and Hillary Clinton are said to have named their daughter Chelsea.

---

2. The 2004 Grammy for Record of the Year went to a duet by Ray Charles and:

a. Tim McGraw
b. Norah Jones
c. 50 Cent
d. John Mayer

GAME 57 Q1 ANSWER d

Written by R&B king Otis Redding, "Respect" was Franklin's first #1 pop hit in 1967 and remains her signature song. Considered one of the all-time R&B classics, this song was even sung by a nun in the 1979 spoof movie *Airplane!* In 1987, Aretha Franklin was also the first woman to be inducted into the Rock and Roll Hall of Fame.

---

2. What famous record producer helped shape The Beatles' sound?

a. Clive Davis
b. Jack Nietzsche
c. George Martin
d. Andrew Loog Oldham

GAME 77 Q1 ANSWER b

After leaving Roxy Music in 1973, Eno recorded several solo albums before starting his career as a producer for Obscure records, which he founded. He has been credited with coining the term "ambient music"—low-volume music intended to modify the listener's perception of his surrounding environment.

---

12. Which band is responsible for the albums *Summerteeth* and *Being There*?

a. Wilco
b. Coldplay
c. Old 97's
d. The Milkshakes

Born in Arkansas on February 26, 1932, Johnny Cash first recorded in 1955 on Sun Records—the same label that had signed Elvis Presley. Cash became known as the "The Man in Black" after his first appearance at the Grand Ole Opry in 1956. In 2005, his life story was made into a movie starring Joaquin Phoenix called *Walk the Line*.

12. Who dubbed Tuesday Weld's singing voice in the movie *Rock, Rock, Rock*?

a. Connie Francis
b. Doris Day
c. Jo Stafford
d. Rosemary Clooney

Written by folk singer, songwriter, and political activist Pete Seeger, the lyrics to The Byrds' hit came from the Biblical book of Ecclesiastes. "Turn, Turn, Turn" was both the title and the first track of The Byrds' second album. The song is commonly interpreted as a plea for world peace.

12. Which Australian group recorded the 1982 #1 hit song "Down Under"?

a. Men at Work
b. Counting Crows
c. INXS
d. Midnight Oil

"Daily Nightly" is Mike's song from The Monkees' fourth album—*Pisces, Aquarius, Capricorn, & Jones, Ltd.* (1967). I had the first Moog synthesizer on the West Coast at that time, and we decided to use it somewhere on the album. We featured it on "Daily Nightly" and again on the album's last song, "Star Collector."

12. Whose 1997 free concert was dubbed the "Million Decibel March"?

a. Metallica
b. Pearl Jam
c. Smashing Pumpkins
d. Red Hot Chili Peppers

"Hippy Hippy Shake" was written and first recorded in 1959 by American rocker Chan Romero. Some time later, while hosting a "Tuesday Night Guest" show at Liverpool's Cavern Club, The Swinging Blue Jeans heard this song performed by none other than The Beatles! They decided to record their own version of the song, and it was a hit.

1. Which of these groups did *not* perform at Woodstock in 1969?

a. The Doors

b. Jefferson Airplane

c. Jimi Hendrix

d. Crosby, Stills, & Nash

The answer to this question is on:

page 104, top frame, right side.

---

1. Who wrote Judy Collins' 1967 hit "Both Sides Now"?

a. Joni Mitchell

b. Laura Nyro

c. Joan Baez

d. Carole King

The answer to this question is on:

page 104, second frame, right side.

---

1. Which song earned Aretha Franklin her first of many Grammy Awards?

a. "Chain of Fools"

b. "Freeway of Love"

c. "Natural Woman"

d. "Respect"

The answer to this question is on:

page 104, third frame, right side.

---

1. Which Grammy-winning producer co-founded and played keyboards for Britain's Roxy Music?

a. Quincy Jones

b. Brian Eno

c. Dave Grusin

d. David Foster

The answer to this question is on:

page 104, bottom frame, right side.

GAME 5

Punk Rock

*Turn to page 109
for the first question.*

GAME 4 Q12 ANSWER a
Lead singer-songwriter Jeff Tweedy has always been the one constant in the band's ever-changing lineup. Winner of two Grammys (Best Packaging and Best Alternative Album) in 2005 for *A Ghost Is Born*, Wilco's incredible live show can be heard best on its double-disc live concert album, *Kicking Television: Live in Chicago*.

GAME 25

Spinal Tap

*Turn to page 109
for the first question.*

GAME 24 Q12 ANSWER a
Connie Francis provided the pretty singing voice for Weld's 1956 motion picture debut. Appearing in the film as Weld's love interest was Teddy Randazzo, who sang with The Three Chuckles (they had a Top 20 hit in 1953 with "Runaround"). Randazzo went on to co-write several hit songs for Little Anthony & the Imperials.

GAME 45

The Rolling Stones

*Turn to page 109
for the first question.*

GAME 44 Q12 ANSWER a
Men at Work's debut album, *Business as Usual*, charted at #1 for fifteen weeks. Along with "Down Under," the group had a #1 hit that year with "Who Can It Be Now?" The MTV videos for these songs were very popular. By 1985, after their third album, *Two Hearts*, was released, Men at Work decided to stop working— as a group, that is.

GAME 65

Irish Musicians

*Turn to page 109
for the first question.*

GAME 64 Q12 ANSWER a
Roughly 40,000 fans attended the concert in the parking lot of the CoreStates complex in Philadelphia. The location was chosen specifically by the group's fans, who were given the opportunity to make suggestions through a toll-free number. Later that year, Metallica was named Billboard's Rock and Roll Artist of the Year.

GAME 17

Woodstock '69

*Turn to page 106
for the first question.*

Turn to page 106
for the first question.

GAME 16 Q12 ANSWER c
The Platters are best remembered for the songs "Only You," "The Great Pretender," and their #1 hit recording of Jerome Kern's ballad "Smoke Gets in Your Eyes" (1959). Zola Taylor was one of three women married to Lymon before he died in 1968. Halle Berry played Taylor in the 1998 Frankie Lymon biopic *Why Do Fools Fall in Love*.

GAME 37

They Write the Songs

*Turn to page 106
for the first question.*

Turn to page 106
for the first question.

GAME 36 Q12 ANSWER c
Sting made his film debut in 1979's *Quadrophenia*, a British film based on The Who's 1979 album of the same name. Later film appearances were made in *Brimstone and Treacle* (1982), *Dune* (1984), *Plenty* (1985), *The Bride* (1985), and *The Adventures of Baron Munchausen* (1988).

GAME 57

Grammy Winners

*Turn to page 106
for the first question.*

Turn to page 106
for the first question.

GAME 56 Q12 ANSWER d
As with so many Michael Jackson hits, his videos are just as popular as the songs. "Black or White" was directed by Jon Landis (he also directed Jackson's classic 1983 "Thriller" video), and features a Macaulay Culkin cameo. "Remember the Time" features cameos by Eddie Murphy and fashion model Iman, who married David Bowie in 1992.

GAME 77

Producers

*Turn to page 106
for the first question.*

Turn to page 106
for the first question.

GAME 76 Q12 ANSWER b
Released in 1987, *Permanent Vacation* was a comeback album for Aerosmith. It featured the popular hits "Rag Doll," "Angel," and "Dude (Looks Like a Lady)." *Toys in the Attic* came out in 1975, and featured the well-known songs "Walk This Way" and "Sweet Emotion." *Get a Grip* was released in 1993, and *Honkin' on Bobo* hit stores in 2004.

GAME 5	**1.** Which band returned to the stage after nineteen years with its Filthy Lucre Tour? **a.** Dead Kennedys **b.** Sex Pistols **c.** Dead Milkmen **d.** The Ramones	The answer to this question is on: **page 111, top frame, right side.**
GAME 25	**1.** In *This Is Spinal Tap*, which monument is used as a motif for the band's show? **a.** Taj Mahal **b.** Rome Coliseum **c.** Leaning Tower of Pisa **d.** Stonehenge	The answer to this question is on: **page 111, second frame, right side.**
GAME 45	**1.** All of these people are or were members of The Rolling Stones except: **a.** Mick Jagger **b.** Keith Richards **c.** Bill Wyman **d.** Keith Relf	The answer to this question is on: **page 111, third frame, right side.**
GAME 65	**1.** Eithne Ni Bhraonain is the birth name of which Irish musician? **a.** Van Morrison **b.** Bono **c.** Enya **d.** Sinead O'Connor	The answer to this question is on: **page 111, bottom frame, right side.**

12. Zola Taylor, the only female singer in The Platters, was once married to:

a. Chuck Berry

b. Little Anthony

c. Frankie Lymon

d. Tony Williams

GAME 16 Q11 ANSWER a
Singer-songwriter Barrett Strong did more than forty takes to nail the sound of this 1960 single. Although it was his only major hit as a singer, Strong also co-wrote such soul classics as "I Heard It Through the Grapevine" and "Papa Was a Rolling Stone." The Beatles recorded a popular version of "Money" in 1963.

12. What rock star played the ultra-cool mod leader in the film *Quadrophenia*?

a. Sid Vicious

b. Pete Townshend

c. Sting

d. Bono

GAME 36 Q11 ANSWER c
Although Robertson sang only a few songs with The Band, he was the group's primary songwriter. In the years after his 1976 split from the group, he released several solo albums as well as supervising the musical soundtracks for a number of Martin Scorsese films, including *Raging Bull*.

12. "Black or White" and "Remember the Time" were hit songs from which Michael Jackson album?

a. *Bad*

b. *Thriller*

c. *Off the Wall*

d. *Dangerous*

GAME 56 Q11 ANSWER a
Released during the huge popularity of the *Moonlighting* TV show, this bluesy single saw high chart success, giving Willis the chance to create an alter ego musician named Bruno Radolini. Willis played his "Bruno" persona in a 1988 HBO special called *The Return of Bruno*. It featured a good-natured cameo by former Beatle Ringo Starr.

12. Which of these Aerosmith albums is from the '80s?

a. *Honkin' on Bobo*

b. *Permanent Vacation*

c. *Get a Grip*

d. *Toys in the Attic*

GAME 76 Q11 ANSWER a
Gary Lewis (son of comedian Jerry) and The Playboys hit #1 with "This Diamond Ring" in 1965. In 1968, Gary Puckett's popular "Young Girl" and "Lady Willpower" got only as high as #2 on the charts. Gary Numan's New Wave hit "Cars" reached #9 in 1979. Actor Gary Cooper never had a hit, but the *High Noon* theme song won an Oscar in 1952.

GAME 5	**2.** Steve Diggle and Pete Shelley are two members of which veteran punk band? **a.** Clash **b.** Buzzcocks **c.** Ramones **d.** Sex Pistols	**GAME 5 Q1 ANSWER b** Organized as a six-month world tour in 1996, the mainstream success and acceptance of the Filthy Lucre Tour was a far cry from the chaos and social outrage that surrounded the Sex Pistols on its first tour of England in 1976. Since 1996, the group toured again in the US on the equally successful Piss Off Tour of 2003.
GAME 25	**2.** Which band member's girlfriend nearly destroys Spinal Tap? **a.** David St. Hubbins **b.** Nigel Tufnel **c.** Derek Smalls **d.** Viv Savage	**GAME 25 Q1 ANSWER d** Spinal Tap is one of my favorite "fake/real" rock groups. In one of this film's many funny scenes, lead guitarist Nigel (played by Christopher Guest) draws a blueprint on a napkin for a Stonehenge monument at eighteen inches rather than the intended eighteen feet. Watch for Angelica Huston's cameo as "the Stonehenge artist."
GAME 45	**2.** From what did The Rolling Stones get its name? **a.** A Bob Dylan song **b.** A group member who collected moss **c.** A Muddy Waters song **d.** A TV show	**GAME 45 Q1 ANSWER d** Relf, who died in 1976 from electrocution while playing an ungrounded electric guitar, was lead singer and harmonica player for The Yardbirds. In addition to founding member Brian Jones and guitarist Mick Taylor, bassist Bill Wyman also left the Stones. As a metal detecting enthusiast, however, Wyman leaves no stone unturned.
GAME 65	**2.** Which band's debut album was titled *Everybody Else Is Doing It, So Why Can't We?* **a.** Oasis **b.** The Sundays **c.** Creed **d.** The Cranberries	**GAME 65 Q1 ANSWER c** The artist chose "Enya" to approximate the sound of the Irish name "Eithne." Before going solo, Enya provided backing vocals and played keyboard for Clannad—a band composed of three of her siblings and two of her uncles. She achieved a breakthrough in her solo career in 1988, with the album *Watermark*.

11. Which Motown song recorded by Barrett Strong is subtitled "That's What I Want"?

a. "Money"

b. "Love"

c. "Fame"

d. "Peace"

GAME 16 Q10 ANSWER c
Although Barry, Maurice, and Robin Gibb wanted Andy to become part of the Bee Gees, he was much younger than the others and preferred to go solo. By 1978, he had become the first male solo artist in the US to have three consecutive #1 singles. He died in March 1988 of heart disease at age thirty.

---

11. Which ex-member of The Band had the hit song "Somewhere Down That Crazy River" in 1988?

a. Garth Hudson

b. Rick Danko

c. Robbie Robertson

d. Levon Helm

GAME 36 Q10 ANSWER a
These boys from Philly had their first #1 hit in 1976 with "Rich Girl." A string of #1 hits followed in the early '80s: "Kiss On My List," "Private Eyes," and "I Can't Go For That (No Can Do)" in 1981; "Maneater" in 1982; and "Out of Touch" in 1984. This string of six #1 hits over an eight-year period remains a remarkable feat.

---

11. Which of these actors had a Top 10 hit in 1987 called "Respect Yourself"?

a. Bruce Willis

b. John Travolta

c. William Shatner

d. Keanu Reeves

GAME 56 Q10 ANSWER b
After cracking the Top 10 in 1986 with a rap version of Aerosmith's "Walk This Way," Run DMC recorded this Michael Nesmith song from our second album, *More of the Monkees* (1967). This version of the song is featured on the group's 1988 album *Tougher Than Leather*. Run DMC retired in 2002 after the death of their DJ, Jam Master Jay.

---

11. Which "Gary" is the only one to have a #1 hit song?

a. Gary Lewis

b. Gary Numan

c. Gary Puckett

d. Gary Cooper

GAME 76 Q10 ANSWER b
Recorded by the Fab Four and included on their 1965 album Beatles for Sale, "Words of Love" features George Harrison's note-for-note guitar solo that is identical to Buddy Holly's own version. The Rolling Stones recorded "Not Fade Away" in 1964, and Linda Ronstadt had hits in the mid-'70s with "It's So Easy" and "That'll Be the Day."

---

3. Who was the lead singer for the 1970s punk band the Plasmatics?

a. Wendy O. Williams
b. Stiv Bators
c. Jello Biafra
d. Rat Scabies

GAME 5 Q2 ANSWER b
After hearing the Sex Pistols play a London concert in February 1976, friends Pete Shelley and Howard Devoto joined with fellow musicians Steve Diggle and John Maher and performed as Buzzcock, opening for the Sex Pistols' in July 1976. The group broke up in 1981 after only three albums.

3. What was the nickname of original Spinal Tap drummer John Pepys?

a. Bambi
b. Stumpy
c. Ducky
d. Pepe

GAME 25 Q2 ANSWER a
David's girlfriend "Janine" proceeds to join the group on tambourine after Nigel (Christopher Guest) leaves the group following a gig at a military base. Great moments include her mistaking "Doubly" for the "Dolby" sound process, and her booking of the band at a venue that gives the day's top billing to a puppet show.

3. Before joining The Rolling Stones in 1976, Ron Wood played with The Faces along with:

a. Eric Clapton
b. Jerry Garcia
c. David Lee Roth
d. Rod Stewart

GAME 45 Q2 ANSWER c
In 1962, Brian Jones formed The Rolling Stones with Mick Jagger and Keith Richards. The group took its name from a lyric in the Muddy Waters blues classic "Mannish Boy." Bob Dylan's song "Like a Rolling Stone" didn't appear until 1965. The Rolling Stones finally did a cover of Dylan's song for the 1995 live album *Stripped*.

3. Which Dublin-born singer played the role of Pink in the film *Pink Floyd The Wall*?

a. Bob Geldof
b. Peter Gabriel
c. Sting
d. George Michael

GAME 65 Q2 ANSWER d
The Cranberries formed in 1990—although originally, the group called itself The Cranberry Saw Us, as a pun on "cranberry sauce." Their 1993 debut album, featuring lyrics by lead singer Dolores O'Riordan, was a huge hit in both the US and the UK, and launched the hit singles "Linger" and "Dreams."

10. Which Gibb brother was *not* a member of The Bee Gees?

a. Barry Gibb
b. Maurice Gibb
c. Andy Gibb
d. Robin Gibb

GAME 16 Q9 ANSWER a
This song from the band's Grammy-winning second album, *A Rush of Blood to the Head,* won the Grammy for Record of the Year in 2004. "Clocks" was also featured in the movie trailer for the 2003 live-action film of *Peter Pan,* and has been heard in episodes of both NBC's hospital show *ER* and HBO's popular mob drama *The Sopranos.*

10. What vocal duo has had the most #1 hits?

a. Hall & Oates
b. Sonny & Cher
c. The Everly Brothers
d. Simon & Garfunkel

GAME 36 Q9 ANSWER a
Tug of War was McCartney's first official solo album after the dissolution of Wings. The duet "Ebony and Ivory," performed with Stevie Wonder, received critical acclaim when it was released in March 1982, and was a #1 hit worldwide. When the album was released a month later, it, too, rose to #1.

10. Which Monkees' song did rap group Run DMC do a cover version of in the '80s?

a. "(I'm Not Your) Stepping Stone"
b. "Mary Mary"
c. "Last Train to Clarksville"
d. "Words"

GAME 56 Q9 ANSWER a
Written by music producer Frederick Knight, this song went to #1 in the US in 1979. By year's end, it had also reached #1 in Canada, Britain, Central America, South Africa, and even Israel! This instant success was short-lived, however—by 1980, disco was out and New Wave was coming in. And lo, another one-hit wonder was born . . .

10. Which Buddy Holly song did The Beatles cover on one of their albums?

a. "Not Fade Away"
b. "Words of Love"
c. "It's So Easy"
d. "That'll Be the Day"

GAME 76 Q9 ANSWER a
Between 1972 and 1973, Jim Croce recorded three fantastic albums that launched the hit singles "Time in a Bottle," "You Don't Mess Around With Jim," "Operator (That's Not the Way It Feels)," and "Bad Bad Leroy Brown," which reached #1 only months before he died in a plane crash on September 20, 1973.

4. Which British punk band had Captain Sensible and Rat Scabies as founding members?

a. Buzzcocks

b. The Clash

c. The Sex Pistols

d. The Damned

GAME 5 Q3 ANSWER a
Wendy Orlean Williams was one of punk's most outrageous performers, often playing guitars with chainsaws and blowing up cars live onstage. In 1981, she was arrested in Cleveland, Ohio, for performing in public covered only in shaving cream. Amidst all this wildness, she was nominated for a Grammy in 1985 for Best Rock Vocal.

4. Which of these songs is *not* an original Spinal Tap tune?

a. "Plaster Caster"

b. "Sex Farm"

c. "Big Bottom"

d. "Heavy Duty"

GAME 25 Q3 ANSWER b
Pepys was replaced by "Stumpy Joe" Childs and then Peter "James" Bond (Ed Begley, Jr.). Bond's death from a bizarre gardening accident begins the group's dreaded drummer curse. By film's end, drummer Mick Shrimpton has spontaneously combusted on stage and been replaced by Joe "Mama" Besser for the group's big tour of Japan.

4. What was The Rolling Stones' first Top 10 hit in the United States?

a. "(I Can't Get No) Satisfaction"

b. "Start Me Up"

c. "Time Is on My Side"

d. "Jumpin' Jack Flash"

GAME 45 Q3 ANSWER d
The Faces started out as The Small Faces in the '60s. After the original line-up disbanded, Ron Wood joined in 1970 along with vocalist Rod Stewart. Stewart had been the singer for the Jeff Beck Group, which broke up in 1969. The Faces also included Kenny Jones, who later joined The Who. The Faces disbanded in 1974.

4. Prior to his solo career, Van Morrison was a member of which band?

a. Yes

b. Them

c. Jethro Tull

d. Rolling Stones

GAME 65 Q3 ANSWER a
Roger Waters, who wrote the 1982 film's screenplay, originally considered taking on the lead role. Finally, though, the film starred Bob Geldof, whose character Pink is based on the lives of both Waters and former group member Syd Barrett. Waters was disappointed with the final product, but many fans consider the film a powerful work.

9. Which piano-driven rock melody from Coldplay ponders life's big questions?

a. "Clocks"

b. "Cannonball"

c. "Carnival"

d. "Closing Time"

GAME 16 Q8 ANSWER a
Reaching #1 in the fall of 1960, "Stay" was written and recorded by doo-wop great Maurice Williams with The Zodiacs. At only one minute, thirty-six seconds long, it remains the shortest #1 US pop single. After being featured in the 1987 hit movie *Dirty Dancing*, this recording of "Stay" enjoyed a new surge in popularity.

9. Which Paul McCartney album features the duet "Ebony and Ivory"?

a. *Tug of War*

b. *Pipes of Peace*

c. *Press to Play*

d. *Flowers in the Dirt*

GAME 36 Q8 ANSWER a
Both works were composed by The Who's Pete Townshend, with "Won't Get Fooled Again" first appearing in 1971, and "Who Are You," in 1978. Eventually, "Who Are You" became the theme song of the hit TV show *CSI: Crime Scene Investigation*, while "Won't Get Fooled Again" became the theme song of *CSI: Miami*.

9. Anita Ward had her one and only hit with which loony tune?

a. "Ring My Bell"

b. "I'm Your Boogie Man"

c. "Clean-Up Woman"

d. "It's Raining Men"

GAME 56 Q8 ANSWER c
For many, original vocalist Natalie Merchant *was* 10,000 Maniacs. When she left to pursue a solo career in 1993, the group hired Mary Ramsey to take over vocal duties. They released two albums with her: *Love Among the Ruins* in 1997 and *The Earth Pressed Flat* in 1999. Mary Ramsey and guitarist John Lombardo left the group in 2002.

9. Who displayed his folksy rock sound in the posthumous 1973 hit single "I'll Have to Say I Love You in a Song"?

a. Jim Croce

b. Cat Stevens

c. Al Stewart

d. Kenny Loggins

GAME 76 Q8 ANSWER d
David Lee Roth sang on "Me Wise Magic" for *The Best of Van Halen, Vol. 1*, but quit the group (or was fired) after a backstage fight during an MTV awards show. Gary Cherone joined in 1997 and left in 1999. In 1996, after recording the song "Humans Being" for the movie *Twister*, Sammy Hagar either quit (or was fired) from the group.

GAME 5

5. After leaving The Clash, Mick Jones went on to form which band?

a. Home Sweet Homicide

b. Fine Young Cannibals

c. Hanoi Rocks

d. Big Audio Dynamite

GAME 5 Q4 ANSWER d
In 1976, The Damned was the first of the English punk rock groups to actually release a single ("New Rose") and an album called *Damned Damned Damned*. Before taking up music, lead singer Dave Vanian was a gravedigger. This, coupled with his vampiric persona, helped establish The Damned as founders of gothic rock.

GAME 25

5. *Smell the Glove* was the followup to which critically-panned Spinal Tap LP?

a. *Heavy Metal Memories*

b. *Intravenus De Milo*

c. *Shark Sandwich*

d. *Break Like the Wind*

GAME 25 Q4 ANSWER a
Written by KISS frontman Gene Simmons for the group's 1977 *Love Gun* album, "Plaster Caster" is about an inventive late '60s groupie sometimes known as Cynthia Plaster Caster who used to approach rock stars with her plaster of Paris molds and ask for much more than just an autograph. She still has not called Spinal Tap.

GAME 45

5. The concert film *Let's Spend the Night Together* covers a tour supporting which album?

a. *Get Yer Ya-Ya's Out*

b. *Let It Bleed*

c. *Sticky Fingers*

d. *Tattoo You*

GAME 45 Q4 ANSWER c
"Time Is on My Side" is on the Stones' 1964 album *12 x 5*. Two versions of this song exist—one with an organ intro, another with a guitar intro. John Lennon and Paul McCartney gave The Rolling Stones one of its first hits with "I Wanna Be Your Man." The Stones' version of the song went to #12 on the UK charts in November 1963.

GAME 65

5. Liam Ó'Maonlai was the voice behind what Dublin-based band?

a. The Lemonheads

b. The Smiths

c. Hothouse Flowers

d. Supertramp

GAME 65 Q4 ANSWER b
The Northern Irish band Them formed in 1963, and in addition to Morrison, featured Billy Harrison, Eric Wrixen, Alan Henderson, and Ronnie Millings. The band's greatest hit was the rock standard "Gloria." Written by Morrison, it was released in 1964 and has since been performed by thousands of bands.

Answers are in right-hand boxes on page 119.

8. Which #1 song has the shortest running time?

a. "Stay"

b. "She Loves You"

c. "Dizzy"

d. "Rise"

GAME 16 Q7 ANSWER c
British singer Seal (Seal Henry Samuel) had his first #1 Grammy-winning hit in 1995 with "Kissed by a Rose," which was featured in the popular summer film *Batman Forever*. Before recording his album *Seal IV*, Seal recorded and then shelved an entire album called *Togetherland*. In March 2005, Seal married supermodel Heidi Klum.

8. Which band recorded the songs "Won't Get Fooled Again" and "Who Are You"?

a. The Who

b. The Beatles

c. The Monkees

d. The Rolling Stones

GAME 36 Q7 ANSWER a
This Swedish group first hit the US pop charts with "Waterloo" in 1974. Although the members gradually drifted apart in the early 1980s, ABBA was so successful that their songs live on not only in their albums, but also on the soundtrack of the 1994 film *Muriel's Wedding* and the score of the musical *Mamma Mia!*

8. In the mid-1990s, Mary Ramsey took on the duties of lead singer for which group?

a. Cranberries

b. En Vogue

c. 10,000 Maniacs

d. Hole

GAME 56 Q7 ANSWER a
"Yakety-Yak" was a big R&B hit in 1958 for The Coasters. Meanwhile, Lloyd Price had three #1 R&B hit singles in 1959— "Stagger Lee," "Personality," and "I'm Gonna Get Married." Based on an old blues song about a killer in the 1890s, Price's version of "Stagger Lee" had to be changed to be performed on TV's *American Bandstand*.

8. Which Van Halen song and Van Halen vocalist is a mismatch?

a. "Without You"/Gary Cherone

b. "Jump"/David Lee Roth

c. "When It's Love"/Sammy Hagar

d. "Me Wise Magic"/Gary Cherone

GAME 76 Q7 ANSWER a
After "Something in the Way" ends on the *Nevermind* CD, ten minutes of silence go by before "Endless Nameless" starts. The track is nearly seven minutes long. On European versions of the band's *In Utero* (1993), there is another hidden track called "Gallons of Rubbing Alcohol Flow Through the Strip"—it's almost twenty-four minutes long!

6. Which female rocker was the vocalist for the punk band X?

a. Lene Lovich
b. Exene Cervenka
c. Wendy O. Williams
d. Patti Smith

GAME 5 Q5 ANSWER d
The best (and last) year for The Clash was 1982. Its album *Combat Rock* had spawned a Top 10 single ("Rock the Casbah"), and the group opened for The Who during their Farewell Tour. By 1985, Mick Jones decided to start Big Audio Dynamite, while his Clash chum Joe Strummer produced the album *Hell's Ditch* for The Pogues.

6. Which TV talk-show host was tricked into thinking that Spinal Tap was a real group?

a. Dick Cavett
b. Johnny Carson
c. Joe Franklin
d. David Letterman

GAME 25 Q5 ANSWER c
In yet another classic cameo from the film, Fran Drescher of *Nanny* fame plays an annoying rock publicist called Bobbie Fleckman. It's her job to tell the band that their new album, *Smell the Glove*, has been banned in all stores because of its "sexist" cover. Nigel's classic response? "What's wrong with being sexy?"

6. Which of the following live concert albums does *not* feature The Rolling Stones?

a. *Got Live If You Want It!*
b. *At Budokan*
c. *Get Yer Ya-Ya's Out!*
d. *Love You Live*

GAME 45 Q5 ANSWER d
Hal Ashby directed this 1983 concert film of the Stones' 1981 Tattoo You Tour. A smart director and Oscar-winning film editor, Ashby was also a Rolling Stones fan. In his 1978 Vietnam anti-war classic *Coming Home*, Ashby featured Stones' classics like "Out of Time," "Ruby Tuesday," "No Expectations," and "Sympathy for the Devil."

6. Paddy Moloney is the longtime leader of what Irish act?

a. The Chieftains
b. Fairport Convention
c. Steeleye Span
d. The Irish Rovers

GAME 65 Q5 ANSWER c
Hothouse Flowers formed when Liam Ó Maonlai and Fiachna o Braonain, who played together as street musicians, were joined by Peter O'Toole. In 1986, Bono saw the group perform on television and offered his support. This ultimately resulted in a record contract and the 1988 album *People*, which climbed to #1 in Ireland and #2 in England.

GAME 16

7. Who sings about love's healing powers on "Love's Divine"?

a. Dave Matthews
b. Lenny Kravitz
c. Seal
d. Michael Bolton

GAME 16 Q6 ANSWER a
Sung by Stevie Nicks, "Dreams" is Fleetwood Mac's only #1 hit single to date. It came from the group's 1977 super-hit album, *Rumours,* which spent thirty-one big weeks at #1 on the US pop album charts. In 1986, Van Halen also had a hit song called "Dreams" (it went to #22 on the charts) from *5150*—the group's first #1 album.

GAME 36

7. "Take a Chance on Me," "Fernando," and "Dancing Queen" were all hits for which European rock band?

a. ABBA
b. Scorpions
c. Roxy Music
d. Kraftwerk

GAME 36 Q6 ANSWER c
Michael Stipe was born in Decatur, Georgia on January 4, 1960. In 1980, Stipe was studying photography and painting at the University of Georgia when he met Peter Buck, Bill Berry, and Mike Mills. The four college students formed R.E.M., with Stipe as lead vocalist.

GAME 56

7. Which song was *not* made famous by Lloyd Price?

a. "Yakety-Yak"
b. "Stagger Lee"
c. "Personality"
d. "I'm Gonna Get Married"

GAME 56 Q6 ANSWER b
After The Go-Go's broke up in 1985, Carlisle embarked on a successful solo career. Her other '80s solo singles include the #1 hit "Heaven Is a Place on Earth;" the Top 10 hit "Circle in the Sand;" and "Leave a Light On," which went to #11. In 2001, The Go-Go's reunited and put out the new album *God Bless the Go-Go's.*

GAME 76

7. What is the name of the notorious "hidden track" on Nirvana's 1991 album *Nevermind*?

a. "Endless Nameless"
b. "Scentless Apprentice"
c. "Tourette's"
d. "Something in the Way"

GAME 76 Q6 ANSWER b
The song, written by singer-songwriter Bill Withers, was a #1 hit in 1972. Popular '80s R&B group Club Nouveau recorded its version of the song in 1987, and once again it shot to #1, earning Withers his third Grammy as a songwriter. The song enjoyed further popularity in the 1989 film *Lean on Me,* starring Morgan Freeman.

<table>
<tr><td>

GAME 5

7. *Mirage, Huevos, and Monsters* are all albums by which hardcore punk band?

a. Bad Brains

b. Replacements

c. Meat Puppets

d. Husker Du

</td><td>

GAME 5 Q6 ANSWER b

Cervenka's given first name is "Christine" and she was married from 1980 to 1985 to the band's guitarist John Doe—yep, that's his real name. Doors' keyboardist Ray Manzarek came aboard to produce three of X's best albums in the '80s, while Exene Cervenka got married again—this time, to actor Viggo Mortensen from 1987 to 1992.

</td></tr>
<tr><td>

GAME 25

7. What is a former name of the heavy metal band Spinal Tap?

a. The Double Deckers

b. The Old Originals

c. Piccadilly Circus Clowns

d. The Thamesmen

</td><td>

GAME 25 Q6 ANSWER c

Joe Franklin had interviewed nearly 300,000 performers since first going on the air in 1951. By 1984, it was forgivable for him not to know that the heavy metal band he was interviewing was in fact composed of American actors using fake British accents. You can see the Joe Franklin segment on the *This Is Spinal Tap* DVD.

</td></tr>
<tr><td>

GAME 45

7. For which album did The Rolling Stones win its first Grammy for Best Rock Album?

a. *Steel Wheels*

b. *Voodoo Lounge*

c. *Beggars Banquet*

d. *It's Only Rock and Roll*

</td><td>

GAME 45 Q6 ANSWER b

At Budokan is a live album released by Cheap Trick in 1978. Although technically considered a concert album, *Got Live If You Want It!* features two songs that were recorded in a studio and not in a live concert. Both "Fortune Teller" and "I've Been Loving You Too Long" had audience overdubs added by recording studio engineers.

</td></tr>
<tr><td>

GAME 65

7. What quartet was pushed into the spotlight by its debut album *Forgiven, Not Forgotten*?

a. The Wallflowers

b. Crash Test Dummies

c. The Corrs

d. Oasis

</td><td>

GAME 65 Q6 ANSWER a

Formed in 1962, The Chieftains are known for performing traditional Irish music. Band leader and founder Paddy Moloney—who plays traditional instruments such as the Uilleann pipes and the bodhran—composes and/or arranges most of The Chieftains' music. The group has won six Grammy awards and been nominated eighteen times.

</td></tr>
</table>

6. Who had a #1 hit in 1977 with the song "Dreams"?

GAME 16

a. Fleetwood Mac

b. Marvin Gaye

c. Debby Boone

d. Lionel Richie

GAME 16 Q5 ANSWER a
After a string of hits throughout the 1980s, Billy Joel decided he wanted to be the first rock act to play in Russia since the Berlin Wall went up in 1961. Six live shows were pulled together into a double-album that reached #38 on the US pop album charts. A big show favorite was Joel's cover of The Beatles' "Back in the USSR."

---

6. Which of these famous rockers was *not* born in England?

GAME 36

a. Eric Clapton

b. Peter Gabriel

c. Michael Stipe

d. Paul McCartney

GAME 36 Q5 ANSWER a
Gene Vincent and The Blue Caps had their biggest US chart hit in 1956 with "Be-Bop-A-Lula." That same year in England, a fourteen-year-old Paul McCartney first saw a sixteen-year-old John Lennon sing this song with his group The Quarrymen. Lennon later recorded the song for his 1975 album *Rock 'n' Roll*.

---

6. Which former lead singer of The Go-Go's had a hit with "I Get Weak"?

GAME 56

a. Susanna Hoffs

b. Belinda Carlisle

c. Joan Jett

d. Chynna Phillips

GAME 56 Q5 ANSWER c
This song remains one of the best ever written for The Kinks by lead singer Ray Davies. It was released on the group's 1967 album *Something Else By the Kinks*, and went to #2 on the UK charts. Rumor has it that the song is about a real-life romantic encounter between actors Terence Stamp and Julie Christie, but Davies denies it.

---

6. Which song was a #1 hit in both the 1970s and 1980s?

GAME 76

a. "Take My Breath Away"

b. "Lean on Me"

c. "On My Own"

d. "Greatest Love of All"

GAME 76 Q5 ANSWER b
Raised in the "Hell's Kitchen" section of Manhattan, Orlando was best friends with comic Freddie Prinze. Although he began as a crooner in the early '60s, Orlando didn't have success until a decade later with his backup group Dawn. Their hits were "Candida," "Knock Three Times," and "Tie a Yellow Ribbon 'Round the Old Oak Tree."

<table>
<tr><td>

8. Which of the following is *not* a song by Dead Kennedys?

a. "Chemical Warfare"

b. "Anarchy in the UK"

c. "Holiday in Cambodia"

d. "Let's Lynch the Landlord"

</td><td>

GAME 5 Q7 ANSWER c

Hardcore punk emerged in the US in the early '80s, but never really hit the mainstream. It did, however, mix a bit with heavy metal. The result? Speed metal, defined best by such groups as Anthrax, Megadeth, and the Grammy-winning Metallica. The classic hardcore punk sound was reinvented in the '90s by Green Day.

</td></tr>
<tr><td>

8. Which psychedelic tune from Spinal Tap is a hit from the Summer of Love?

a. "Hell Hole"

b. "Stonehenge"

c. "Flower People"

d. "The Sun Never Sweats"

</td><td>

GAME 25 Q7 ANSWER d

David St. Hubbins was first with a group called The Creatures, and Nigel Tufnel was in Lovely Lads. The two joined together and started The Originals in 1964, but changed to The New Originals when they learned that another group already had their name. Later, as The Thamesmen, they had a minor hit with "Gimme Some Money."

</td></tr>
<tr><td>

8. Which female vocalist sang a duet with Mick Jagger on the 1978 song "Beast of Burden"?

a. Carly Simon

b. Marianne Faithfull

c. Bette Midler

d. Tina Turner

</td><td>

GAME 45 Q7 ANSWER b

Thirty-two years after it began, The Rolling Stones were finally given some satisfaction by the music biz with this first Grammy win. *Voodoo Lounge* was produced by Don Was of the '80s band Was (Not Was). Mick Jagger and Keith Richards were also named as producers under the name "The Glimmer Twins."

</td></tr>
<tr><td>

8. Blues guitarist Rory Gallagher recorded three albums with which band prior to its breakup?

a. Foghat

b. Taste

c. Big Star

d. Fleetwood Mac

</td><td>

GAME 65 Q7 ANSWER c

Consisting of three sisters and one brother, The Corrs formed to audition for the 1991 film *The Commitments* and, during the audition, captured the interest of their future manager, John Hughes. The group's 1995 album *Forgiven, Not Forgotten* first did well only in Australia, France, and Ireland, but eventually won global success.

</td></tr>
</table>

GAME 16

5. Whose 1987 tour of the Soviet Union resulted in the double album *Kohyept*?

a. Billy Joel
b. Scorpions
c. David Lee Roth
d. Billy Graham

GAME 16 Q4 ANSWER d
Released two years before Seattle grunge led to strong debut albums by Nirvana (*Nevermind*) and Pearl Jam (*Ten*) in 1991, *Louder than Love* set the stage for Soundgarden's classic albums *Badmotorfinger* and Grammy-winning *Superunknown*. Led by Evan Dando, the Lemonheads released its first major-label album, *Lovey*, late in 1990.

GAME 36

5. What rocker was the featured member of The Blue Caps?

a. Gene Vincent
b. Eddie Cochran
c. Bill Haley
d. Duane Eddy

GAME 36 Q4 ANSWER d
A solo hit by former Wham! member George Michael, "Faith" is the title track of Michael's 1987 debut album. The album *Faith* has the distinction of being the first album by a white solo artist to rise to #1 on the R&B charts, while the song became one of Michael's most popular recordings.

GAME 56

5. Which British Invasion band scored a big hit in the UK with "Waterloo Sunset"?

a. The Rolling Stones
b. The Dave Clark Five
c. The Kinks
d. The Animals

GAME 56 Q4 ANSWER c
Formed in 1961, this UK band had an instantly recognizable sound in the electric keyboard of Rod Sargent. The Zombies three Top 10 hits were "She's Not There" (1964), "Tell Her No" (1965), and "Time of the Season" (1969). Ignored when first released in 1968, the group's last album, *Odessey and Oracle,* is now considered a classic.

GAME 76

5. What pop singer was born Michael Cassavitis in New York City in 1944?

a. Roy Orbison
b. Tony Orlando
c. Tom Jones
d. Elton John

GAME 76 Q4 ANSWER b
The group started the RCA-distributed Grunt Records in 1971 when singer Marty Balin and drummer Spencer Dryden quit. They put out two albums of their own—*Bark* (1971) and *Long John Silver* (1972)—as well as albums by fiddler Papa John Creach and Hot Tuna, a side project of Jefferson Airplane's Jack Casady and Jorma Kaukonen.

GAME 5

9. From 1974 to 1975, The Ramones were the house band at what famous New York City club?

a. Wetlands

b. Bowery Ballroom

c. CBGB's

d. Radio City Music Hall

GAME 5 Q8 ANSWER b

Hailing from San Francisco in the late '70s, Dead Kennedys was in many ways America's answer to the Sex Pistols. Frontman, Jello Biafra, used humorous lyrics to satirize people and situations. The group's first single in 1979, "California Über Alles," took aim at the policies of then-California governor Jerry Brown.

GAME 25

9. Which Spinal Tap track is found on their *Break Like the Wind* album?

a. "Cups and Cakes"

b. "The Majesty of Rock"

c. "Big Bottom"

d. "Gimme Some Money"

GAME 25 Q8 ANSWER c

The sitar solo quotes Mozart and features a very strategically placed "wrong" note that further satirizes the group's pompous methods of music making. This scene is a total rip on all of the late '60s bands, including The Monkees.

GAME 45

9. Along with Mick Jagger, which Rolling Stones' member appears in the movie *The Rutles: All You Need Is Cash*?

a. Charlie Watts

b. Ron Wood

c. Bill Wyman

d. Keith Richards

GAME 45 Q8 ANSWER c

Recorded for her 1983 album *No Frills*, the "Divine Miss M" and Mick Jagger deliver a powerhouse duet on this Stones' song that became one of the album's highlights. The video for this song was also popular with MTV fans. In 1986, Jagger performed the theme song for the Bette Midler/Danny DeVito comedy hit, *Ruthless People*.

GAME 65

9. This brother of Irish singing legend Christy Moore, born Barry Moore, is better known as:

a. Billy Bragg

b. Luka Bloom

c. Joe Cocker

d. Beck

GAME 65 Q8 ANSWER b

Established in 1966 by renowned Irish blues/rock guitarist Rory Gallagher, Taste recorded two studio albums and made two live recordings. The band is best remembered for its 1970 appearance at the Isle of Wight Festival, where Taste played eight encores before the audience finally allowed the group to leave the stage.

GAME 16

4. *Louder than Love* was a 1989 album release of which grunge band?

a. Nirvana
b. Pearl Jam
c. Lemonheads
d. Soundgarden

GAME 16 Q3 ANSWER d
Jethro Tull's first album *This Was* was released in 1968. After its 1971 hit *Aqualung,* the group began further experimentation. The 1972 album *Thick as a Brick* had only one song, while the group's 1973 *A Passion Play* featured a single song interrupted by a fairy tale called "The Story of the Hare Who Lost His Spectacles."

GAME 36

4. Which of these #1 hit songs was *not* a duet?

a. "Say, Say, Say"
b. "Ebony and Ivory"
c. "Up Where We Belong"
d. "Faith"

GAME 36 Q3 ANSWER b
Creedence Clearwater Revival—frequently referred to as CCR, or simply Creedence—had its first hit single in 1968 with the Dale Hawkins swamp-rock classic "Suzie Q." "Proud Mary" became the group's second hit in 1969, after which CCR recorded a series of successful tunes, including 1969's "Bad Moon Rising."

GAME 56

4. Which of these negative songs was a hit for The Zombies in 1965?

a. "I'm Not Your Clown"
b. "The Twelfth of Never"
c. "Tell Her No"
d. "Not a Second Time"

GAME 56 Q3 ANSWER b
The Yardbirds had prepared new material to play when filmed in this movie. But director Michelangelo Antonioni wanted the group to perform its version of the '50s song "The Train Kept a-Rollin'." Unable to secure permission to use that song in the film, the group changed the words and renamed the song "Stroll On."

GAME 76

4. In the 1970s, which San Francisco-based band formed its own custom label, Grunt Records?

a. The Grateful Dead
b. Jefferson Airplane
c. Moby Grape
d. Journey

GAME 76 Q3 ANSWER b
Ian had her first hit at age fifteen with "Society's Child," which reached the Top 20 in 1967. "At Seventeen," with its poignant take on teenage angst, struck a nerve with the public and became a big hit. It reached #3 on the pop charts, and won the Grammy for Best Female Pop Vocal. In addition to songs, Ian also writes sci-fi novels.

10. Mission of _____ was a popular post-punk band in the early 1980s.

a. Survival

b. Toledo

c. Cornwall

d. Burma

Strangely enough, CBGB's is short for "Country BlueGrass Blues." Opened in 1973 by Hilly Kristal, CBGB's almost immediately became home to the growing punk scene in New York City. The Ramones' sets usually lasted around twenty minutes, producing a barrage of two-minute songs almost without interruption.

---

10. In which city was Spinal Tap playing when they got lost backstage?

a. Detroit

b. Boston

c. Cleveland

d. Los Angeles

During the tour for this album, Spinal Tap lead guitarist Nigel Tufnel played an electric guitar that was in the shape of a Marshall amplifier stack. In a joke on Jimmy Page's technique of using a violin bow on the strings of his guitar, Nigel instead rubbed a violin against the guitar.

---

10. Which Rolling Stones' song was featured in the 1987 film *Full Metal Jacket*?

a. "Paint It Black"

b. "(I Can't Get No) Satisfaction"

c. "Jumpin' Jack Flash"

d. "Tell Me"

Monty Python's Eric Idle had already done some Rutles spoofs on *Saturday Night Live* in 1976. The Rolling Stones had also been on the show around that time. *SNL* producer Lorne Michaels decided to produce a Rutles movie, which featured Mick Jagger and Ron Wood, along with Paul Simon and actual Beatle George Harrison in a cameo.

---

10. What U2 song is a tribute to Martin Luther King, Jr.?

a. "Sunday Bloody Sunday"

b. "New Year's Day"

c. "Pride (In the Name of Love)"

d. "With or Without You"

To avoid comparisons with sister Christy, Luka Bloom took his first name from a Suzanne Vega song and his second name from the James Joyce novel *Ulysses*. Bloom is known for his distinctive style of guitar playing—a strumming style he adopted when tendonitis forced him to abandon his original fingerpicking technique.

---

3. *Thick as a Brick* and *A Passion Play* were popular albums by which '70s British band?

a. Moody Blues

b. Fleetwood Mac

c. Emerson, Lake, & Palmer

d. Jethro Tull

GAME 16 Q2 ANSWER d
In 1971, Bryan Ferry paired up with fellow art student and electronic music pioneer Brian Eno to start Roxy Music. The group had its first big hit in 1975 with "Love Is the Drug," but Eno had left the group by then. In 1982, Roxy Music had a hit song and MTV video with "More Than This" from its final studio album, *Avalon*.

---

3. "Suzie Q" was the first hit single from which group's debut album?

a. The Coasters

b. CCR

c. Chicago

d. The Commodores

GAME 36 Q2 ANSWER b
In the summer of 1970, "All Right Now" rose to #1 in the UK and #4 in the US. Because the band broke up soon after this hit, Free is considered a one-hit wonder. But "All Right Now" became nationally famous in 1972, when the Stanford University Band adopted it as its official tune, playing it at that year's Rose Bowl halftime show.

---

3. Which '60s British rock group appears in the 1966 film *Blow-Up*?

a. The Kinks

b. The Yardbirds

c. The Animals

d. The Hollies

GAME 56 Q2 ANSWER d
Written by songwriters Mort Garson and Bob Hilliard, this song was a #1 hit in 1963 for Ruby & the Romantics. Led by singer Ruby Nash Curtis, this group, which had only the one hit, broke up in 1971. "Our Day Will Come" is heard in the films *Shag* and *She's Out of Control*, featuring my daughter, Ami Dolenz, in her movie debut.

---

3. Which singer won a Grammy for her 1975 song "At Seventeen"?

a. Olivia Newton-John

b. Janis Ian

c. Joan Baez

d. Helen Reddy

GAME 76 Q2 ANSWER b
Bad Company was a '70s British supergroup that featured players from King Crimson, Free, and Mott The Hoople. The group was one of the first signed to Led Zeppelin's own independent record label, Swan Song, in 1974. In 1984, four years after Led Zeppelin folded, Page went on to start The Firm with Bad Company lead singer Paul Rodgers in 1984.

---

11. Which punk band's songs include such gems as "Now I Wanna Sniff Some Glue"?

a. The Police

b. Wham!

c. Baker Street

d. The Ramones

GAME 5 Q10 ANSWER d
This Boston-based group was the most promising new punk group of 1983 with the release of *Vs*, its debut album. Then the band broke up and didn't record another album for twenty-two years—during which time Pearl Jam released its own album named *Vs*. Back with a new album titled *Onoffon* in 2004, the Mission of Burma continues.

11. What is one of Nigel Tufnel's most prized possessions in *This Is Spinal Tap*?

a. Mini Steinway piano

b. Guitar pick made of gold

c. Triple-necked guitar

d. Amp that goes to 11

GAME 25 Q10 ANSWER c
There's no sadder (or funnier!) moment in *This Is Spinal Tap* than when bassist Derek Smalls calls out "Hello, Cleveland! Hello, Cleveland!" in anticipation of hitting the stage . . . only to never find the stage. For rock musicians, this is almost as painfully comical as the group's record store appearance that no fans attend.

11. The Rolling Stones' 2002 greatest hits collection is titled *Forty* _____.

a. *Rocks*

b. *Stones*

c. *Licks*

d. *Hits*

GAME 45 Q10 ANSWER a
Director Stanley Kubrick deliberately chose to have "Paint It Black" playing on the film's soundtrack just as the screen goes black and the end credits begin. Francis Ford Coppola also set a certain mood with "(I Can't Get No) Satisfaction" in his 1979 film *Apocalypse Now*, while director Hal Ashby used "Jumpin' Jack Flash" in *Coming Home* (1978).

11. Shane MacGowan of Ireland was a leading force behind which punk-folk act?

a. Television

b. Teenage Fanclub

c. Soundgarden

d. The Pogues

GAME 65 Q10 ANSWER c
The first single launched from the 1984 album *Unforgettable Fire*, "Pride (In the Name of Love)" is one of U2's best-known songs. A major chart success and a U2 concert favorite, it is credited with introducing the band to a broader audience, and has been called a modern rock classic.

2. The multifaceted rock group Roxy Music was the brainchild of which English art student?

a. Peter Gabriel

b. Ray Davies

c. Brian May

d. Bryan Ferry

GAME 16 Q1 ANSWER d
Released in 1994 as a labor of love by these punk pioneers, *Acid Eaters* features sped-up covers of songs by The Rolling Stones ("Out of Time"), Jefferson Airplane ("Somebody to Love"), and The Who ("Substitute") among others. Listen closely on "Substitute" for the backing vocals by Who guitarist Pete Townshend!

2. Which British band hit the Top 10 only once with "All Right Now" in 1970?

a. Blind Faith

b. Free

c. Badfinger

d. Moody Blues

GAME 36 Q1 ANSWER a
The Supremes racked up a total of twelve #1 hits between 1964 and 1969. Beginning as The Primettes in 1959, the group changed its name to The Supremes after signing with Motown in 1961. Once the trio achieved success with Diana Ross as lead singer, Motown president Berry Gordy rechristened it Diana Ross & The Supremes.

2. Which '60s pop song was featured in two 1989 Hollywood movies?

a. "Another Saturday Night"

b. "It's My Party"

c. "He's So Fine"

d. "Our Day Will Come"

GAME 56 Q1 ANSWER d
This song was a 1996 hit for Garbage, featuring lead singer Shirley Manson. Thirty years earlier, in 1966, The Rolling Stones had its own song called "Stupid Girl." It was the second track on the *Aftermath* UK album, which includes classics like "Mother's Little Helper," "Lady Jane," and "Under My Thumb."

2. Guitarist Jimmy Page was *not* a member of:

a. Led Zeppelin

b. Bad Company

c. The Firm

d. The Yardbirds

GAME 76 Q1 ANSWER b
Status Quo first made its way into The Guinness Book of World Records' for these four concerts, which here held in Glasgow, Sheffield, Birmingham, and Wembley respectively. The group went on to set another Guinness World Record in 2005 for recording sixty-one hit singles—the most that any band has ever had in UK chart history.

12. This bassist for The Clash is smashing his guitar on the cover of *London Calling:*

a. Joe Strummer
b. Ronnie Van Zant
c. Ray Manzarek
d. Paul Simonon

GAME 5 Q11 ANSWER d
With classic song titles like "I Wanna Be Sedated," "Judy Is a Punk," and "Gimme Gimme Shock Treatment," it seems clear that The Ramones were never ones for subtlety. The group's bare-bones approach to music is what made it stand out. The quartet was inducted into the Rock and Roll Hall of Fame in 2002.

12. Which of these actors was *not* part of the cast of *This Is Spinal Tap?*

a. Ben Stiller
b. Michael McKean
c. Harry Shearer
d. Christopher Guest

GAME 25 Q11 ANSWER d
Saying that "these go to 11" has become code language for most guitarists. Another of Nigel's favorite things is his cherryburst Gibson Les Paul electric guitar that's "famous for its sustain." In the film, Nigel also displays a custom t-shirt that shows the exact skeletal structure of his body—including his *green* blood.

12. Which Rolling Stones' song was the first to reach #1 on the Billboard charts?

a. "Time Is on My Side"
b. "Tell Me"
c. "It's All Over Now"
d. "(I Can't Get No) Satisfaction"

GAME 45 Q11 ANSWER c
Though now considered the band's definitive greatest hits collection, this forty-song CD is *not* the only one the group has ever made. In 1972, *Hot Rocks* became one of the most popular Stones' "best-of" compilations available. Before that, there was *Big Hits (High Tide and Green Grass)* in 1966, and *Through the Past Darkly* in 1969.

12. The Chieftains won an Oscar for their soundtrack to which Stanley Kubrick film?

a. *The Shining*
b. *Barry Lyndon*
c. *2001: A Space Odyssey*
d. *A Clockwork Orange*

GAME 65 Q11 ANSWER d
Originally called Pogue Mahone, which is Gaelic for "kiss my backside," The Pogues formed in 1982. The group's politically tinged music first featured only traditional Irish instruments, but later included electronic instruments as well. The Pogues' commercial success hit its peak in the late '80s—shortly before MacGowan left the group.

GAME 16

1. *Acid Eaters* is an album of 1960s favorites by which band?

a. The Rolling Stones

b. Jefferson Airplane

c. The Who

d. The Ramones

The answer to this question is on:

page 130, top frame, right side.

GAME 36

1. Which was the first American group to have five consecutive #1 hits?

a. The Supremes

b. The Jackson Five

c. The Eagles

d. The Beach Boys

The answer to this question is on:

page 130, second frame, right side.

GAME 56

1. Who released the rock recording "Stupid Girl"?

a. No Doubt

b. Smashing Pumpkins

c. Nine Inch Nails

d. Garbage

The answer to this question is on:

page 130, third frame, right side.

GAME 76

1. In 1991, which rock group held four charity concerts in four British cities in twelve hours in 1991?

a. Scorpions

b. Status Quo

c. Steeler

d. Kansas

The answer to this question is on:

page 130, bottom frame, right side.

GAME 6

The '50s

*Turn to page 135
for the first question.*

*Turn to page 135
for the first question.*

GAME 5 Q12 ANSWER d

The image on the cover of this explosive 1979 double-album signaled the moment when punk became respectable. It was also Simonon's tribute to fellow English rocker Pete Townshend, who smashed guitars with The Who in the '60s. Simonon's broken electric bass guitar is on display at the Rock and Roll Hall of Fame.

GAME 26

The Beach Boys

*Turn to page 135
for the first question.*

*Turn to page 135
for the first question.*

GAME 25 Q12 ANSWER a

Director Rob Reiner also appears as Marty DiBergi, director of this "mockumentary." There are many small cameos in the film, including Howard Hesseman of *WKRP in Cincinnati* fame; Billy Crystal and Dana Carvey as arguing mime caterers; and Bruno Kirby as Spinal Tap's Sinatra-loving limo driver Tommy Pischedda.

GAME 46

The Doors

*Turn to page 135
for the first question.*

*Turn to page 135
for the first question.*

GAME 45 Q12 ANSWER d

According to Keith Richards, he came up with the "Satisfaction" riff late one night in a hotel room during the Stones' 1965 US Tour. Mick Jagger then wrote lyrics for it, and a demo was recorded in May 1965. The demo was released by London Records and quickly reached #1. *Rolling Stone* magazine named it the best rock song ever.

GAME 66

1990s Love Songs

*Turn to page 135
for the first question.*

*Turn to page 135
for the first question.*

GAME 65 Q12 ANSWER b

The Chieftains got their major break in the US when they were asked to provide traditional Irish pieces for Kubrick's 1975 film *Barry Lyndon*. Although the film wasn't a great commercial success, The Chieftains were—especially Sean Ó Riada's original composition "Women of Ireland," which received heavy radio play on certain stations.

GAME 16

GRAB BAG

*Turn to page 132
for the first question.*

GAME 15 Q12 ANSWER b
A crucial pioneer of thrash metal, Pantera, which was formed in 1981, hailed from Dallas, Texas. Fellow metal bands Megadeth and Metallica emerged from the West Coast and Anthrax came from New York. After Pantera disbanded in 2003, the Abbotts formed a new band named Damageplan.

GAME 36

GRAB BAG

*Turn to page 132
for the first question.*

GAME 35 Q12 ANSWER a
This song rose to #1 on the Modern Rock chart, but achieved a more modest #68 on the Hot 100. Along with the single "Ocean Breathes Salty," "Float On" was first released on the group's 2004 album *Good News for People Who Love Bad News*—Modest Mouse's fourth full-length album.

GAME 56

GRAB BAG

*Turn to page 132
for the first question.*

GAME 55 Q12 ANSWER a
To indicate his bitterness about being contractually shackled to Warner Brothers, Prince went out in public with the word "slave" printed on his cheek. When released from the contract in 1996, Prince released *Emancipation*. At three hours, this album holds the Guinness World Record for the longest album of all time.

GAME 76

GRAB BAG

*Turn to page 132
for the first question.*

GAME 75 Q12 ANSWER a
John Lee Hooker turns up in this film, performing the song "Boom Boom" in his trademark half-spoken vocal style. Hooker was joined in the film by fellow R&B legends Ray Charles, Aretha Franklin, Chaka Khan, and James Brown. Scat singing legend Cab Calloway was even shown in the film singing his classic "Minnie the Moocher."

GAME 6

1. What is the literal translation of the musical term "a cappella"?

a. "with voices"

b. "with leads"

c. "as in church"

d. "without music"

The answer to this question is on:

page 137, top frame, right side.

GAME 26

1. What was the first #1 hit recorded by The Beach Boys?

a. "Surfin' USA"

b. "I Get Around"

c. "Good Vibrations"

d. "California Girls"

The answer to this question is on:

page 137, second frame, right side.

GAME 46

1. Along with "Light My Fire," what song did The Doors perform on *The Ed Sullivan Show*?

a. "People Are Strange"

b. "Love Me Two Times"

c. "Hello, I Love You"

d. "Break on Through"

The answer to this question is on:

page 137, third frame, right side.

GAME 66

1. Who reached the top of the charts with "Vision of Love" on her debut album?

a. Mariah Carey

b. Celine Dion

c. Whitney Houston

d. Sheryl Crow

The answer to this question is on:

page 137, bottom frame, right side.

12. Brothers Darrell and Vinnie Paul Abbott formed which heavy metal band?

a. Megadeth
b. Pantera
c. Slaughter
d. King Diamond

GAME 15 Q11 ANSWER a
In 1975, Lemmy Kilmister started a rock band that would play faster and louder than any other. Motörhead's first album was released in 1977 and its extreme sound influenced groups like Metallica. Thirty years after Motorhead began, it won a 2005 Best Metal Performance Grammy for its cover of Metallica's "Whiplash."

12. Who floated onto the Billboard charts with "Float On" in 2004?

a. Modest Mouse
b. The Killers
c. Jet
d. Son Volt

GAME 35 Q11 ANSWER c
Featured on the band's 2003 album *Welcome Interstate Managers*, the song describes a school boy's adolescent fantasies about a female friend's mother. Part of the hit song's popularity was due to the video, which features several scenes in which supermodel Rachel Hunter portrays the title character.

12. The *Emancipation* album refers to Prince's freedom from which record company?

a. Warner Brothers
b. Virgin
c. Epic
d. Capitol

GAME 55 Q11 ANSWER d
"Alphabet St." is a Top 10 hit from Prince's 1988 album *Lovesexy*. This popular soundtrack album by Prince & The Revolution spent twenty-four weeks on top of the US album charts, and won the 1985 Oscar for Best Original Score. A prolific songwriter and bold musician, Prince was inducted into the Rock and Roll Hall of Fame in 2004.

12. Which of these blues greats appeared in the 1980 film *The Blues Brothers*?

a. John Lee Hooker
b. B.B. King
c. Muddy Waters
d. Lonnie Brooks

GAME 75 Q11 ANSWER c
Buddy Guy has been a hero to rock guitar icons since he started playing at Chess Records in 1959. Although Jimi Hendrix popularized the practice of playing the guitar behind one's back, he learned it from seeing Guy perform live. In 2005, Buddy Guy was inducted into the Rock and Roll Hall of Fame by Eric Clapton and B.B. King.

2. "Yakety Yak" and "Charlie Brown" were hit singles in the late '50s for which group?

a. The Clovers
b. The Orioles
c. The Coasters
d. The Del Vikings

GAME 6 Q1 ANSWER c
The term means to sing without instrumental accompaniment. Throughout the centuries, it has been customary to hear unaccompanied singing in many European churches. Here in the US, church singing—Southern gospel music, especially—figured prominently in the style of early rockers like Elvis and Little Richard.

---

2. With which song did The Beach Boys hit the charts in 1988 on the soundtrack of the film *Cocktail?*

a. "Darlin'"
b. "Kokomo"
c. "Good Vibrations"
d. "In My Room"

GAME 26 Q1 ANSWER b
With Mike Love in the lead, "I Get Around" hit the top spot in June 1964. Earlier singles of this California group that were big hits, but failed to reach #1, included "Surfer Girl," "Surfin' USA," "Little Deuce Coupe," "Be True to Your School," and "In My Room."

---

2. Which is the only Doors' album with no bass player?

a. *The Doors*
b. *Strange Days*
c. *Morrison Hotel*
d. *The Soft Parade*

GAME 46 Q1 ANSWER a
While most people remember The Doors performed its #1 hit "Light My Fire" on *The Ed Sullivan Show* in September of 1967, many forget that the group first performed its Top 30 hit "People Are Strange" on that same show. The Doors also performed "People Are Strange" on *Murray the K in New York* later that same year.

---

2. What tender ballad is found on the Extreme album *Pornograffiti?*

a. "Tears in Heaven"
b. "More Than Words"
c. "Lips Like Sugar"
d. "There She Goes"

GAME 66 Q1 ANSWER a
"Vision of Love" was one of four singles launched by Carey's 1990 self-titled album, which climbed to the top of the charts. Co-written by Carey, "Vision of Love" was first recorded on the artist's demo tape—a tape that was heard by record exec Tommy Mottola, who not only signed Carey, but also married her. They were divorced in 1997.

---

11. Bassist Lemmy Kilmister is the leader of which group?

a. Motörhead
b. Thin Lizzy
c. Humble Pie
d. Anthrax

GAME 15 Q10 ANSWER a
In most metal bands, the guitarist gets all of the attention. However, guitarist Mick Mars remains the most subdued and least-known member of Mötley Crüe. While his bandmates have consistently made headlines for womanizing, car crashes, street brawls, and near-death overdoses, Mick Mars has pretty much stayed off the radar.

11. Who, according to Fountains of Wayne, has it "goin' on"?

a. Our Boy Dom
b. Chaka Khan
c. Stacy's Mom
d. Jennifer Aniston

GAME 35 Q10 ANSWER a
A Tex-Mex rock group from San Angelo, Texas, Los Lonely Boys—brothers Henry, Jojo, and Ringo Garza—released their debut album in 2004. Their hit single "Heaven," featured on that album, not only reached #16 on the Billboard Hot 100, but also won a Grammy Award for Best Pop Performance by a Duo or Group with Vocal.

11. Which of the following songs is *not* from Prince's smash *Purple Rain* album?

a. "I Would Die 4 U"
b. "Let's Go Crazy"
c. "When Doves Cry"
d. "Alphabet St."

GAME 55 Q10 ANSWER a
"When You Were Mine" was featured on Lauper's wildly popular 1983 debut album, *She's So Unusual*, which reached #4 in the US. By 1984, this album had provided four Top 5 hit singles—"She Bop," "Time After Time," "Girls Just Want to Have Fun," and "All Through the Night."

11. Which blues legend was the house guitarist at Chess Records for much of the 1960s?

a. B.B. King
b. Albert King
c. Buddy Guy
d. Jimmy Reed

GAME 75 Q10 ANSWER a
Buddy Holly recorded a revved-up version of this classic Chuck Berry song in early 1957. It wasn't released to the public until 1963—four years after his death in that fateful plane crash. Chuck Berry remains a crucial figure in rock-and-roll history, inspiring bands like The Beatles, The Beach Boys, and The Rolling Stones.

3. Which rock-and-roll star gave Waylon Jennings his big break in the late 1950s?

a. Elvis Presley
b. Roy Orbison
c. Buddy Holly
d. Eddie Cochran

GAME 6 Q2 ANSWER c
Originally called The Robins before changing its name in 1955, this beloved quartet also had hits with "Searchin'," "Along Came Jones," "Poison Ivy," and "Young Blood," a song The Beatles often performed. In 1987, The Coasters was the first vocal group to be inducted into the Rock and Roll Hall of Fame.

3. In "California Girls," The Beach Boys hail southern girls for the way they:

a. Smile
b. Laugh
c. Kiss
d. Talk

GAME 26 Q2 ANSWER b
Written by Mike Love, Scott MacKenzie, Terri Melcher, and John Phillips, "Koko-mo" was the only Beach Boys #1 hit that was *not* written or co-written by Beach Boy Brian Wilson. Besides being featured in the film *Cocktail*, the song was released on the album *Still Cruisin'*.

3. How many #1 hits did The Doors have?

a. Three
b. Two
c. One
d. None

GAME 46 Q2 ANSWER a
When recording *The Doors* in 1967, Ray Manzarek played keyboards and bass simultaneously. He played a Vox Continental electric piano with his right hand, while playing a Rhodes piano bass (stacked on top of the Vox) with his left hand. Though they used bassists on later albums, Manzarek kept playing both instruments in concert.

3. What pop-rock band rose to the top of the charts in 1992 with "To Be With You"?

a. Tesla
b. Faster Pussycat
c. Motley Crue
d. Mr. Big

GAME 66 Q2 ANSWER b
Extreme enjoyed fame as a heavy metal band in the late '80s. In the group's 1990 album *Pornograffiti*, the romantic ballad "More Than Words" surprised Extreme's audience by departing from the band's usual style. The song raced to the #1 spot on the Hot 100, bringing the group its first mainstream success in the US.

10. "Loud rude aggressive guitarist available" read the ad that got Mick Mars a gig with:

a. Mötley Crüe
b. Twisted Sister
c. Poison
d. Warrant

GAME 15 Q9 ANSWER c
Before Machine Head was formed in 1992, its name was better known in metal history as the title of Deep Purple's classic 1971 album. Although it is considered a "thrash" metal band, the group itself rejects that label. Machine Head had the bad luck of releasing a video, "Crashing Around You," just after 9/11.

---

10. In their breakthrough hit, Los Lonely Boys want to know how far ____ is.

a. Heaven
b. Hope
c. Insanity
d. Desperation

GAME 35 Q9 ANSWER a
"Maybelline," a unique version of the Bob Wills hit song "Ida Red," was named after a line of cosmetics. Released as a single in July 1955, the Chuck Berry recording peaked at #1 on the R&B charts in August, ending the eleven-week reign of Fats Domino's "Ain't That a Shame."

---

10. Which song did Prince write for '80s icon Cyndi Lauper?

a. "When You Were Mine"
b. "She Bop"
c. "Time After Time"
d. "Girls Just Want to Have Fun"

GAME 55 Q9 ANSWER a
In a career comeback of sorts, Tom Jones paired with '80s techno group The Art of Noise to produce a version of "Kiss" that went to #31 on the pop charts. Prince's funky version of his own song was one of the biggest hit singles of 1986. Good news for Prince, since his second feature film *Under a Cherry Moon* was a box-office dud.

---

10. Buddy Holly covered which of the following Chuck Berry hits?

a. "Brown Eyed Handsome Man"
b. "Too Much Monkey Business"
c. "Johnny B. Goode"
d. "Sweet Little Sixteen"

GAME 75 Q9 ANSWER d
Fats Domino was born Antoine Dominique Domino in New Orleans in 1928. His recording of "The Fat Man" is considered by many to be the first rock-and-roll record. Drawing on a robust style of boogie-woogie piano playing, Domino had thirty-five Top 40 singles, including "I'm Walkin'," "Ain't That a Shame," and his version of "Blueberry Hill."

---

4. Which song was *not* a #1 hit during the 1950s?

a. "Smoke Gets in Your Eyes"
b. "Tammy"
c. "My Girl"
d. "Teddy Bear"

GAME 6 Q3 ANSWER c
Fellow Texan Buddy Holly produced Jennings' single "Jole Blon" in 1958, and used Jennings as a bassist. In 1959, Jennings gave up his seat to JP Richardson (The Big Bopper) on the fateful plane that crashed and killed the Bopper, Buddy Holly, and Richie Valens. Waylon was inducted into the Country Music Hall of Fame in 2001.

4. According to "Surfin' USA," who should be told that The Beach Boys are out riding waves?

a. The lifeguard
b. Their parents
c. Their teacher
d. Their girlfriends

GAME 26 Q3 ANSWER d
Not playing favorites, this 1965 song—written by Brian Wilson and Mike Love—praises east coast girls for their hip style; mid-west farmer's daughters for the way they make you feel; northern girls for the way they kiss; and west coast girls for their great tans.

4. Jim Morrison's father served in which branch of the US military?

a. Army
b. Marines
c. Navy
d. Air Force

GAME 46 Q3 ANSWER b
The group's first #1 hit was "Light My Fire," which was on the pop charts for three weeks in the summer of 1967. A year passed before "Hello, I Love You" reached the top of the charts in August 1968. By May 1971, The Doors' final hit, "Riders on the Storm," reached #14. Jim Morrison died two months later.

4. The Proclaimers' hit "I'm Gonna Be (500 Miles)" is on what film's soundtrack?

a. *The Mask*
b. *Benny & Joon*
c. *Sleepless in Seattle*
d. *Pretty Woman*

GAME 66 Q3 ANSWER d
The US band Mr. Big was formed in 1988 by Billy Sheehan, who is considered one of the top bassists of rock. After a disappointing response to its debut album, the band enjoyed a breakthough with its second album, 1991's *Lean Into It*, whose ballad "To Be With You" rose to #1 on the Billboard Hot 100.

9. Robb Flynn is the vocalist and guitarist for which metal group?

a. Napalm Death
b. White Zombie
c. Machine Head
d. Slayer

GAME 15 Q8 ANSWER d
Mixing heavy metal with a grotesque comic-book look, this British band debuted the "Eddie" mascot on its first album, *Iron Maiden*, in 1980. That same year, on the record sleeve for the group's *Sanctuary* EP, Eddie was shown slashing Prime Minister Margaret Thatcher with a knife. The controversy only made the group more popular.

9. "Maybellene" was the first hit song for which artist?

a. Chuck Berry
b. Bo Diddley
c. Little Richard
d. Fats Domino

GAME 35 Q8 ANSWER d
Perkins' song, which was released in 1956 on the Sun Records label, was based on an actual incident he witnessed during one of his gigs. Although it was the only Perkins' tune that made it into the pop Top 40, "Blue Suede Shoes" not only helped establish rockabilly music, but also propelled Sun Records to national prominence.

9. In 1988, who had a hit single with "Kiss" only two years after Prince took it to #1 on the charts?

a. Tom Jones
b. Rod Stewart
c. "Weird Al" Yankovic
d. Lou Reed

GAME 55 Q8 ANSWER c
Following the amazing success of the 1984 *Purple Rain* album and feature film, "Raspberry Beret" headed straight to the top of the charts (it eventually went to #2). However, *Around the World in a Day* was very different in sound and presentation from *Purple Rain*. The diehard fans followed, but pop chart addicts soon went elsewhere.

9. Which musical legend made his debut in 1949 with the song "The Fat Man"?

a. Fatty Arbuckle
b. Fats Waller
c. Minnesota Fats
d. Fats Domino

GAME 75 Q8 ANSWER d
Little Richard (born Richard Wayne Penniman) sang with a wilder, more electrifying voice than perhaps even Elvis Presley. His hit "Long Tall Sally" had a big effect on The Beatles, especially Paul McCartney. Little Richard suddenly quit rock 'n roll during a 1957 tour and became a minister. He returned to performing in 1962.

5. Greasy revival band Sha Na Na performed which '50s classic for the '69 Woodstock crowd?

a. "Sea Cruise"

b. "Rockin' Robin"

c. "At the Hop"

d. "Tears on My Pillow"

GAME 6 Q4 ANSWER c
The great Miracles' singer Smokey Robinson co-wrote "My Girl," which was a #1 hit for The Temptations in 1965. Although "Smoke Gets in Your Eyes" was a hit for The Platters in 1959, it was actually first written back in 1933 by Jerome Kern and Otto Harbach for the musical *Roberta*.

---

5. Which of the following surfing songs was *not* a hit for The Beach Boys?

a. "Surfin' Safari"

b. "Surfin' USA"

c. "Surfer Girl"

d. "Surf City"

GAME 26 Q4 ANSWER c
"Surfin' USA" was the title track of the 1963 album credited with breaking The Beach Boys' career wide open. The fuller sounding vocals (created by simply doubling them) and Brian Wilson's growing songwriting abilities were two of the elements that propelled the album to gold record status.

---

5. What word in "Light My Fire" was Jim Morrison told *not* to sing on *The Ed Sullivan Show* in 1967?

a. "Higher"

b. "Wire"

c. "Pyre"

d. "Night"

GAME 46 Q4 ANSWER c
James Douglas Morrison was one of three children born to Admiral George Stephen Morrison and his wife, Clara. Both of Morrison's parents were employed by the US Navy, which meant that Jim and his younger siblings, Anne and Andrew, spent a number of years moving from naval base to naval base throughout the country.

---

5. Which sultry singer hit #1 in early 1999 with the single "Angel of Mine"?

a. Toni Braxton

b. Monica

c. Aaliyah

d. Janet Jackson

GAME 66 Q4 ANSWER b
The song first appeared on The Proclaimers' 1988 album *Sunshine on Leith*, and was subsequently released as a single. Then in 1993, it became the theme song to the romantic comedy *Benny & Joon*. In Scotland, the home country of Proclaimers' Charlie and Craig Reid, "I'm Gonna Be (500 Miles)" is considered an unofficial National Anthem.

GAME 15

8. Eddie is a psychotic mascot created by which band?

a. Van Halen
b. Judas Priest
c. Mötley Crüe
d. Iron Maiden

GAME 15 Q7 ANSWER a
Formed in 1969, this heavy metal quintet from Hanover, Germany, only started to enjoy radio hits in the '80s with songs such as "No One Like You" and the great metal anthem "Rock You Like a Hurricane." Known for its always-tasteless album covers, Scorpions was also the first heavy metal band to play in the former USSR in 1988.

GAME 35

8. "Blue Suede Shoes" was the first hit single for which of the following singers?

a. Elvis Presley
b. Bobby Vee
c. Del Shannon
d. Carl Perkins

GAME 35 Q7 ANSWER a
"Don't Make Me Over" was only a moderate hit, and the followups were unsuccessful. But 1964's "Anyone Who Had a Heart" did well, and "Walk on By" became a major hit, launching Warwick's career. All three songs, as well as most of Warwick's other successful recordings of the '60s, were written by Burt Bacharach and Hal David.

GAME 55

8. The 1985 hit single "Raspberry Beret" comes from which Prince album?

a. *Diamonds and Pearls*
b. *Purple Rain*
c. *Around the World in a Day*
d. *1999*

GAME 55 Q7 ANSWER b
When Prince met actress/model Denise Matthews in 1982, he felt that looking at her was like looking into a mirror. He gave her the name "Vanity," and made her the lead singer of a group called Vanity 6. She left Prince in 1983 after landing a record deal with Motown Records, so he cast Apollonia Kotero in *Purple Rain* instead.

GAME 75

8. When did Little Richard give up rock 'n roll to become a Pentecostal minister?

a. 1986
b. 1976
c. 1962
d. 1957

GAME 75 Q7 ANSWER b
Johnson remains the most famous and influential Delta blues guitarist who ever lived. According to legend, in exchange for skill on the guitar, Johnson gave the devil his soul at the crossroads of US Highways 61 and 49 in Mississippi. Bob Dylan's song title "Highway 61 Revisited" is a reference to this longstanding blues legend.

---

6. What was the biggest hit for the 1950s R&B band The Cadillacs?

a. "Silhouettes on the Shade"

b. "Speedo"

c. "Shop Around"

d. "Get a Job"

GAME 6 Q5 ANSWER c
Originally a #1 hit for Danny & the Juniors in 1958, Sha Na Na's version of "At the Hop" at Woodstock set the stage for the resurgence of '50s music that soon took place. The mid-'70s success of ABC's *Happy Days* boosted Sha Na Na's popularity, and by 1978, the group had appeared in the film *Grease* and also had its own TV show.

6. Brian Wilson released a long-lost Beach Boys' album in 2004. What was its name?

a. *Dance*

b. *Smile*

c. *Laugh*

d. *Sing*

GAME 26 Q5 ANSWER d
Brian Wilson and Jan Berry—of Jan and Dean fame—collaborated on a number of hits, including "Surf City," which was recorded by Jan and Dean and rose to #1 status in 1963. Although Jan and Dean formed before The Beach Boys got together, they became best known for the surf music inspired by the second group.

6. Why was Jim Morrison arrested on stage during a Doors' concert in 1967?

a. Public indecency

b. Inciting a riot

c. Fighting with a security guard

d. Firing a gun

GAME 46 Q5 ANSWER a
Morrison was instructed to replace "Girl, we couldn't get much *higher*" to "Girl, we couldn't get much *better*." Morrison sang the word on the live show anyway, which caused a bit of a controversy. The Rolling Stones had a similar experience when asked to sing "Let's spend *the night* together" as "Let's spend *some time* together."

6. The Cure's Robert Smith is in love on what day of the week?

a. Sunday

b. Monday

c. Wednesday

d. Friday

GAME 66 Q5 ANSWER b
Monica Denise Arnold—better known as Monica—enjoyed triple-platinum success with her 1995 debut album *Miss Thang*. Then in 1998, she released her second album *The Boy Is Mine*, which featured not only "Angel of Mine," but also "The Boy Is Mine"—the artist's popular duet with Brandy. The result was another triple-platinum hit.

GAME 15

7. Which heavy metal band recorded the 1980s albums *Blackout* and *Animal Magnetism*?

a. Scorpions
b. Judas Priest
c. Motorhead
d. Iron Maiden

GAME 15 Q6 ANSWER a
Although Tool was formed in 1990, it hit it big only after playing the main stage during the 1993 Lollapalooza Tour. In addition to its incredibly intense live concerts and atmospheric metal-influenced music, Tool has also won diehard fans through its stop-motion animation videos created by the band's guitarist, Adam Jones.

GAME 35

7. 1962's "Don't Make Me Over" was the first hit for which singer?

a. Dionne Warwick
b. Lesley Gore
c. Dusty Springfield
d. Cilla Black

GAME 35 Q6 ANSWER c
The Miracles—who later became known as Smokey Robinson and the Miracles—were the first successful group act for Motown Records. Written by Bill "Smokey" Robinson and Berry Gordy, "Shop Around" was not only the group's first Motown hit, but also the first Motown song to rise to #1 on the R&B charts.

GAME 55

7. Which of the following Prince-discovered artists did *not* appear in the 1984 film *Purple Rain*?

a. Apollonia
b. Vanity
c. Wendy & Lisa
d. Doctor Fink

GAME 55 Q6 ANSWER d
Reaching #6 on the pop charts, "Little Red Corvette" came from Prince's album *1999,* and moved him from cult status to the mainstream. The album's title track went to #12 in the charts, while the album's third single, "Delirious," made it to #8. *1999* was actually Prince's fifth album—the first, *For You,* was released in 1978.

GAME 75

7. This blues guitarist was rumored to have sold his soul to the devil:

a. Charley Patton
b. Robert Johnson
c. Skip James
d. Kokomo Arnold

GAME 75 Q6 ANSWER c
The blues has always differed a bit from place to place. "Delta" blues was the most basic, with harmonica and acoustic slide guitar; "Memphis" blues started rock's tradition of a rhythm and lead guitarist; "Texas" blues had a looser sound derived from New Orleans jazz; and "Chicago" blues featured electric guitar and the saxophone.

7. Bill Haley & the _____ was a successful '50s rock group.

a. Playboys
b. Crickets
c. Comets
d. Moonbeams

GAME 6 Q6 ANSWER b
Racing to the top of the charts in 1955, "Speedo" featured the vocals of Earl "Speedo" Carroll. A sequel was released in 1958 called "Speedo Is Back," but wasn't as successful. Martin Scorsese featured "Speedo" in the opening scenes of his 1990 gangster film, *GoodFellas*.

7. In 1985, which Beach Boys' song provided David Lee Roth with a Top 5 US single?

a. "California Girls"
b. "Good Vibrations"
c. "Surfin' USA"
d. "Wouldn't It Be Nice"

GAME 26 Q6 ANSWER b
Originally called *Dumb Angel, Smile* was created in 1967, but was shelved due to both resistance from the group and Brian Wilson's personal problems. The 2004 album *Smile*—a rerecorded version of the previously cancelled album—was released to rave reviews and sparked a world tour.

7. Which is the only Doors' song to feature a lead vocal by guitarist Robby Krieger?

a. "Love Her Madly"
b. "Tell All the People"
c. "Queen of the Highway"
d. "Runnin' Blues"

GAME 46 Q6 ANSWER a
Morrison's onstage arrest occurred in New Haven, Connecticut, and was captured on film. He had been arrested three times prior to this incident—the first was in September 1963 in Tallahassee, Florida, for "drunkedness and petty larceny." In 1969, he was arrested once again for alleged indecent exposure during a concert in Miami.

7. What British band invaded the US charts with the majestic ballad "Wonderwall"?

a. Blur
b. Pulp
c. Oasis
d. Suede

GAME 66 Q6 ANSWER d
"Friday I'm in Love," a hook-laden offering from the 1992 album *Wish*, rose to #1 on the Modern Rock Tracks chart, while the album reached the #2 position on the Billboard 200. Like the other tracks on the album, this love song was penned by Cure members Perry Bamonte, Simon Gallup, Robert Smith, Porl Thompson, and Boris Williams.

6. *AEnima* is a best-selling album by which metal rock group?

a. Tool
b. Godsmack
c. Filter
d. Helmet

GAME 15 Q5 ANSWER a
Although most consider Osbourne the best Black Sabbath singer, Dio did incredible work on two of the best Black Sabbath albums to date: *Heaven and Hell* (1980) and *Mob Rules* (1981). In 1983, ex-Deep Purple lead vocalist Ian Gillan joined Black Sabbath.

6. The 1960 song "Shop Around" was the first hit for what Motown superstars?

a. The Four Tops
b. The Temptations
c. The Miracles
d. The Supremes

GAME 35 Q5 ANSWER c
"Do It Again" was featured on Steely Dan's 1972 debut album *Can't Buy a Thrill*, which went gold, rising to #17 on the charts. The album also yielded "Reeling in the Years," which rose to #11. ("Do It Again" peaked at #6.) All of the songs on the LP were written by Walter Becker and Donald Fagen.

6. Which "Little Red" car drove Prince to his first Top 10 hit?

a. Thunderbird
b. Mustang
c. Volkswagen
d. Corvette

GAME 55 Q5 ANSWER b
Prince performed "Partyup" during his first *SNL* appearance (on that same show, cast member Charles Rocket slipped and said "the F word"). On SNL's 15th Anniversary Special in 1989, Prince performed "Batdance" from his *Batman* album. Twenty-five years after his first appearance on the show, Prince returned to *SNL* in February 2006.

6. The Muddy Waters Band exemplified which type of blues?

a. Texas
b. Delta
c. Chicago
d. Memphis

GAME 75 Q5 ANSWER a
Why "Lucille," you ask? Well, the story goes that a fight started between two men during one of King's early gigs in 1949. The building caught fire during the fight, which forced an evacuation. King went back in to get his Gibson guitar and almost died. He later heard the two men were fighting over a woman named Lucille . . .

8. Which '50s rock star had a hit with the song "Great Balls of Fire"?

a. The Big Bopper

b. Bill Haley

c. Jerry Lee Lewis

d. Fats Domino

Bill Haley & the Comets recorded "Rock Around the Clock" on April 12, 1954. After the song was used in the opening credits of *The Blackboard Jungle* (1955), it became a #1 hit. George Lucas used it during the credits of *American Graffiti* (1973); and it was the theme song during the first season of TV's *Happy Days*.

---

8. What was the subject of The Beach Boys' hit song "Shut Down"?

a. Movie theater

b. Car race

c. Beach closing

d. Date refusal

While still a member of Van Halen, David Lee Roth released a solo EP of offbeat standards, which included both The Beach Boys' "California Girls" and Louis Prima's "Just a Gigolo/I Ain't Got Nobody." Both singles were hits, as was the album.

---

8. What was The Doors' last studio album before Jim Morrison's death in 1971?

a. *Morrison Hotel*

b. *The Doors*

c. *Waiting for the Sun*

d. *L.A. Woman*

A strange mix of country and jazz, "Runnin' Blues" is a Robby Krieger song from the group's most elusive album, *The Soft Parade* (1969). Though Jim Morrison is frequently cited for his poetic lyrics, it was Krieger who wrote "Light My Fire" along with other classic tunes like "Love Me Two Times," "Touch Me," and "Love Her Madly."

---

8. In 1996, what folk-rock band further established its popularity with "Crash Into Me"?

a. Dave Matthews Band

b. Spin Doctors

c. Blues Traveler

d. Ben Folds Five

"Wonderwall" helped the 1996 album *(What's the Story) Morning Glory?* rocket to #1 in England, and proved to be the group's American breakthrough hit, as well. Taking its name from George Harrison's 1968 solo album *Wonderwall Music*, "Wonderwall" is perhaps Oasis's most popular song, and appears on many "best of" singles polls.

---

5. Who replaced Ozzy Osbourne as lead singer of Black Sabbath in 1979?

a. Ronnie James Dio
b. Vince Neal
c. David Lee Roth
d. Robert Plant

GAME 15 Q4 ANSWER c
In 1976, the outspoken bassist from KISS saw the group perform at LA's Starwood Club and made the initial investment in producing a first demo. Not long after, they were signed by Warner Brothers Records and released their debut album in 1978. That same year, Van Halen opened for Black Sabbath on their Never Say Die! Tour.

5. With which of the following tunes did Steely Dan score its first hit single?

a. "Deacon Blues"
b. "Kid Charlemagne"
c. "Do It Again"
d. "Peg"

GAME 35 Q4 ANSWER a
In the 1970s, Heart, with lead singer Ann Wilson, was a hugely successful hard rock band. In 1976, their song "Crazy on You" reached #35 on the charts, to be followed later that year by "Magic Man," which rose to #9.

5. When did Prince first appear as the musical guest on *Saturday Night Live*?

a. 1979
b. 1981
c. 1999
d. 2006

GAME 55 Q4 ANSWER a
"U Got It Bad" is a #1 single by R&B singer-songwriter Usher from his album *8701*. Usher also wrote and released a song called "U-Turn" from that same album. Prince has a real thing for replacing the word "You" with the letter "U"—he even did it in 1990 when he wrote the hit song "Nothing Compares 2 U" for Sinead O'Connor.

5. What name does blues guitarist B.B. King give to all his guitars?

a. "Lucille"
b. "Maybelline"
c. "Donna"
d. "Riley"

GAME 75 Q4 ANSWER a
While Billie Holliday's singing voice offered a soft and haunted tone, Dinah Washington sang with a strength and intensity that earned her the nickname of "Queen of the Blues." Her best-known song, "What a Diff'rence a Day Makes," went to #8 in the pop charts and won her a Grammy for Best R&B Performance in 1959. She died in 1963.

GAME 6

9. Which song tried to provide an etiquette manual for lovestruck teens of the 1950s?

a. "The Ten Commandments of Love"

b. "A Lover's Question"

c. "The Book of Love"

d. "No, Not Much"

GAME 6 Q8 ANSWER c
For The Monkees 1969 TV special *33 1/3 Revolutions Per Monkee*, we were able to get Jerry Lee Lewis, Fats Domino, and Little Richard to appear on the program. Jerry Lee gave an especially inspired performance on that show, but most people didn't see it because the networks put it up against the Oscars.

GAME 26

9. In "Little Deuce Coupe," The Beach Boys claim they have all of these items except:

a. A flat head mill

b. A 409 engine

c. Four on the floor

d. A competition clutch

GAME 26 Q8 ANSWER b
Written by Brian Wilson and Roger Christian, "Shut Down" is a classic song about drag racing. One of The Beach Boys' many car songs, it was released on the 1963 album *Surfin' USA*, and tells the story of a fuel-injected Corvette Stingray that leaves a superstock Dodge in the dust.

GAME 46

9. Which of the following songs is *not* from The Doors' first album?

a. "Take It as It Comes"

b. "Soul Kitchen"

c. "Indian Summer"

d. "20th Century Fox"

GAME 46 Q8 ANSWER d
In the lyrics of "L.A. Woman," Morrison cleverly turned his name "Jim Morrison" by way of anagram into the song's own "Mr. Mojo Risin.'" He also recorded nearly all of the album's vocals in the studio bathroom to get that classic "reverb" sound. Oliver Stone filmed Val Kilmer singing "L.A. Woman" that way in his 1991 film *The Doors*.

GAME 66

9. In 1995, "Only Wanna Be With You" was a major hit for what band?

a. Geggy Tah

b. Dave Matthews Band

c. Hootie & the Blowfish

d. Better Than Ezra

GAME 66 Q8 ANSWER a
Early in its career, the Dave Matthews Band built a big following by touring college campuses, but 1996's *Crash* was the album that really put the group on the map. The band's best-selling album, it featured not only "Crash Into Me," but also the Grammy-winning "So Much to Say" and favorites such as "Two Step."

Answers are in right-hand boxes on page 153.   **151**

GAME 15

4. Which established rocker financed Van Halen's first demo tape?

a. Peter Frampton
b. Ozzy Osbourne
c. Gene Simmons
d. Eric Clapton

GAME 15 Q3 ANSWER b
The plaintiffs in this case alleged that Judas Priest had encouraged their sons to kill themselves by placing the words "do it" subliminally into the song "Better By You, Better Than Me" from the band's 1978 album, *Stained Class*. After five years of legal proceedings, a judge finally dismissed the charges in 1990.

GAME 35

4. Which female-led band's first hit was "Crazy on You"?

a. Heart
b. The Pretenders
c. Missing Persons
d. Martha and the Vandellas

GAME 35 Q3 ANSWER a
Although Diamond's "Solitary Man" was not a tremendous hit when it was released in January 1966, it paved the way for "Cherry, Cherry," which met with instant success when it was released later that same year. Several hits followed—including "I'm a Believer," which topped the charts for The Monkees.

GAME 55

4. Which of these "U" songs is *not* by Prince?

a. "U Got It Bad"
b. "Take Me With U"
c. "Do U Lie?"
d. "U Got the Look"

GAME 55 Q3 ANSWER d
Prince played the part of "Camille" in this 1987 song by speeding up his recorded voice to sound more feminine. The "Camille" persona was created a year earlier when Prince recorded eight songs with the sped-up voice. Although the *Camille* album was never released, three songs from those sessions turned up on *Sign 'O' the Times*.

GAME 75

4. Which of these singers was born Ruth Lee Jones?

a. Dinah Washington
b. Odetta
c. Nina Simone
d. Billie Holiday

GAME 75 Q3 ANSWER c
In the late '50s, James Brown created a wild and crazy stage presence. During the Monkees' 1967 tour, I used to perform a song on my own in homage to "the Godfather of Soul." I'd even drop to the floor like he used to, and Mike would come out on stage to wrap me in a cloak (another James Brown-ism). I really got into character!

10. Which starlet of the 1950s married singer Bobby Darin?

a. Liz Taylor
b. Ann-Margret
c. Sandra Dee
d. Annette Funicello

The Monotones belong to that lovable group known to trivia mavens as "one-hit wonders." Formed in 1955, the six-member doo-wop group came from the same Newark, New Jersey housing project. They recorded "The Book of Love" in 1957, and it became a Top 10 hit when released in 1958. By 1962, The Monotones had split up.

10. What country music great played bass guitar for The Beach Boys in 1965?

a. Waylon Jennings
b. Roy Orbison
c. Glen Campbell
d. Wilson Pickett

"Little Deuce Coupe" was the title track of a 1963 album. The car referred to is a Ford Model B. The 1932 version, commonly called a "deuce coupe," was popular with hot-rodders because it was readily available, and could be easily stripped of extra weight and souped up.

10. What's the name of The Doors' second album?

a. *Axis: Bold As Love*
b. *Disraeli Gears*
c. *Strange Days*
d. *Paranoid*

"Indian Summer" was one of the first songs written by Robby Krieger and Jim Morrison for The Doors as a band. It was first recorded on an early demo tape in 1965, but the group felt it was not as strong as other material. The song finally appeared on the 1970 album, *Morrison Hotel*. It remains one of their most beautiful songs.

10. What movie featured Bryan Adams' 1991 hit "(Everything I Do) I Do It For You"?

a. *Notting Hill*
b. *Robin Hood*
c. *Sleepy Hollow*
d. *Mansfield Park*

Hootie & the Blowfish's 1994 debut album, *Cracked Rear View*, was an instant success, eventually selling over 16 million copies in the US. The album launched five hit singles, including the love song "Only Wanna Be With You," as well as "Hold My Hand," "Let Her Cry," "Drowning," and "Time."

GAME 15

3. Which band was sued by two families for causing their sons' suicides in 1985?

a. Metallica
b. Judas Priest
c. Slayer
d. KISS

GAME 15 Q2 ANSWER d
Although Metallica's . . . *And Justice for All* album was also nominated for the 1989 Best Hard Rock Performance Grammy, it lost to Jethro Tull's synth-laden *Crest of a Knave*. Metallica did, however, win Grammys for Best Metal Performance both in 1989 and 1990, and then won Best Metal Recording in 1991 with its self-titled album.

GAME 35

3. Which singer's first hit was "Solitary Man" in 1966?

a. Neil Diamond
b. Barry Manilow
c. B.J. Thomas
d. Neil Sedaka

GAME 35 Q2 ANSWER b
Orbison wrote "Only the Lonely" for Elvis Presley and also offered it to the Everly Brothers before recording it himself. Released as a single in 1960, the song—which was written by Orbison and Joe Melson—rose to #2 on the US Billboard pop music charts and #1 in the UK.

GAME 55

3. What is the name of Prince's alter ego, who is credited with the lead vocal on the song "If I Was Your Girlfriend"?

a. Cynthia
b. Candace
c. Catherine
d. Camille

GAME 55 Q2 ANSWER c
"U Got the Look" is featured on Prince's 1987 double-album *Sign 'O' the Times*. The song's drum part was played by Prince protégé Sheila E., who had a Top 10 hit in 1984 with "The Glamorous Life." Prince first worked with Easton that same year, writing her provocative song "Sugar Walls" under the pseudonym of Alexander Nevermind.

GAME 75

3. Whose red satin and rhinestone tuxedo jacket is on display at the Rock and Roll Hall of Fame?

a. Junior Wells
b. Leadbelly
c. James Brown
d. Wynonie Harris

GAME 75 Q2 ANSWER b
Dixon helped define Chicago's electric blues music in the '50s. Though a great bassist and accomplished music producer, Dixon's true genius was songwriting. The Doors covered Dixon's "Back Door Man" on their 1967 debut album, while Led Zeppelin did versions of "You Shook Me" and "I Can't Quit You Baby" on their first album in 1969.

11. "Summertime Blues" was the only Top 10 hit for which rockabilly star of the '50s?

a. Ricky Nelson

b. Roy Orbison

c. Eddie Cochran

d. Dale Hawkins

GAME 6 Q10 ANSWER c
Born as Alexandra Zuck in 1942, Sandra Dee had already won a Golden Globe for "Most Promising Newcomer" in 1958 before marrying Bobby Darin in 1960. Darin's first hits on the pop charts were the rock 'n roll classics "Splish Splash" in 1958 and "Dream Lover" in 1959.

---

11. What was the first Beach Boys' album to be produced by Brian Wilson?

a. *Surfer Girl*

b. *Surfin' USA*

c. *Surfin' Safari*

d. *Little Deuce Coupe*

GAME 26 Q10 ANSWER c
In 1958, Arkansas native Campbell moved to Los Angeles and became a session musician—a musician available for hire. During this period, Campbell played not only with The Beach Boys, but also with Bobby Darin, Rick Nelson, Elvis Presley, Merle Haggard, The Mamas and the Papas, *and* The Monkees.

---

11. Which Doors' album features the song "Waiting for the Sun"?

a. *The Soft Parade*

b. *Waiting for the Sun*

c. *Morrison Hotel*

d. *L.A. Woman*

GAME 46 Q10 ANSWER c
Many songs from *Strange Days* were written before the Doors' first album, including "When the Music's Over." The group first recorded this song without Jim Morrison, who hadn't shown up that day. The other "second" album choices are by Jimi Hendrix (*Axis: Bold As Love*), Cream (*Disraeli Gears*), and Black Sabbath (*Paranoid*).

---

11. Whose 1995 debut album includes the hit single "You Were Meant for Me"?

a. Jewel

b. Spice Girls

c. The Fugees

d. Beth Orton

GAME 66 Q10 ANSWER b
Co-written and performed by Adams for *Robin Hood: Prince of Thieves,* the song was initially disliked by the film company, and was buried at the end of the credits. Yet it became a worldwide success, spending seven weeks at #1 in the US, and breaking records in the UK by remaining in the #1 position for sixteen weeks.

GAME 15

2. Whose songs "One" (1989) and "Stone Cold Crazy" both won Grammys for Best Metal Performance?

a. Aerosmith

b. Nine Inch Nails

c. Stone Temple Pilots

d. Metallica

GAME 15 Q1 ANSWER d
Founded in Birmingham, England in 1969 under the name Earth, Black Sabbath remains the first group whose slow, ominous riff-based music would become universally known as "heavy metal." With legendary frontman Ozzy Osbourne at the helm, Sabbath created such occult-tinged metal classics as "N.I.B.," "War Pigs," and "Iron Man."

GAME 35

2. Which of the following was Roy Orbison's first Top 10 hit single?

a. "Pretty Woman"

b. "Only the Lonely"

c. "Cryin'"

d. "Dream Baby"

GAME 35 Q1 ANSWER c
That same year, Tom Jones also scored hits with the themes to the movies *What's New, Pussycat* and *Thunderball*. By 1970, Jones had sold over 30 million discs and was the world's highest-paid TV star, with his show *This Is Tom Jones* airing in both the UK and the US.

GAME 55

2. The song "U Got the Look" is a duet featuring Prince and:

a. Patti LaBelle

b. Anne Murray

c. Sheena Easton

d. Cyndi Lauper

GAME 55 Q1 ANSWER a
Born in Minneapolis, Minnesota, in 1958, Prince was given this royal name because his father, John Nelson, played in a jazz group called The Prince Rogers Trio at that time. Over the years, Prince has adopted a number of pseudonyms, including Paisley Park, Joey Coco, and Christopher Tracy.

GAME 75

2. Which bluesman wrote classics "Back Door Man" and "Little Red Rooster"?

a. Memphis Slim

b. Willie Dixon

c. Muddy Waters

d. John Lee Hooker

GAME 75 Q1 ANSWER b
Bo Diddley (born Othas Ellas Bates) changed rock guitar with a unique playing style that emphasized heavy, chugging rhythms rather than melody. In 1955, Diddley was the first African-American to appear on *The Ed Sullivan Show*, and his songs have been covered by dozens of rockers, including Buddy Holly, The Who, and George Thorogood.

12. Best known as an actor, he had a #1 hit with "Young Love" in 1957:

a. Bobby Rydell
b. Fabian
c. Tab Hunter
d. Frankie Avalon

GAME 6 Q11 ANSWER c
Born in Albert Lee, Minnesota in 1938, Eddie Cochran got his first acclaim when he performed his song "Twenty Flight Rock" in the 1956 Jayne Mansfield movie *The Girl Can't Help It*. Before "Summertime Blues," he had a Top 20 hit with "Sittin' in the Balcony" in 1957. Cochran was killed in a car crash in 1960.

12. Who was the only member of The Beach Boys who surfed?

a. Brian Wilson
b. Carl Wilson
c. Murry Wilson
d. Dennis Wilson

GAME 26 Q11 ANSWER a
In 1963, The Beach Boys' popularity was so high that when *Surfer Girl* was released almost simultaneously with *Little Deuce Coupe*—another Brian Wilson-produced effort—both albums hit the Top 10. Both albums include the hallmark Beach Boys mix of songs about surfing, cars, and girls.

12. Which song by The Doors is the longest?

a. "When the Music's Over"
b. "The End"
c. "The Soft Parade"
d. "L.A. Woman"

GAME 46 Q11 ANSWER c
This one's tricky. Although their 1968 album is called *Waiting for the Sun*, The Doors did not release a song with that title until two years later on *Morrison Hotel* (1970). *Waiting for the Sun* also features a track called "Not to Touch the Earth," in which Morrison calls himself "The Lizard King" for the first time.

12. Which R&B singer is known for love ballads such as "No One Else Comes Close"?

a. Tyrese
b. Joe
c. Usher
d. Sisqo

GAME 66 Q11 ANSWER a
Jewel cut her debut album *Pieces of You* when she was only nineteen, and it sold over 11 millions copies in the US, making it one of the best-selling debut albums ever. Although most of the album's songs were written solely by Jewel, "You Were Meant for Me" was co-written by friend Steve Poltz, founding member of The Rugburns.

1. Who recorded such hit albums as *Paranoid* and *Master of Reality*?

a. Blue Oyster Cult

b. Jethro Tull

c. Pink Floyd

d. Black Sabbath

The answer to this question is on:

page 156, top frame, right side.

1. Who had his first hit in 1965 with "It's Not Unusual"?

a. Neil Diamond

b. Wayne Newton

c. Tom Jones

d. Gary US Bonds

The answer to this question is on:

page 156, second frame, right side.

1. What is Prince's real name?

a. Prince Rogers Nelson

b. Prince Gordon Sumner

c. Prince Vincent Furnier

d. Prince Stanley Eisen

The answer to this question is on:

page 156, third frame, right side.

1. Who became a blues and rock legend in the '50s with his square-shaped electric guitars?

a. Jerry Lee Lewis

b. Bo Diddley

c. Wayne King

d. Little Willie John

The answer to this question is on:

page 156, bottom frame, right side.

GAME 7

The '60s

*Turn to page 161
for the first question.*

Turn to page 161
for the first question.

GAME 6 Q12 ANSWER c
Tab Hunter's recording of "Young Love" replaced Sonny James' version on the charts in February 1957. Hunter's version stayed at #1 for six weeks, while his other single, "Ninety-Nine Ways," went to #11. Hunter's career was revived in the '80s with a small role in *Grease II*, and his work with camp film director John Waters.

GAME 27

Shooting Stars

*Turn to page 161
for the first question.*

Turn to page 161
for the first question.

GAME 26 Q12 ANSWER d
Although surfing themes were prominent in the early Beach Boys' songs, Dennis Wilson was the sole surfer of the group, and the one who suggested that they capitalize on the southern California surfing craze. Murry, by the way, was the father of Brian, Carl, and Dennis, and not a member of The Beach Boys.

GAME 47

Different Drums

*Turn to page 161
for the first question.*

Turn to page 161
for the first question.

GAME 46 Q12 ANSWER b
"The End" from the group's 1967 debut album is its longest song at eleven minutes, thirty-five seconds. "When the Music's Over" clocks in at ten minutes, fifty-nine seconds, while "The Soft Parade" sneaks into third place at eight minutes, thirty-six seconds. "L.A. Woman" is seven minutes, fifty-three seconds long.

GAME 67

"Day" Songs

*Turn to page 161
for the first question.*

Turn to page 161
for the first question.

GAME 66 Q12 ANSWER b
Joe Thomas—usually credited as simply Joe—released his album *All That I Am* in 1997 after signing a contract with Jive Records. This was the artist's breakthrough album, and included not only "No One Else Comes Close," but also the hits "All the Things (Your Man Won't Do)," "Don't Wanna Be a Player," and "The Love Scene."

GAME 15
Heavy Metal

Turn to page 158
for the first question.

GAME 14 Q12 ANSWER b
Adams formed this alternative country group in 1994 in Raleigh, North Carolina. Praised for its unique sound and lyrics, the group released three albums before disbanding in 1999. Ryan Adams put out his first solo LP, *Heartbreaker*, in 2000. Between making albums, Adams has performed live with Elton John and Willie Nelson.

GAME 35
Their First Hits

Turn to page 158
for the first question.

GAME 34 Q12 ANSWER a
With lyrics by Bernie Taupin, this song was recorded by John in 1984 and released on his album *Breaking Hearts*. The single of "Sad Songs (Say So Much)" never made it to #1, rising to #7 on the UK charts and #5 on the US charts.

GAME 55
Prince

Turn to page 158
for the first question.

GAME 54 Q12 ANSWER c
This final song on Simon's 1983 album *Hearts and Bones* memorializes both legendary blues guitarist Johnny Ace and ex-Beatle John Lennon, who had been assassinated by Mark David Chapman just three years earlier. Paul Simon was living in England in 1964 when Beatlemania first hit the US.

GAME 75
Pioneers and Precursors

Turn to page 158
for the first question.

GAME 74 Q12 ANSWER a
Seven Mary Three formed in Williamsburg, Virginia in 1992. Although people often assume that the group's name refers to the Trinity, founder Jason Ross traces it to a call sign used on the TV series *ChiPs*. The group's success with the single "Cumbersome" opened the door to a contract with the Mammoth record label.

1. Which city is considered the birthplace of the psychedelic rock scene?

a. Chicago

b. Los Angeles

c. San Francisco

d. New York City

The answer to this question is on:

page 163, top frame, right side.

1. Which Buddy Holly song hit the charts first?

a. "That'll Be the Day"

b. "Peggy Sue"

c. "Maybe Baby"

d. "Oh Boy"

The answer to this question is on:

page 163, second frame, right side.

1. Who was the drummer for Led Zeppelin?

a. Paul Cook

b. Larry Mullen, Jr.

c. Ron Bushy

d. John Bonham

The answer to this question is on:

page 163, third frame, right side.

1. Which song did Prince write for The Bangles?

a. "Blue Monday"

b. "I Don't Like Mondays"

c. "Monday, Monday"

d. "Manic Monday"

The answer to this question is on:

page 163, bottom frame, right side.

12. Before going solo, which North Carolina singer-songwriter led the band Whiskeytown?

a. Ian Matthews
b. Ryan Adams
c. Joe Henry
d. Ron Sexsmith

GAME 14 Q11 ANSWER b
The group, famous for its dueling guitarists Dan Baird and Rick Richards, was formed in 1980. *Keep the Faith,* its first recorded album, was made independently in 1985. "Keep Your Hands to Yourself" from the group's self-titled debut LP, reached #2 on the pop charts in 1987.

12. Which of these songs by Elton John was *not* a #1 hit in the 1970s?

a. "Sad Songs (Say So Much)"
b. "Crocodile Rock"
c. "Bennie and the Jets"
d. "Island Girl"

GAME 34 Q11 ANSWER c
Because John again collaborated with longtime lyricist Bernie Taupin on this album, and also brought back former band members such as Nigel Olsson, some critics said that *Songs From the West Coast* returned John to his musical roots. Although the album received good reviews, it did not fare well in sales.

12. Which of the following Paul Simon songs is from his solo career?

a. "Cecilia"
b. "Fakin' It"
c. "The Late Great Johnny Ace"
d. "So Long, Frank Lloyd Wright"

GAME 54 Q11 ANSWER a
Phil and Don Everly had a big influence on Paul Simon's music and the harmonies he first sang with Art Garfunkel while performing "Hey, Schoolgirl" back in 1958. They appear on this Grammy-winning album along with the celebrated South African chorus group Ladysmith Black Mambazo and Tex-Mex rock band Los Lobos.

12. Which group topped the rock charts in 1996 with the single "Cumbersome"?

a. Seven Mary Three
b. Ben Folds Five
c. 3LW
d. S Club 7

GAME 74 Q11 ANSWER b
Although 1984's "Pride (In the Name of Love)" did not win a Grammy for U2, it is one of their best-known songs. Written for Martin Luther King, Jr., "Pride" became the band's first Top 5 hit in the UK, and first Top 40 hit in the US. The song also marks the band's shift from a sound of overall stridency to one of greater subtlety.

GAME 7

2. Which "Brothers" group had a hit with "Time Has Come Today"?

a. The Chambers Brothers
b. The Righteous Brothers
c. The Isley Brothers
d. The Statler Brothers

GAME 7 Q1 ANSWER c
The seeds of psychedelia were first sown back in the San Francisco of the 1950s, where Beat poet Allan Ginsberg first read his classic poem "Howl" and fellow poet Lawrence Ferlinghetti opened City Lights Bookstore. By 1966, both The Grateful Dead and Jefferson Airplane were making music in San Fran's Haight-Asbury section.

GAME 27

2. In "Purple Haze," Jimi Hendrix asks to be excused while he:

a. Kisses the sky
b. Says goodbye
c. Starts to die
d. Eats some pie

GAME 27 Q1 ANSWER a
"That'll Be the Day" was released in 1957, becoming a #1 seller. The title came from John Wayne's oft-repeated line in the film *The Searchers*. "Peggy Sue" and "Oh Boy" hit the charts later that year, and "Maybe Baby" was released in 1958.

GAME 47

2. Who played drums for The Police?

a. Roger Taylor
b. Stewart Copeland
c. Jon Moss
d. Clem Burke

GAME 47 Q1 ANSWER d
Known as "Bonzo," John Bonham bashed skins for Led Zeppelin from 1969 until he died in 1980. He was the loudest drummer in England, playing with the heaviest drumsticks around (he called them "trees"). His passionate drumming was crucial to the Zeppelin sound, and he received a posthumous Lifetime Achievement Grammy in 2005.

GAME 67

2. Which song is by U2?

a. "Any Old Sunday"
b. "Sunday Morning"
c. "Sunday Bloody Sunday"
d. "Hello Sunday Hello Road"

GAME 67 Q1 ANSWER d
Written under the pseudonym Christopher Tracy, this 1986 song was The Bangles' first hit. It went to #2 on the pop charts, behind Prince's own single "Kiss." Later in 1986, The Bangles had its first of two #1 hits with "Walk Like an Egyptian." The group's second #1 song was 1988's "Eternal Flame," co-written by Bangles' lead singer Susanna Hoffs.

---

11. Which country-oriented rock group had a hit with "Keep Your Hands to Yourself"?

a. ZZ Top
b. Georgia Satellites
c. Charlie Daniels Band
d. Fabulous Thunderbirds

GAME 14 Q10 ANSWER c
Led by brothers Chris and Rich Robinson, The Black Crowes has sold over 5 million albums since the release of *Shake Your Money Maker*. The album's tracks "Hard to Handle" and "She Talks to Angels" cracked the Top 30 pop charts that same year. In 2000, lead singer, Chris Robinson, married Goldie Hawn's daughter, Kate Hudson.

---

11. Elton John's 2001 album was entitled *Songs From the ____*.

a. Sahara
b. Steppes
c. West Coast
d. North Pole

GAME 34 Q10 ANSWER c
A big sports fan, John was thrilled to meet tennis pro Billie Jean King at a party. When King gave John a customized track suit, John showed his appreciation by writing the song "Philadelphia Freedom," named after the tennis team that King coached. Single copies bear the dedication to "B.J.K."

---

11. Who sings backup on Paul Simon's song "Graceland"?

a. The Everly Brothers
b. Linda Ronstadt
c. The Four Tops
d. The Jordanaires

GAME 54 Q10 ANSWER a
This reunion song, which rose to #9 on the charts, was written by Paul Simon and appeared on both his album *Still Crazy After All These Years* and Art Garfunkel's album *Breakaway*. Just five years earlier, Simon and Garfunkel had gone their separate ways after recording the Grammy-winning Best Album *Bridge Over Troubled Water*.

---

11. For which of these songs did U2 *not* earn a Grammy Award?

a. "Walk On"
b. "Pride"
c. "Beautiful Day"
d. "Elevation"

GAME 74 Q10 ANSWER d
This was The Jackson 5's debut album with Motown. Although both the album title and the liner notes suggest that Ross discovered the group, that story was actually manufactured as a public relations stunt. The Gary, Indiana group had really been discovered by Motown stars Gladys Knight and Bobby Taylor.

---

3. Which psychedelic rock band of the '60s was led by Arthur Lee?

a. Love

b. The Beau Brummels

c. The Amboy Dukes

d. Canned Heat

GAME 7 Q2 ANSWER a
Released in the mad season of war protest and assassinations that was 1968, "Time Has Come Today" was a breakthrough hit for The Chambers Brothers. This trippy song went as high as #11 for the soul group from Mississippi. Unlike other so-called "brothers" acts, George, Joe, Lester, and Willie Chambers were actual brothers.

3. With which tune did Janis Joplin have a posthumous #1 hit?

a. "Piece of My Heart"

b. "Ball and Chain"

c. "Me and Bobby McGee"

d. "Red Rubber Ball"

GAME 27 Q2 ANSWER a
The meaning and origin of the phrase "kiss the sky" has been widely debated. Some say it refers to drugs—specifically, LSD. Some say it was taken from a science fiction novel by Philip Jose Farmer. Some have misheard it as "kiss this guy." Hendrix once explained that the 1967 song is about love—not about drugs.

3. Who played drums for Cream?

a. Ginger Baker

b. Vinnie Appice

c. John Densmore

d. Levon Helm

GAME 47 Q2 ANSWER b
The youngest child of a CIA agent, Stewart Copeland spent his early years living in the Middle East before moving to England in 1975. He founded The Police with Sting in 1977, and is known for his use of unusual percussive rhythms in rock. He is also a film director—his Police documentary, *Everyone Stares,* was released in 2006.

3. "Another Saturday Night" was a big hit for this quintessential soul man:

a. Sam Cooke

b. Solomon Burke

c. Wilson Pickett

d. Jackie Wilson

GAME 67 Q2 ANSWER c
Written by Bono in 1983, U2's song responds to two deadly clashes between British and Irish factions in Northern Ireland. The first incident took place in 1920, and the second was in 1972—and both are known as "Bloody Sunday." After the 1972 conflict, John Lennon and Yoko Ono also wrote a song called "Sunday Bloody Sunday."

GAME 14

10. *Shake Your Money Maker* was the hit 1990 debut album of which group?

a. Smashing Pumpkins
b. Blind Melons
c. Black Crowes
d. Los Lobos

GAME 14 Q9 ANSWER d
Hailing from Tennessee, Kings of Leon is led by the Followill brothers—Caleb on lead vocals and rhythm guitar; Jared on bass; and Nathan on drums. The group is named after the Followill's father and grandfather, both named Leon. Kings of Leon got a big career boost when it was chosen to open for U2's Vertigo Tour in 2005.

GAME 34

10. For which professional athlete did Elton John write his 1975 hit "Philadelphia Freedom"?

a. Julius Erving
b. Pete Rose
c. Billie Jean King
d. Bobby Hull

GAME 34 Q9 ANSWER b
Five songs from this 1994 Disney animated feature film were composed by John and Rice. The soundtrack of *The Lion King* was a huge success, and the John-Rice song "Can You Feel the Love Tonight" was the biggest hit that Elton John had enjoyed in years.

GAME 54

10. Paul Simon reunited with Art Garfunkel in 1975 to record which song?

a. "My Little Town"
b. "The Sound of Silence"
c. "The Boxer"
d. "Mrs. Robinson"

GAME 54 Q9 ANSWER a
Phoebe and Paul got together on "Gone at Last," which made the Top 40 in 1975. Although he did not do anything on the record, Paul Simon's longtime friend Chevy Chase lip-synched the lyrics in the 1987 video for "You Can Call Me Al." The video was nominated that year for Best Male Video at the now-annual MTV Video Music Awards.

GAME 74

10. Which of these songs is featured on the 1969 album *Diana Ross Presents The Jackson 5*?

a. "Sugar Daddy"
b. "Show You the Way to Go"
c. "Never Can Say Goodbye"
d. "I Want You Back"

GAME 74 Q9 ANSWER b
"A Day in Erotica" is a track on the album *Sixteen Tambourines* by The Three O'-clock—a so-called Paisley Underground Band that performed in the mid-'80s. The well-known band Three Dog Night performed between 1969 and 1975, scoring a succession of twenty-one hits, the most famous of which is 1971's "Joy to the World."

4. Who recorded the lengthy 1969 psychedelic song "In-A-Gadda-Da-Vida"?

a. The Grateful Dead
b. Iron Butterfly
c. Moby Grape
d. Jefferson Airplane

GAME 7 Q3 ANSWER a
This LA band's first album was the 1966 self-titled *Love*. Although popular in its own time, Love is perhaps known better now for sharing the bill with The Doors at the legendary LA rock club Whiskey A-Go-Go the night that Jim Morrison threw Oedipal references into their classic song "The End" . . . and got the group fired!

4. Which city was the site of the last concert featuring Jim Morrison and The Doors?

a. Cleveland
b. Miami
c. New Orleans
d. Naples

GAME 27 Q3 ANSWER c
The Joplin recording—featured on the 1971 *Pearl* album, which she was working on at the time of her death—was the second posthumous #1 hit in rock and roll history. The first was Otis Redding's 1968 "(Sittin' On) The Dock of the Bay," which was released shortly after Redding's death in a plane crash.

4. Who is the drummer for Def Leppard?

a. Frank Beard
b. Rick Allen
c. Liberty DeVito
d. Tommy Lee

GAME 47 Q3 ANSWER a
Born Peter Edward Baker in London in 1939, "Ginger" Baker joined Eric Clapton and Jack Bruce to form Cream in 1966. His playing is heavily influenced by jazz rhythms and improvisation. Baker was one of the first rock-and-roll drummers to use two bass drums on his set.

4. "Friday I'm in Love" is a song by which forerunners of goth-rock?

a. The Sex Pistols
b. Black September
c. The Smashing Pumpkins
d. The Cure

GAME 67 Q3 ANSWER a
This jam reached #1 on the R&B charts and #10 on the pop charts. It was released as a single in 1963 and also appeared on Cooke's 1964 album *Ain't That Good News*. Cooke was killed in 1964 at the peak of his career, but his songs live on. "Another Saturday Night," for example, was remade by both Jimmy Buffett and Cat Stevens.

Answers are in right-hand boxes on page 169.

9. *Aha Shake Heartbreak* is an album by which Southern quartet?

a. Franz Ferdinand
b. Papa Roach
c. Blue Rodeo
d. Kings of Leon

GAME 14 Q8 ANSWER b
Written as a retort and defense of the South, Lynyrd Skynyrd's 1974 anthem makes a lyrical reference to Canadian rocker Neil Young and his anti-racism 1970 protest song "Southern Man." By the way, Young's full name is Neil Percival Kenneth Robert Ragland Young. Pretty hard to mention all that in a song . . .

9. On which of the following musicals did Elton John collaborate with Tim Rice?

a. *Beauty and the Beast*
b. *The Lion King*
c. *The Little Mermaid*
d. *Aladdin*

GAME 34 Q8 ANSWER c
Elton John's performance wasn't the only one to enliven the 1975 movie of the rock opera *Tommy*. The film also features acclaimed performances by Eric Clapton (in "Eyesight to the Blind") and Tina Turner (in "Acid Queen"). And, of course, there's The Who.

9. Other than Art Garfunkel, with which singer did Paul Simon record a hit duet?

a. Phoebe Snow
b. Billy Idol
c. David Bowie
d. Olivia Newton-john

GAME 54 Q8 ANSWER a
This semi-autobiographical 1980 film saw Simon playing Jonah Levin, an aging rock star whose career and marriage are both failing. Although it featured great actors like Rip Torn, Blair Brown, and Allen Garfield in the cast, the movie was a bit of a dud. It did, however, yield the great Paul Simon song "Late in the Evening."

9. Which of these songs is *not* a Three Dog Night recording?

a. "Eli's Coming"
b. "A Day in Erotica"
c. "Black and White"
d. "Joy to the World"

GAME 74 Q8 ANSWER a
Hailing from Atlanta, Georgia, 112 is rooted in gospel, soul, and hip-hop, and is the most successful urban vocal group to emerge from Sean "P. Diddy" Combs' Bad Boy Entertainment records. The group is best known for such hit singles as "Anywhere," "Dance With Me," and the Grammy-winning "I'll Be Missing You."

5. Which psychedelic band's albums include *Surrealistic Pillow*?

a. Pink Floyd
b. Jefferson Airplane
c. Moby Grape
d. The Electric Prunes

GAME 7 Q4 ANSWER b
This classic acid-rock tune is almost seventeen minutes long, and features a two-and-a-half minute drum solo by Ron Bushy. Legend has it that Doug Ingle, lead singer and keyboardist, was really singing "In the Garden of Eden," but his slurred words came out sounding . . . a bit different. A *lot* of that was going on in the '60s!

5. Which song is a single from Aaliyah's self-titled 2001 album?

a. "Back & Forth"
b. "Angel of Mine"
c. "We Need a Resolution"
d. "At Your Best"

GAME 27 Q4 ANSWER c
The 1970 New Orleans concert was a disaster, with Morrison smashing his microphone into the stage, throwing the stand into the audience, and finally slumping down, motionless. Just a few months later, in July 1971, Morrison's girlfriend found him dead in a bathtub in his Paris apartment.

5. Who was the drummer for Hole?

a. Phil Rudd
b. Charlie Benante
c. Patty Schemel
d. Sean Kinney

GAME 47 Q4 ANSWER b
Rick Allen was only fifteen years old when he joined Def Leppard in 1978. Following the tremendous success of the group's 1983 album, *Pyromania,* Allen was involved in a New Year's Eve car accident that cost him his left arm. The group stuck by their drummer, though, and Allen learned to play a custom-made drum kit.

5. Which of these songs was on The Monkees' first album?

a. "Tuesday Afternoon"
b. "Saturday's Child"
c. "Rainy Days and Mondays"
d. "Day Tripper"

GAME 67 Q4 ANSWER d
"Halo" and "Scared as You" are companion songs on the extended single for this 1992 Top 20 hit by gothic rock band The Cure. "Friday I'm in Love," appears on *Wish,* the group's ninth studio album, which also includes the hits "High" and "A Letter to Elise." A successful tour followed this album's release.

8. Who is referred to in Lynyrd Skynyrd's classic song "Sweet Home Alabama"?

a. Randy Newman

b. Neil Young

c. Lyndon Baines Johnson

d. Don Henley

GAME 14 Q7 ANSWER c
Street Survivors is a Lynyrd Skynyrd album released in 1977 after the fatal plane crash that claimed the lives of group members Ronnie Van Zant, Steve Gaines, and Cassie Gaines. This album's original cover showed the group surrounded in flames, but it was later changed.

8. Elton John's rendition of "Pinball Wizard" helped to make which film a success?

a. *Jesus Christ Superstar*

b. *Buster*

c. *Tommy*

d. *Quadrophenia*

GAME 34 Q7 ANSWER c
In a surprise move, John married Renate Blauel—a German music engineer—on Valentine's Day of 1984. The wedding, which took place four days after John's proposal of marriage, was held in Sydney, Australia. The couple was divorced four years later.

8. Paul Simon wrote and starred in which film?

a. *One Trick Pony*

b. *Less Than Zero*

c. *New York Stories*

d. *Shampoo*

GAME 54 Q7 ANSWER b
"The Boxer" was a Top 10 hit from this album, which earned three Grammy Awards in 1970, including Album of the Year. "Leaves That Are Green" comes from the 1966 album *Sounds of Silence*, while "Cloudy" appeared that same year on *Parsley, Sage, Rosemary and Thyme*. "Overs" was featured on the 1968 album *Bookends*.

8. What numerical group's #1 hits include "Only You," "It's Over Now," and "Peaches & Cream"?

a. 112

b. SR-71

c. 98 Degrees

d. All-4-One

GAME 74 Q7 ANSWER c
Formed in 1996 from members of several local high school bands, Sum 41 includes Deryck Whibley, Dave Baksh, Jason McCaslin, and Steve Jocz. The band won its 2000 contract with Island Records by submitting demo tapes along with video footage of themselves doing zany things, like robbing a pizza parlor with water guns.

6. Skip Spence was a guitarist for which psychedelic band of the '60s?

a. Steam

b. Ohio Express

c. Canned Heat

d. Moby Grape

GAME 7 Q5 ANSWER b
Together with The Grateful Dead, Jefferson Airplane epitomized the sounds of the 1967 "Summer of Love" with its classic "White Rabbit" and "Somebody to Love." Although popular in the '70s as Jefferson Starship, the group didn't have a #1 hit until "We Built This City" in 1985—at which time the group was called simply Starship.

6. Besides chantilly lace, the Big Bopper wanted all these in a girl except:

a. A ponytail

b. A giggle

c. A pretty face

d. A bright smile

GAME 27 Q5 ANSWER c
"We Need a Resolution" was released in April 2001, four months before the release of the *Aaliyah* album. Later that year, it was decided that the album's second single would be "Rock the Boat." After filming the "Rock the Boat" video in the Bahamas, Aaliyah Dana Haughton died in a plane crash while en route to Miami, Florida.

6. Which of the following female performers is *not* a drummer?

a. Karen Carpenter

b. Sheila E.

c. Gina Schock

d. Susanna Hoffs

GAME 47 Q5 ANSWER c
Schemel took over for Hole's former drummer Caroline Rue, and played on the albums *Live Through This* (1994) and *Celebrity Skin* (1998). Although Hole officially disbanded in 2002, Schemel also played drums on Courtney Love's first solo album, *America's Sweetheart.*

6. "Love You Till _____" is a David Bowie song.

a. Monday

b. Tuesday

c. Wednesday

d. Thursday

GAME 67 Q5 ANSWER b
Written by Bread's David Gates, this song mentions all the days of the week. Two other "day" songs are found on our hit debut album: "Tomorrow's Gonna Be Another Day" and "This Just Doesn't Seem to Be My Day." I sang "Saturday's Child" and "Tomorrow's Gonna Be Another Day;" Davy sang "This Just Doesn't Seem to Be My Day."

7. Which of the following albums was *not* recorded by Tom Petty and the Heartbreakers?

a. *Damn the Torpedoes*
b. *Hard Promises*
c. *Street Survivors*
d. *Long After Dark*

GAME 14 Q6 ANSWER c
Jacksonville, Florida, is also home to other classic Southern rock groups such as Lynyrd Skynyrd and .38 Special. Formed in 1975, Molly Hatchet is allegedly named after a Southern prostitute who was said to mutilate and behead her paying customers.

7. To which of the following women was Elton John briefly married?

a. Sheila Dwight
b. Kiki Dee
c. Renate Blauel
d. Madonna

GAME 34 Q6 ANSWER a
The show was named after John's lacquered Yamaha grand piano. Described as being "jaw dropping" and "eye popping," Red Piano features Elton John and his band, along with video montages, short films, and other elements that work together to detail John's musical journey.

7. Which of the following songs is from Simon & Garfunkel's final album, *Bridge Over Troubled Water*?

a. "Overs"
b. "The Boxer"
c. "Cloudy"
d. "Leaves That Are Green"

GAME 54 Q6 ANSWER b
Annie Hall, Woody Allen's 1977 Oscar-winning gem, features Paul Simon as LA-based musician Tony Lacey. Garfunkel's first two film roles came through director Mike Nichols, who knew him from working on *The Graduate.* First came *Catch-22* in 1970, followed a year later by *Carnal Knowledge,* starring my old buddy Jack Nicholson.

7. Heavy-metal guitar and wild percussion are typical of Sum 41, a Canadian ____.

a. Duo
b. Trio
c. Quartet
d. Quintet

GAME 74 Q6 ANSWER c
Born in Jamaica, Queens, rapper 50 Cent experienced his first commercial success with his 2003 debut album, *Get Rich or Die Tryin'.* The release skyrocketed to #1 on the charts, selling 11 million copies worldwide. As a result, 50 Cent was given his own record label, G-Unit Records, which was established in 2003.

7. Which psychedelic frontman was backed by the Magic Band?

a. Screamin' Jay Hawkins
b. Dr. John
c. Howlin' Wolf
d. Captain Beefheart

This guy's choice of instrument is kind of like what happened to me with The Monkees . . . but in reverse! I auditioned for The Monkees on guitar, but was later put on drums. Skip Spence first played drums for Jefferson Airplane in 1966, but quickly left the group to play guitar with Moby Grape. By 1968, Skip had left the group.

---

7. Which song was John Lennon's first posthumous #1 hit?

a. "Imagine"
b. "(Just Like) Starting Over"
c. "Give Peace a Chance"
d. "Woman"

Jiles Perry Richardson, Jr., known as the Big Bopper, was a disc jockey who became a rock-and-roll star. His hit "Chantilly Lace" reached #16 on the pop charts in the summer of 1958. Six months later, the Bopper died in a plane crash along with Buddy Holly and Ritchie Valens.

---

7. Which of the following bands does *not* feature two drummers?

a. The Allman Brothers
b. The Grateful Dead
c. The Outlaws
d. Deep Purple

Lead singer for The Bangles, Susanna Hoffs also plays rhythm guitar. Karen Carpenter sang and played drums while brother Richard played the piano. Gina Schock is the drummer for The Go-Gos, while Sheila E. was discovered by Prince in the '80s.

---

7. The title track on the soundtrack for the 1995 film *Friday* was recorded by the film's co-writer:

a. Chris Tucker
b. LL Cool J
c. Ice Cube
d. Ice-T

This was a track on Bowie's self-titled 1967 debut album. Over the years, Bowie has embodied many a pop persona, from Major Tom of "Space Oddity" fame to The Thin White Duke in the late '70s. His real name is David Jones, but he changed it (perhaps to avoid being mistaken for another singer with that same name . . .).

6. Which city does the Southern rock band Molly Hatchet call home?

a. Milwaukee

b. New Orleans

c. Jacksonville

d. Birmingham

GAME 14 Q5 ANSWER d
Led by brothers Tom and John Fogerty, CCR represented "the Southern" sound at Woodstock. The group's strident sound on songs like "Fortunate Son" signaled a mounting frustration with the Vietnam war. "Fortunate Son" was redone by Wyclef Jean for *The Manchurian Candidate* (2004).

6. What is the name of Elton John's glitzy stage show at Caesars Palace?

a. Red Piano

b. Blue Note

c. White Curtain

d. Velvet Chair

GAME 34 Q5 ANSWER a
The song was originally a track on the 1972 album *Honky Chateau*. Written by Elton John and Bernie Taupin, "Rocket Man" is loosely based on Ray Bradbury's short story of the same name from Bradbury's collection *The Illustrated Man*.

6. Which film does *not* feature Art Garfunkel in a supporting role?

a. *Boxing Helena*

b. *Annie Hall*

c. *Catch-22*

d. *Carnal Knowledge*

GAME 54 Q5 ANSWER d
Garfunkel earned his master's in mathematics from Columbia University. Education has always been one of his deep passions. In fact, Garfunkel even has a website that lists every book he has read since 1968. To date, that number is well over a thousand!

6. What is the real name of rapper 50 Cent?

a. Paul Hewson

b. Marshall Mathers

c. Curtis James Jackson

d. Dwayne Johnson

GAME 74 Q5 ANSWER d
Hassan plays percussion and trombone; Brown, drums; and Travers, saxophone. Other UB40 members include Ali Campbell, Robin Campbell, and Earl Falconer, who play guitar; and Astro, who plays percussion and trumpet. The band is said to have purchased its first instruments with money Ali Campbell received as compensation after a bar fight.

8. Popping pills is a central theme of which psychedelic rock song?

a. "Union of the Snake"

b. "Karma Chameleon"

c. "White Rabbit"

d. "See You Later Alligator"

GAME 7 Q7 ANSWER d
Captain Beefheart was born Don Vliet in 1941, and became friends with Frank Zappa in high school. Back in 1969, Zappa decided to produce Vliet's first album. The album, *Trout Mask Replica*, remains one of the most bizarre rock recordings ever made. I still don't know what "fast and bulbous" means . . .

8. How were Allman Brothers Band members Duane Allman and Berry Oakley both killed?

a. Plane crashes

b. Drug overdoses

c. Drownings

d. Motorcycle accidents

GAME 27 Q7 ANSWER b
"(Just Like) Starting Over" was a single from Lennon's 1980 comeback album *Double Fantasy*. The single had begun climbing the charts when, on the morning of December 8, 1980, Lennon was fatally shot in front of his New York City apartment building. By Christmas, the song had reached #1.

8. Which of the following drummers did *not* play with Frank Zappa?

a. Neil Peart

b. Jimmy Carl Black

c. Aynsley Dunbar

d. Terry Bozzio

GAME 47 Q7 ANSWER d
Ian Paice has been the drummer for British metal pioneer Deep Purple since 1968. The Allman Brothers feature both Butch Trucks and Jai Johanny "Jaimoe" Johanson on drums, while The Grateful Dead had both Bill Kreutzmann and Mickey Hart as drummers. The Outlaws had two drummers (Monte Yoho and David Dix) and *three* guitarists.

8. "Fell on Black Days" is by which Seattle grunge band?

a. Alice in Chains

b. Pearl Jam

c. Mudhoney

d. Soundgarden

GAME 67 Q7 ANSWER c
Ice Cube also plays the film's main character, Craig Jones. At one point in the film, the characters played by Ice Cube and Chris Tucker are watching a music video on television. The song in the video is by Ice Cube's long-time friend and fellow rapper K-Dee, and the video was directed by none other than Ice Cube himself.

5. Who had a hit song in the 1970s with "Born on the Bayou"?

a. Lynyrd Skynyrd
b. The Charlie Daniels Band
c. The Marshall Tucker Band
d. Creedence Clearwater Revival

The group's only hit single (#2 on the charts), "Ramblin' Man" was written by Dickey Betts for the 1973 album *Brothers and Sisters*. It was released after the deaths of band members Berry Oakley and Duane Allman. In 1979, Willie Nelson recorded Gregg Allman's "Midnight Rider" for the Robert Redford film *The Electric Horseman*.

---

5. "I Think It's Gonna Be a Long, Long Time" is the subtitle of which Elton John hit?

a. "Rocket Man"
b. "I Want Love"
c. "Your Song"
d. "Someone Saved My Life"

Elton John and John Lennon collaborated on several works. John, for instance, co-wrote Lennon's #1 comeback single "Whatever Gets You Through the Night," and they even performed on stage together at Madison Square Garden. When Lennon was killed in 1980, John mourned the loss in "Empty Garden (Hey Hey Johnny)."

---

5. Art Garfunkel has a master's degree in what subject?

a. English
b. Physical education
c. Economics
d. Mathematics

Graceland is Simon's biggest critical and commercial hit to date. However, it isn't his only album to win a Grammy. In 1976, the equally popular *Still Crazy After All These Years* also won an Album of the Year Grammy. That same year, Simon sang that album's title track on *Saturday Night Live* while dressed in a chicken suit.

---

5. Keyboards are the specialty of which UB40 member?

a. Norman Hassan
b. Jim Brown
c. Brian Travers
d. Mickey Virtue

In My Tribe, 10,000 Maniacs' 1987 breakthrough album, rose to #37 on the Billboard 200 chart and received great critical acclaim. This was the first album for which singer-lyricist Natalie Merchant wrote the songs without John Lombardo, who left the band in 1986. Instead, Merchant started new songwriting partnerships.

GAME 7

9. Which group's classic psychedelic tunes include "Monterey" and "Sky Pilot"?

a. Blue Cheer

b. Moby Grape

c. Eric Burdon & The Animals

d. Country Joe and the Fish

GAME 7 Q8 ANSWER c
Written by Jefferson Airplane's lead singer, Grace Slick, this song is influenced by literature (Lewis Carroll's *Alice in Wonderland*) and chemicals (LSD). Although its call to "Feed your head" sounded like an ad for acid in 1967, "White Rabbit" now sounds more like a warning against the dangers of drug use. Just ask Alice . . .

GAME 27

9. In what was assumed to be his suicide note, Kurt Cobain quoted a lyric written by:

a. John Lennon

b. Bob Dylan

c. Elton John

d. Neil Young

GAME 27 Q8 ANSWER d
Duane Allman was killed in a motorcycle accident in Macon, Georgia in 1971, during a break from touring. A year later, Berry Oakley died in an accident just a few blocks from where Allman had been killed. The bandmates were buried side by side in Macon's Rose Hill Cemetary.

GAME 47

9. Which drummer is a mismatch with its '80s glam metal band?

a. Bobby Blotzer/Ratt

b. Frankie Banali/Quiet Riot

c. A.J. Pero/Dokken

d. Rikki Rockett/Poison

GAME 47 Q8 ANSWER a
Neil Peart plays drums for Canadian rock trio Rush. Jimmy Carl Black was the first drummer in Zappa's Mothers of Invention. He was followed by Aynsley Dunbar, who almost played drums for the Jimi Hendrix Experience. Terry Bozzio played with Zappa from the '70s to the early '80s, after which he started the group Missing Persons.

GAME 67

9. Which rap song is by Ludacris?

a. "Saturday Love"

b. "Saturday Nite"

c. "Saturday (Oooh Oooh!)"

d. "Saturday Evening"

GAME 67 Q8 ANSWER d
This song is a single from *Superunknown*, the 1994 album that debuted at #1. Different versions of the "Fell on Black Days" single were released in different countries, each also with a different B-side song. An alternate version of the song was used for both the music video and 1995's *Songs from the Superunknown*.

GAME 14

4. "Ramblin' Man" was a big hit for which band?

a. Molly Hatchet
b. The Allman Brothers Band
c. Lynyrd Skynyrd
d. .38 Special

GAME 14 Q3 ANSWER a
The Van Zant brothers are a big part of Southern rock. Donnie led .38 Special to big hits in the early '80s with songs like "Hold on Loosely" and "Caught Up in You." Ronnie was the lead vocalist for Lynyrd Skynyrd until he died in the group's 1977 plane crash. Johnny became Lynyrd Skynyrd's singer in 1987.

GAME 34

4. Which of the following songs is Elton John's tribute to John Lennon?

a. "The Last Song"
b. "Your Song"
c. "Empty Garden"
d. "Sad Songs"

GAME 34 Q3 ANSWER b
The lyrics of "Tiny Dancer" were inspired by the first wife of Elton John's longtime lyricist Bernie Taupin. As the song recounts, Maxine Feibelman was at one time actually a dancer on Elton John's tour. A later song, "Between Seventeen and Twenty," refers to Bernie and Maxine's divorce.

GAME 54

4. Which of the following Paul Simon efforts earned a Grammy for Album of the Year?

a. *Graceland*
b. *The Paul Simon Song Book*
c. *Hearts and Bones*
d. *Live Rhymin'*

GAME 54 Q3 ANSWER b
Simon's third solo album sold over a million copies when released in 1973. Both "Kodachrome" and "Loves Me Like a Rock" went to #2 on the singles charts, but Simon would not have his first #1 solo single until "Fifty Ways to Leave Your Lover" from the album *Still Crazy After All These Years* hit the airwaves in 1975.

GAME 74

4. Which numerical group released the album *In My Tribe*?

a. 2 Live Crew
b. Thrice
c. 10,000 Maniacs
d. 3rd Bass

GAME 74 Q3 ANSWER b
"Stay Together for the Kids" is a single from the 2001 album *Take Off Your Pants and Jackets*. Written by Blink-182's singer-guitarist Tom Delonge, it is about the divorce of Delonge's parents during the artist's teen years. The album also launched the singles "First Date" and "The Rock Show."

10. A psychedelic _____ became a trademark of Beatle legend John Lennon.

a. Stratocaster guitar
b. Rolls-Royce
c. Lear jet
d. Steinway piano

GAME 7 Q9 ANSWER c
Rock and Roll Hall of Famer Eric Burdon was lead singer for the British group The Animals from 1962 to 1967. After Burdon left the group for a solo career, his fellow Animals band member Chas Chandler became Jimi Hendrix's manager after hearing him play in a New York club. The Animals reunited in 1975, and again in 1983.

10. Stevie Ray Vaughan, who died in 1992, was famous for playing the:

a. Piano
b. Saxophone
c. Guitar
d. Trumpet

GAME 27 Q9 ANSWER d
Penned in 1994, Cobain's note quoted Young's lyric, "It's better to burn out than to fade away" from the song "My My, Hey Hey (Out of the Blue)." This had a profound effect on Young, who recorded portions of his 1994 album _Sleeps With Angels_ in Cobain's memory.

10. Who was the _first_ drummer for KISS?

a. Eric Carr
b. Anton Fig
c. Peter Criss
d. Eric Singer

GAME 47 Q9 ANSWER c
A.J. Pero was the drummer for Twisted Sister. It was Mick Brown who played drums for Dokken. Frankie Banali is the drummer for Quiet Riot, whose 1983 single "Cum on Feel the Noize" was the first metal song to make the Top 5 in the pop charts.

10. "Blue Monday" was the breakthrough hit for which British group?

a. New Order
b. Roxy Music
c. Depeche Mode
d. Duran Duran

GAME 67 Q9 ANSWER c
This Atlanta-based rapper is part of the "Dirty South" rap explosion that began in 2000. "Saturday (Oooh Oooh!)" is from his third album, 2001's _Word of Mouf_. Ludacris has been nominated for twelve Grammys to date. He won his first Grammy in 2005 for Best Rap/Sung Collaboration with Lil Jon and Usher on the song "Yeah."

GAME 14

3. For which Southern rock band is Donnie Van Zant the lead singer?

a. .38 Special
b. The Allman Brothers Band
c. The Marshall Tucker Band
d. Blackfoot

GAME 14 Q2 ANSWER b
Also called "That Little ol' Band from Texas," ZZ Top has been together since 1969. Before the band was formed, guitarist Billy Gibbons' group, The Moving Sidewalks, opened for the Jimi Hendrix Experience in 1967. When he appeared on *The Tonight Show*, Hendrix called Billy Gibbons his favorite guitar player.

GAME 34

3. In which song does Elton John sing about a seamstress who will marry a music man?

a. "Nikita"
b. "Tiny Dancer"
c. "Your Song"
d. "Little Jeannie"

GAME 34 Q2 ANSWER a
Written by Elton John and Bernie Taupin, the original version of "Candle in the Wind" appeared on the 1973 album *Goodbye Yellow Brick Road*. In 1997, the song was rewritten as a tribute to Diana, Princess of Wales, and became the best-selling single of all time in the United Kingdom.

GAME 54

3. Which Paul Simon album includes the hits "Koda-chrome" and "Loves Me Like a Rock"?

a. *The Rhythm of the Saints*
b. *There Goes Rhymin' Simon*
c. *You're the One*
d. *Hearts and Bones*

GAME 54 Q2 ANSWER d
The version of this song that reached #1 in January 1966 was actually a remix, with electric guitar added by producer Tom Wilson. It was recorded in February 1964 and featured on Simon & Garfunkel's debut album, *Wednesday Morning, 3 A.M.* While in England, Simon recorded the song alone on his 1965 solo album, *The Paul Simon Song Book*.

GAME 74

3. Which of these groups suggests that you "Stay Together for the Kids"?

a. 311
b. Blink-182
c. Maroon 5
d. 3 Doors Down

GAME 74 Q2 ANSWER a
Levi Stubbs, Abdul "Duke" Fakir, Renaldo "Obie" Benson, and Lawrence Payton formed The Four Aims in high school, but in 1956 changed their name to The Four Tops to avoid confusion with The Ames Brothers. The Motown quartet's hits include "Baby I Need Your Loving," "It's the Same Old Song," and "Reach Out I'll Be There."

11. Who recorded the 1968 psychedelic hit "Magic Carpet Ride"?

a. The Rascals
b. Steppenwolf
c. Jimi Hendrix
d. Donovan

GAME 7 Q10 ANSWER b
Although they gave up touring in 1966 and didn't attend the Monterey Pop Festival in 1967, The Beatles wound up producing the definitive psychedelic album with *Sgt. Pepper's Lonely Hearts Club Band*. John poured flower-power paint on his Rolls-Royce, while George Harrison put it on his Stratocaster guitar . . . and his house!

11. In October 1996, Tupac Shakur's death pushed which album into the Top 10?

a. *Loungin'*
b. *All Eyez On Me*
c. *E. 1999 Eternal*
d. *Beats, Rhymes and Life*

GAME 27 Q10 ANSWER c
Vaughan, a singer and guitarist, formed the blues-rock band Double Trouble in the late 1970s, and soon drew the attention of David Bowie, who featured him on his 1982 *Let's Dance* album. In 1983, Vaughan released *Texas Flood*, his debut album. He continued to tour and record until his tragic 1992 death in a helicopter crash.

11. Who was The Who's *second* drummer?

a. Keith Moon
b. Kenny Jones
c. Simon Phillips
d. Zak Starkey

GAME 47 Q10 ANSWER c
Peter Criss (real name: Peter Criscuola) joined KISS in 1973 when the group was called Wicked Lester. Criss sang the group's 1976 breakthrough hit "Beth," but then quit the group in 1980. He was replaced by Eric Carr, who died in 1991 and was later replaced by Eric Singer. Criss rejoined KISS from 1996 to 2001.

11. The Rolling Stones sing goodbye to this lady:

a. Zazu Thursday
b. Marlow Friday
c. Ruby Tuesday
d. Lulu Wednesday

GAME 67 Q10 ANSWER a
Over seven minutes long, this 1983 single crept up to #5 on the Billboard Dance charts. Formed in 1980, New Order cultivated an image of mystery as it produced one dance classic after another. Over the years, New Order songs have been featured in films like *Pretty in Pink* (1986), *Trainspotting* (1995), and *The Wedding Singer* (1998).

GAME 14

2. Which Texas trio has a guitarist and bassist with enormous beards?

a. Little Feat
b. ZZ Top
c. Dixie Dregs
d. Lynyrd Skynyrd

GAME 14 Q1 ANSWER d

Formed in 1972, this South Carolina band played at the 1977 inauguration of President Jimmy Carter. The group's name came during a rehearsal in a warehouse. While thinking up a name, someone noticed the warehouse key had the name "Marshall Tucker." Mr. Tucker was a blind piano tuner who had previously rented that warehouse.

GAME 34

2. Which Elton John song is a tribute to Marilyn Monroe?

a. "Candle in the Wind"
b. "Blue Eyes"
c. "Empty Garden"
d. "Shine on Through"

GAME 34 Q1 ANSWER b

Along with the hit song "Daniel," "Crocodile Rock" appeared on Elton John's 1973 album *Don't Shoot Me I'm Only the Piano Player*. Written by Elton John and Bernie Taupin, the song, which has a strong honky-tonk rhythm, takes a nostalgic look at early rock and roll.

GAME 54

2. What was Simon & Garfunkel's first #1 hit single?

a. "I Am a Rock"
b. "Cecilia"
c. "The Boxer"
d. "The Sound of Silence"

GAME 54 Q1 ANSWER c

Performing as Tom and Jerry (Garfunkel went by the name "Tom Graph" while Simon used the name "Jerry Landis"), this famous teenage duo from Queens, New York, scored a minor hit with "Hey Schoolgirl" in 1958. They performed this song, which went to #49 on the charts, on Dick Clark's TV show *American Bandstand*.

GAME 74

2. Which quartet was inducted into the Rock and Roll Hall of Fame in 1990?

a. The Four Tops
b. The Four Preppies
c. The Four Aces
d. The Four Clocks

GAME 74 Q1 ANSWER b

Trent Reznor founded Nine Inch Nails in 1988. In fact, he is the only official member of the band, although a backing band accompanies him on live shows. In 2003, Reznor's song "Hurt" was covered by Johnny Cash for what was to be the last hit of Cash's life

12. Which group asked the psychedelic question, "What's the New Mary Jane?"

a. The Beatles

b. The Temptations

c. Cat Stevens

d. The Grateful Dead

GAME 7 Q11 ANSWER b

Although this group's first hit, "Born to Be Wild," went to #2 on the charts in 1968 and was immortalized a year later on the soundtrack of Dennis Hopper's 1969 film *Easy Rider*, "Magic Carpet Ride" was an equally successful hit single that rose to #3 on the charts. In 2004, this song was used in Chevy car commercials.

12. "Everything Reminds Me of Her" is a haunting song from which singer-songwriter?

a. Elliott Smith

b. Graham Parsons

c. Warren Zevon

d. Alex Chilton

GAME 27 Q11 ANSWER b

In 1996, hip-hop artist Tupac Shakur—born Lesane Parish Crooks—was killed in a drive-by shooting in Las Vegas, Nevada. Although theories regarding Shakur's death abound, his murder remains unsolved. Shortly after his death, the sales of *all* his albums surged.

12. Who was the *third* drummer of The Ozzy Osbourne Band?

a. Lee Kerslake

b. Tommy Aldridge

c. Randy Castillo

d. Bill Ward

GAME 47 Q11 ANSWER b

After Keith Moon died before he "got old" at age thirty-two in 1978, The Who hired ex-Faces drummer Kenny Jones. While Moon could be erratic, Jones was rock-solid. He recorded two albums with The Who in the '80s—*Face Dances* and *It's Hard*. Simon Phillips played live with The Who before Ringo Starr's son Zak Starkey joined in 1996.

12. According to the Elton John song, "Saturday Night's Alright for _____."

a. Fighting

b. Sleeping

c. Shooting

d. Dancing

GAME 67 Q11 ANSWER c

This #1 hit from the 1967 album *Between the Buttons* features the Rolling Stones at their most melodic. Its unusual sound showcases band member Brian Jones's recorder and piano playing. "Ruby Tuesday" is featured on the soundtrack to the 2001 film *The Royal Tenenbaums*, along with another 1967 Stones' song, "She Smiled Sweetly."

GAME 14

1. Which Southern band had a 1977 hit with "Heard It in a Love Song"?

a. Dixie Dregs

b. The Allman Brothers Band

c. Little Feat

d. The Marshall Tucker Band

The answer to this question is on:

page 182, top frame, right side.

GAME 34

1. With which 1973 song did Elton John first reach #1 on the pop singles chart?

a. "Island Girl"

b. "Crocodile Rock"

c. "Goodbye Yellow Brick Road"

d. "Rocket Man"

The answer to this question is on:

page 182, second frame, right side.

GAME 54

1. Paul Simon and Art Garfunkel teamed up in high school, calling themselves:

a. Sylvester and Tweety

b. Popeye and Bluto

c. Tom and Jerry

d. Rocky and Bullwinkle

The answer to this question is on:

page 182, third frame, right side.

GAME 74

1. Which singer-keyboardist forms the backbone of Nine Inch Nails?

a. Adam Clayton

b. Trent Reznor

c. Cory Wells

d. Joe Perry

The answer to this question is on:

page 182, bottom frame, right side.

184

GAME 8

GRAB BAG

Turn to page 187 for the first question.

GAME 7 Q12 ANSWER a

Aside from the obvious marijuana reference in the song title, it's hard to know what this heavily experimental track is about. Available on The Beatles' *Anthology 3* CD, this song was a kind of warm-up for John and Yoko's larger sound montage "Revolution 9." It ends as John says, "Let's hear it, before we get taken a-[way]!"

GAME 28

GRAB BAG

Turn to page 187 for the first question.

GAME 27 Q12 ANSWER a

"Everything Reminds Me of Her" comes from Smith's 2000 album *Figure 8*. Smith—who battled depression, alcoholism, and drug addiction for years—died under mysterious circumstances in 2003 at the age of thirty-four. Although the death was originally reported as a suicide, the autopsy raised questions about this conclusion.

GAME 48

GRAB BAG

Turn to page 187 for the first question.

GAME 47 Q12 ANSWER c

Bill Ward was the drummer when Ozzy Osbourne was in Black Sabbath. For Ozzy's first album, *Blizzard of Ozz*, Osbourne hired Lee Kerslake, who was formerly with Uriah Heep. Tommy Aldridge then played on Osbourne's second album, *Diary of a Madman*. Randy Castillo joined Ozzy's band for *Bark at the Moon* and continues to play with the group.

GAME 68

GRAB BAG

Turn to page 187 for the first question.

GAME 67 Q12 ANSWER a

This song can be found on 1973's *Goodbye Yellow Brick Road*, Elton John's first double album and one in a string of seven consecutive #1 albums. It has been covered by Queen, The Who, and Nickelback. Nickelback's version, featuring Kid Rock, appears on the *Charlie's Angels: Full Throttle* soundtrack.

GAME 14

Southern Rock

Turn to page 184
for the first question.

GAME 13 Q12 ANSWER a
First heard on their 1966 album *Parsley, Sage, Rosemary & Thyme,* Simon & Garfunkel's "Scarborough Fair/Canticle" and its images of soldiers cleaning their guns and fighting a meaningless war evoked thoughts of the Vietnam War. The duo chose to close this LP with another anti-war song, "Seven O'Clock News/Silent Night."

GAME 34

Elton John

Turn to page 184
for the first question.

GAME 33 Q12 ANSWER a
Founded in 1978, the British New Wave band Dexys Midnight Runners was named after Dexedrine, a popular recreational drug. Their song "Come on Eileen" rose to #1 in both the US and the UK, but spent only a week at the top before being replaced by Michael Jackson's hit single "Beat It."

GAME 54

Simon & Garfunkel— Old Friends

Turn to page 184
for the first question.

GAME 53 Q12 ANSWER d
In 1976, The Ramones recorded their debut album for Sire Records at a cost of just over $6,000. Sire also signed Talking Heads, The Pretenders, Elvis Costello, and Depeche Mode, among several other important artists in the punk and New Wave scene. As the '80s got started, Sire also signed up Madonna and rapper Ice T.

GAME 74

Numerical Music Groups

Turn to page 184
for the first question.

GAME 73 Q12 ANSWER d
"Evergreen," the love theme from the 1976 film *A Star is Born,* was co-written by Streisand and Paul Williams. In addition to earning the Oscar, the song won three Grammy Awards—the 1977 awards for Song of the Year, Best Pop Vocal Performance, and Best Arrangement Accompanying a Vocalist.

	Question	Answer Location
GAME 8	**1.** Legendary rock-and-roll radio disc jockey Alan Freed is credited with co-writing which Chuck Berry song? **a.** "Maybelline" **b.** "Sweet Little Sixteen" **c.** "Johnny B. Goode" **d.** "School Days"	The answer to this question is on: **page 189, top frame, right side.**
GAME 28	**1.** "Let Your Dim Light Shine" is a 1995 album by which rock group? **a.** Pearl Jam **b.** Soul Asylum **c.** Mavericks **d.** Oasis	The answer to this question is on: **page 189, second frame, right side.**
GAME 48	**1.** Which song was *not* recorded by the Pointer Sisters? **a.** "Neutron Dance" **b.** "Last Dance" **c.** "Jump (For My Love)" **d.** "I'm So Excited"	The answer to this question is on: **page 189, third frame, right side.**
GAME 68	**1.** Which Guns 'N Roses' album came first? **a.** *Use Your Illusion I* **b.** *Use Your Illusion II* **c.** *Appetite for Destruction* **d.** *"The Spaghetti Incident?"*	The answer to this question is on: **page 189, bottom frame, right side.**

12. Which Simon & Garfunkel hit added anti-war protest lyrics to an English folk song?

a. "Scarborough Fair/Canticle"
b. "Homeward Bound"
c. "America"
d. "The Boxer"

GAME 13 Q11 ANSWER c
Written by Carol King and Gerry Goffin, this song was featured on our *Head* soundtrack album. By that time, we were making Monkees music more and more our own. For example, our well-known TV theme song ran during the opening and end credits of season one. But in season two, the end credits played Peter's song "For Pete's Sake."

---

12. Which song ended the seven-week reign of "Billie Jean" on Billboard's Hot 100 chart in 1983?

a. "Come on Eileen"
b. "Every Breath You Take"
c. "Let's Go Crazy"
d. "Beat It"

GAME 33 Q11 ANSWER b
"It's Still Rock and Roll to Me"—Joel's first song to peak at #1 on Billboards Pop Singles chart—appeared on the 1980 album *Glass Houses,* which also included the hits "Don't Ask Me Why" (#19) and "You May Be Right" (#7). The album itself topped the pop albums chart for six weeks.

---

12. The Ramones were the first punk band to sign a contract with which label?

a. Warner Brothers
b. Pioneer
c. Rough Trade
d. Sire

GAME 53 Q11 ANSWER a
Together from 1991 to 2000, this all-woman band took its name from Lucious Brown Jackson, who played for the Philadelphia 76ers in the 1960s. The group's hip-hop dance tracks were popular with alternative music fans. Luscious Jackson released its last studio album, *Electric Honey,* in 1999.

---

12. Barbra Streisand won the Best Song Oscar for "The Way We Were" and what other song?

a. "People"
b. "Don't Rain on My Parade"
c. "Something's Coming"
d. "Evergreen"

GAME 73 Q11 ANSWER c
Lopez's fourth album *Rebirth* was first given the working title *Call Me Jennifer* in an effort to dispel the singer's reputation as a diva. Eventually, though, *Rebirth* was chosen to signal a new beginning after the failure of the artist's 2003 film *Gigli.* Unfortunately, the album, too, was a commercial disappointment.

GAME 8

2. Which song is on the B-side of Queen's "We are the Champions"?

a. "Bohemian Rhapsody"
b. "Under Pressure"
c. "We Will Rock You"
d. "Bicycle Race"

GAME 8 Q1 ANSWER a
Released in 1955, "Maybelline" was Chuck Berry's first hit, reaching #5 on the Billboard charts. Alan "Moondog" Freed was granted co-writer status on this song just because he agreed to play it on the radio. This bribe-based pattern of radio play—known as "payola"—led to a scandal in 1962 that all but destroyed Freed's career.

GAME 28

2. *Private Dancer* and *Break Every Rule* are acclaimed albums from which of the following legends?

a. Tina Turner
b. Patti LaBelle
c. Whitney Houston
d. Bonnie Raitt

GAME 28 Q1 ANSWER b
The Minneapolis band made its album debut in 1984 with *Say What You Will*, and quickly became a mainstay of the Twin Cities music scene. Soul Asylum even performed at the 1993 inauguration of President Bill Clinton. In 2005, after the death of bassist Karl Mueller, the group disbanded.

GAME 48

2. AC/DC member Angus Young wears his old _____ on stage.

a. Kilt
b. Pajamas
c. Bathing suit
d. School uniform

GAME 48 Q1 ANSWER b
"Last Dance" was a 1978 Grammy-winning hit for "Queen of Disco" Donna Summer. The Pointer Sisters—Anita, Bonnie, Ruth, and June—were a quartet until sister Bonnie went solo in 1977. Their two biggest hits to date were the country and western-influenced songs "Fire" (1978) and "Slow Hand" (1981), both of which went to #2 on the pop charts.

GAME 68

2. Which 1960s British Invasion band recorded "I'm Into Something Good"?

a. The Beatles
b. The Dave Clark Five
c. Herman's Hermits
d. The Hollies

GAME 68 Q1 ANSWER c
Released in 1987, this group's ferocious major-label debut produced three Top 10 hits, sold over 25 million copies worldwide, and singlehandedly killed the reign of hair metal in the US. Songs like "Welcome to the Jungle," "Paradise City," and the #1 hit "Sweet Child O' Mine" have ensured Guns 'N Roses a place in rock history.

Answers are in right-hand boxes on page 191.   **189**

11. Which song opens and closes The Monkees' film *Head* (1968)?

a. "(Theme from) The Monkees"

b. "For Pete's Sake"

c. "Porpoise Song"

d. "Zor and Zam"

GAME 13 Q10 ANSWER b
"Epistle to Dippy" was by Donovan, while "The Flower Children" was by Marcia Strassman (yep, of *Welcome Back Kotter* fame!) and "Neon Rainbow" was by The Box Tops. Meanwhile, "The Frodis Caper" was the alternate title for the last *Monkees* TV episode—my first time in the director's chair. The episode's real title is "Mijacogeo."

11. Who sang the #1 hit song "It's Still Rock and Roll to Me"?

a. Paul Mccartney

b. Billy Joel

c. Glenn Frey

d. Elton John

GAME 33 Q10 ANSWER b
Written by Paul Simon in the aftermath of the assassination of President John Kennedy, the song propelled the folk duo to stardom. "The Sound of Silence" did not do well when it was originally released on the pair's 1964 debut album *Wednesday Morning, 3 A.M.*, but topped the charts for two weeks after its 1965 release as a single.

11. The alternative pop band Luscious Jackson took its name from a:

a. Basketball player

b. New Orleans restaurant

c. Blaxploitation film

d. Las Vegas bordello

GAME 53 Q10 ANSWER b
Lead singer/guitarist David Byrne, drummer Chris Frantz, and bassist Tina Weymouth formed Talking Heads and came to New York in 1974. The group landed the plum gig of opening for The Ramones at Manhattan's famous CBGB club. By 1976, they had added Jerry Harrison on keyboards.

11. What's the one-word title of Jennifer Lopez's 2005 album?

a. *Inferno*

b. *Crescendo*

c. *Rebirth*

d. *Independence*

GAME 73 Q10 ANSWER a
The title of Estefan's solo album refers to the "Queen of Latin Pop's" desire to reach both English- and Spanish-speaking fans. The album was Estefan's best-selling work to date, and included hits such as "Don't Wanna Lose You," "Here We Are," "Oye Mi Canto," "Get on Your Feet," and "Cuts Both Ways."

3. "Shut out the Light" and "Pink Cadillac" are B-sides featured on whose boxed set *Tracks*?

a. Bob Seger
b. Rod Stewart
c. Bruce Springsteen
d. Phil Collins

GAME 8 Q2 ANSWER c
Still popular at sporting events, both of these songs are from Queen's 1977 album *News of the World*. The album begins with "We Will Rock You" as the first track, which goes immediately into "We Are the Champions." Nearly all classic rock radio stations air the songs back-to-back.

---

3. "Mess Around" and "What'd I Say" are uptempo classics from which singer?

a. Sammy Davis, Jr.
b. Johnny Mathis
c. Ray Charles
d. Nat King Cole

GAME 28 Q2 ANSWER a
The 1984 album *Private Dancer* rose to #3 on the US pop charts and launched three hit singles: the title track, "What's Love Got to Do With It," and "Better Be Good to Me." The 1986 album *Break Every Rule* was also a success, making it to #4 on the pop charts and launching several hit singles, including "Typical Male."

---

3. The first day MTV aired, it played a video by which of the following early '80s groups?

a. Loverboy
b. Duran Duran
c. Shoes
d. Devo

GAME 48 Q2 ANSWER d
Formed in 1974, AC/DC remains one of the most successful Australian bands. Music is a family affair for the Youngs—Angus plays lead guitar for AC/DC, while his brother Malcolm plays rhythm guitar. Older brother George was in The Easybeats, the first Australian group to have a worldwide hit with "Friday on My Mind" in 1966.

---

3. The Foo Fighters' video for "Big Me" spoofs commercials for which product?

a. Pepsi
b. Mentos Mints
c. M&Ms
d. Hershey's Kisses

GAME 68 Q2 ANSWER c
While I was a child star on TV's *Circus Boy* in the '50s, Herman's Hermits lead singer, Peter Noone, was also a child star on the British TV show *Coronation Street*. The group had two #1 hits in 1965—"Mrs. Brown, You've Got a Lovely Daughter" and "I'm Henry the Eighth, I Am." Noone still tours with a brand-new group of Hermits.

---

10. Which of the following is *not* a real song from 1967?

a. "Epistle to Dippy"
b. "The Frodis Caper"
c. "The Flower Children"
d. "Neon Rainbow"

GAME 13 Q9 ANSWER d
This folk-rock quartet was tearing up the pop charts between 1966 and 1967, just as *The Monkees* went on TV. Although "California Dreamin'" was its first chart hit in 1965 (it went to #4), the Mamas and Papas first (and only) #1 song was "Monday, Monday." The group was the last to perform at the famous Monterey Pop Festival in 1967.

---

10. Which song was Simon & Garfunkel's first #1 hit?

a. "Mrs. Robinson"
b. "The Sound of Silence"
c. "Homeward Bound"
d. "The Boxer"

GAME 33 Q9 ANSWER b
Fabares enjoyed great popularity in her role as daughter Mary Stone in the 1958–1966 family sitcom *The Donna Reed Show*. When the show's producers asked Farbares to work with Colpix Records, the label for Columbia Pictures Corporation, the result was the single "Johnny Angel," which quickly rose to #1 on the charts.

---

10. Members of which band met at the Rhode Island School of Design?

a. The Pixies
b. Talking Heads
c. The Replacements
d. No Doubt

GAME 53 Q9 ANSWER a
In 1979, The Beastie Boys were called The Young Aborigines. They switched to hip-hop in 1984; in 1986, they released *Licensed to Ill*. It was the first rap album to reach #1 on the charts, and featured the group's first Top 10 single "(You Gotta) Fight for Your Right (to Party)." They played punk and funk on *Check Your Head* (1992).

---

10. Which 1989 release was Gloria Estefan's first solo album?

a. *Cuts Both Ways*
b. *Into The Light*
c. *Mi Tierra*
d. *Destiny*

GAME 73 Q9 ANSWER c
The fourth single released from Spears' 2001 album *Britney*, "I Love Rock 'N Roll" was written by Alan Merrill and Jake Hooker, and originally recorded by The Arrows in 1975. Because Spears' version failed to make the Top 10 in most countries, it was considered a commercial failure.

4. Who was the first artist to have #1 albums in the 1960s, 1970s, 1980s and 1990s?

a. Michael Jackson

b. Bob Dylan

c. Barbra Streisand

d. Paul McCartney

GAME 8 Q3 ANSWER c
This sixty-six track, four-disc collection of B-sides and outtakes also contains such little-known tunes as "Seaside Bar Song" and "Janey Don't You Lose Heart." Natalie Cole had a #5 hit with her version of "Pink Cadillac" in 1988. Clint Eastwood starred in a film called *Pink Cadillac* in 1989, but Springsteen's song is not in it.

---

4. "Stir It Up" is one of two of her songs on the *Beverly Hills Cop* soundtrack:

a. Sade

b. Patti LaBelle

c. Carly Simon

d. Tina Turner

GAME 28 Q3 ANSWER c
The 1953 hit "Mess Around" was written for Charles by Atlantic records president and founder Ahmet Ertegun. The 1959 hit "What'd I Say" began as an improvised number designed to lengthen an Atlanta, Georgia performance that was running twenty minutes short.

---

4. Which of the following songs is by The Who?

a. "Long Live Rock"

b. "Rock 'n Roll"

c. "Crocodile Rock"

d. "Rock and Roll All Nite"

GAME 48 Q3 ANSWER c
Shoes was formed in Zion, Illinois, in 1975. Signed to a record contract by Elektra Records in 1979, the group had a minor radio hit with "Too Late" from its album *Present Tense*. "Too Late" was the twenty-third video shown on August 1, 1981, the first day MTV aired. Shoes still releases music through its own label, Black Vinyl.

---

4. Whose "Baby Got Back" was a huge hit during the summer of 1992?

a. Sir Mix-A-Lot

b. MC Hammer

c. Digital Underground

d. Young MC

GAME 68 Q3 ANSWER b
The video for this song, set up as a mock commercial for the make-believe product "Footos," won the 1996 MTV Video Music Award for Best Group Video. "Big Me" also went to #11 on the charts and was the fourth single off the group's 1995 self-titled debut album. On that album, former Nirvana drummer Dave Grohl played nearly every instrument.

GAME 13

9. The Mamas and the Papas made the pop charts for the first time with which song?

a. "Creeque Alley"

b. "I Saw Her Again"

c. "Monday, Monday"

d. "California Dreamin'"

GAME 13 Q8 ANSWER b
Written by P.F. Sloan in 1965, this "protest song" was recorded by The Turtles for its first album. However, it was Barry McGuire's hastily recorded version that got to #1 on the charts. The song caused a furor, and the conservative rock group The Spokesmen fought back with a parody of the song called "The Dawn of Correction."

GAME 33

9. Though primarily an actress, who had a #1 hit with "Johnny Angel" in 1962?

a. Connie Francis

b. Shelley Fabares

c. Ann-Margret

d. Dorothy Provine

GAME 33 Q8 ANSWER b
Houston's second album, *Whitney*, achieved this feat in 1987, also yielding three #1 hit singles. This gave Houston a total of seven consecutive hits in the United States, breaking the previous record of six hits shared by The Beatles and The Bee Gees.

GAME 53

9. On which album did The Beastie Boys first pick up their own instruments and play?

a. *Check Your Head*

b. *Paul's Boutique*

c. *License to Ill*

d. *Hello Nasty*

GAME 53 Q8 ANSWER a
Geffen Records released the album in 1990—the same year it released Nirvana's breakthrough album, *Nevermind*. Formed in 1981 during a ten-day "Noise Fest" held in lower Manhattan's SoHo district, Sonic Youth experimented with alternate guitar tunings and used tools like screwdrivers on their instruments.

GAME 73

9. What '80s anthem does Britney Spears cover on her album *Britney*?

a. "Bette Davis Eyes"

b. "Physical"

c. "I Love Rock 'N Roll"

d. "Centerfold"

GAME 73 Q8 ANSWER a
The chart-topper "I Swear" was recorded in 1994 by country star John Michael Montgomery. All of the remaining hits were released by Dion, who rose from humble beginnings in rural Quebec, Canada to become an internationally known pop star, selling more than 100 million albums worldwide.

5. Which Pink Floyd album stayed on the Billboard charts for over thirteen years?

a. The Wall
b. Wish You Were Here
c. Dark Side of the Moon
d. Obscured by Clouds

GAME 8 Q4 ANSWER c
Streisand set the mark when *Back to Broadway*, a follow-up to 1985's *The Broadway Album* (also a #1), shot to the top of the charts in July 1993. Nearly all of her sixty-one albums have become gold and/or platinum. In 2005, she teamed up again with "Bee Gee" Barry Gibb for *Guilty Pleasures*, a sequel to their 1980 hit album *Guilty*.

5. Which group had a hit album in 1981 with *Dirty Deeds Done Dirt Cheap*?

a. Kansas
b. Queen
c. AC/DC
d. Cheap Trick

GAME 28 Q4 ANSWER b
LaBelle's other song on that album is "New Attitude." The *Beverly Hills Cop* soundtrack—which won a 1986 Grammy Award for Best Album of Original Score Written for a Motion Picture—also features songs by Glenn Frey, Danny Elfman, and the Pointer Sisters.

5. Which '90s singer-songwriter released an album with a ninety-word title?

a. Lisa Loeb
b. Alanis Morrissette
c. Fiona Apple
d. Liz Phair

GAME 48 Q4 ANSWER a
"Long Live Rock" appeared on The Who's 1974 album *Odds and Sods*. On a first listen, it sounds almost like a parody of rock and roll. Listen again, and notice how Pete Townshend's lyrics ponder whether or not rock music had died by becoming a business. This kind of brutal honesty turned The Who into heroes of the '70s punk scene.

5. What was the only #1 hit for the British Invasion band Freddie and the Dreamers?

a. "Ferry Cross the Mersey"
b. "Bits and Pieces"
c. "There's a Kind of Hush"
d. "I'm Telling You Now"

GAME 68 Q4 ANSWER a
This song stayed at #1 for four weeks and earned Sir Mix-A-Lot the 1993 Grammy for Best Rap Solo Performance. It has been used in several movies, including Shrek, Shark Tale, and Charlie's Angels; in Apple's Ipod commercials; and on the TV show Friends. As a rapper, Sir Mix-A-Lot tends not to glamorize gang violence in his music.

GAME 13

8. Which protest song was Barry McGuire's biggest hit?

a. "In the Year 2525"

b. "Eve of Destruction"

c. "Ballad of the Green Berets"

d. "Blowin' in the Wind"

GAME 13 Q7 ANSWER d
Born on January 9, 1941, Joan Baez remains one of the most passionate political activists in American music. In 1963, she sang "We Shall Overcome" during the Martin Luther King civil rights march in Washington, DC. Her 1973 album, *Where Are You Now, My Son?*, featured songs actually recorded during the 1972 US bombings of Hanoi.

GAME 33

8. Who was the first female singer in Billboard chart history to have an album debut at #1?

a. Madonna

b. Whitney Houston

c. Cher

d. Jessica Simpson

GAME 33 Q7 ANSWER a
Former staff sergeant Barry Sandler and author Robin Moore wrote "The Ballad of the Green Berets" in 1966. That year, the song stayed at the top of the charts for five weeks, selling over 9 million singles and albums. The song was also used in the 1968 John Wayne film *The Green Berets*, based on Moore's book of the same name.

GAME 53

8. After a decade of cult status, Sonic Youth broke into the Top 100 with which album?

a. *Goo*

b. *Washing Machine*

c. *Piece of Cake*

d. *Loveless*

GAME 53 Q7 ANSWER a
Formed in 1999, The Strokes became darlings of the Lower East Side club scene almost overnight. Released in the wake of 9/11, *Is This It* originally contained a politically incorrect song called "New York City Cops" that was removed from the album's final track list. Roman Coppola has directed several of the group's videos.

GAME 73

8. Which of these love songs was *not* recorded by Celine Dion?

a. "I Swear"

b. "My Heart Will Go On"

c. "If You Asked Me To"

d. "Because You Loved Me"

GAME 73 Q7 ANSWER a
The 1989 album *Heart of Stone*—which is regarded by many fans as Cher's best work—launched four hit singles: "After All," "If I Could Turn Back Time," "Just Like Jesse James," and "Heart of Stone." Cher and Cetera's rendition of "After All" was included in the soundtrack of the 1989 movie *Chances Are*.

6. Which Bee Gees song was *not* included in the *Saturday Night Fever* hit soundtrack?

a. "Stayin' Alive"

b. "How Deep Is Your Love"

c. "The Woman in You"

d. "Night Fever"

GAME 8 Q5 ANSWER c
Released in 1973, this album stayed on the charts for over 700 weeks. It was recorded in the Abbey Road Studios of Beatles' fame, and Sir Paul even recorded some spoken-word pieces that were not used. The album's original title was *Eclipse,* and the first voice heard on the album is that of the group's road manager, Chris Adamson.

6. Sheb Wooley's only chart hit, a #1 no less, was which colorful song?

a. "Blue Velvet"

b. "The Purple People Eater"

c. "Red Red Wine"

d. "A White Sport Coat"

GAME 28 Q5 ANSWER c
Fans of 1980s music remember AC/DC for its hit "You Shook Me All Night Long," which appeared on the group's most successful album, *Back in Black.* The song was one of the band's few Top 40 singles, and is included in the list of 100 Greatest Rock Songs.

6. Which geographically named band had a Top 10 hit in 1986 with "The Final Countdown"?

a. America

b. Europe

c. Asia

d. Boston

GAME 48 Q5 ANSWER c
The album's full title is *When the Pawn Hits the Conflicts He Thinks Like a King/What He Knows Throws the Blows When He Goes to the Fight/And He'll Win the Whole Thing 'Fore He Enters the Ring/There's No Body To Batter When Your Mind is Your Might/So When You Go Solo, You Hold Your Own Hand . . .* oh, well, I ran out of room!

6. In 1994, who became the first unsigned artist to top the US Billboard singles chart?

a. Jewel

b. Tori Amos

c. Lisa Loeb

d. Fiona Apple

GAME 68 Q5 ANSWER d
In the time of Beatlemania, Freddie and the Dreamers stood out as the first non-Liverpool band to make the UK charts without the assistance of Brian Epstein. Although they had several popular hits in the UK, "I'm Telling You Now" was their only #1 hit single in the US. Their only other US hit was "Do the Freddie," which went to #18.

GAME 13

7. In the 1960s, which singer founded the Institute for the Study of Nonviolence?

a. Diana Ross
b. Art Garfunkel
c. Marvin Gaye
d. Joan Baez

GAME 13 Q6 ANSWER c
In December 1971, Melanie (Safka) had the #1 song in the US with "Brand New Key." Due to the song's repeated mention of "roller skates," it was used in a pivotal scene from the 1997 hit movie *Boogie Nights*, when we learn that a character named Rollergirl *never* takes off her skates . . .

GAME 33

7. A song about which military unit became a #1 hit on the Billboard charts?

a. Green Berets
b. Navy Seals
c. Royal Air Force
d. French Foreign Legion

GAME 33 Q6 ANSWER c
"Rock Around the Clock" was the #1 song in the summer of 1955, staying at the top of the charts for eight weeks. The recording had enjoyed only modest sales after its 1954 release, but its popularity soared after the release of the 1955 film *The Blackboard Jungle*, which used "Rock Around the Clock" in its soundtrack.

GAME 53

7. What is the US debut album of New York City's neo-garage band The Strokes?

a. *Is This It*
b. *Charmed Life*
c. *Baby Jupiter*
d. *Say When*

GAME 53 Q6 ANSWER a
The group changed its name in 1977 after Walter Murphy & the Big Apple Band rose to #1 in 1976 with "A Fifth of Beethoven"—a song that was featured in *Saturday Night Fever* (1977). Guitarist/producer Nile Rodgers had Chic record classic disco songs like "Everybody Dance" and "Le Freak," which reached #1 in 1978.

GAME 73

7. Who pairs with Cher on the "After All" duet from her double-platinum *Heart of Stone* album?

a. Peter Cetera
b. Willie Nelson
c. Mick Jagger
d. Michael Bolton

GAME 73 Q6 ANSWER c
John teamed up with Tina Turner to belt out the John-Taupin hit "The Bitch Is Back." The concert's other songstresses included Cher, LeAnn Rimes, Brandy, Faith Hill, Whitney Houston, Chaka Khan, and Mary J. Blige, but several performers—including Diana Ross—declined to appear because they disliked being called "Divas."

---

7. Which TV show's theme song was a Top 10 hit for The Ventures?

a. *Hawaii Five-O*

b. *Batman*

c. *The Man from UNCLE*

d. *Secret Agent*

GAME 8 Q6 ANSWER c
Popular in the '60s with ballads like "Lonely Days" and "I Started a Joke," The Bee Gees really hit the big time with disco music in the late '70s. The group's classic "Stayin' Alive" was #1 for six weeks in 1978. "The Woman in You" is from *Staying Alive*, the 1983 Sylvester Stallone-directed sequel to *Saturday Night Fever*.

---

7. Who recorded "Do You Believe in Magic?" and "Summer in the City"?

a. The Byrds

b. Iron Butterfly

c. Lovin' Spoonful

d. Jefferson Airplane

GAME 28 Q6 ANSWER b
Besides his career in music, the talented Wooley—who was a cowboy and rodeo rider in his youth—appeared in dozens of western films, the most notable of which is the 1952 movie *High Noon*. He also appeared in a number of television shows, including *Rawhide* and *Hee Haw*.

---

7. What was the real name of Queen's lead singer Freddie Mercury?

a. Farrokh Bulsara

b. Fred Tencic

c. Bob Sutton

d. Declan McManus

GAME 48 Q6 ANSWER b
Hailing from Sweden, this glam-metal quintet went to #1 in twenty-six countries with this song (it went to #8 in the US). The group's power ballad "Carrie" did better, going all the way to #3 on the US pop charts in 1986. Like so many other '80s metal bands, Europe was defeated by the likes of Nirvana and Pearl Jam in the '90s.

---

7. Which US president is heard at the end of Living Colour's song "Cult of Personality"?

a. Franklin D. Roosevelt

b. Richard M. Nixon

c. Ronald W. Reagan

d. George H.W. Bush

GAME 68 Q6 ANSWER c
Loeb and her band Nine Stories made history with the #1 song "Stay (I Missed You)," which was featured on the soundtrack of the 1994 film *Reality Bites*. By the end of '94, Loeb was signed to Geffen Records and released her debut album, *Tails*. In January 2006, she starred in a reality TV show about herself called *#1 Single*.

---

6. Which Woodstock veteran had a big hit with the song "Brand New Key"?

a. Joan Baez
b. Janis Joplin
c. Melanie
d. Grace Slick

GAME 13 Q5 ANSWER b
Many people believed the song's title stood for LSD, but Lennon vehemently denied it. He explained in various interviews how his first son, Julian, had brought home a drawing from school. When Julian called his picture "Lucy in the Sky with Diamonds," Lennon said he immediately wrote a song around the image. You be the judge.

6. Which artist had the first #1 hit on the Billboard charts?

a. Sam Cooke
b. Paul Anka
c. Bill Haley
d. Bobby Vinton

GAME 33 Q5 ANSWER d
The disco hit "Get Down Tonight" hit #1 on the Billboard chart in 1975, and "Shake Your Booty" did the same in 1976. The band also topped the charts with "I'm Your Boogie Man" (1977) and "Please Don't Go" (1979). But when disco declined at the start of the '80s, so did the popularity of KC and The Sunshine Band.

6. Big Apple Band was the original name of which disco-associated group?

a. Chic
b. The Ohio Players
c. Parliament-Funkadelic
d. Mandrill

GAME 53 Q5 ANSWER a
This death-rock classic is peppered with motorcycle roars, screeching tires, and the sound of breaking glass. The song was covered twice by none other than heavy metal group (and fellow New York band) Twisted Sister, whose first version was recorded in 1982. The second version showed up on the 1985 *Come Out and Play* album.

6. What song did honorary diva Elton John perform at the 1999 VH1 Divas Concert?

a. "Island Girl"
b. "Candle in the Wind"
c. "The Bitch Is Back"
d. "Honky Cat"

GAME 73 Q5 ANSWER c
Written by Linda Perry, "Beautiful" appeared on Aguilera's second full-length English album, *Stripped*. The song—which rose to #1 on the Adult Contemporary, Top 40 Mainstream, and Top 40 Tracks charts—was praised for its theme of self-acceptance, and won Aguilera a Grammy in the Best Pop Female Vocal category.

GAME 8	**8.** To date, which of the following actors did *not* write and perform a hit song? **a.** Patrick Swayze **b.** Irene Cara **c.** Don Johnson **d.** Keith Carradine	**GAME 8 Q7 ANSWER a** With hits like "Walk, Don't Run" and "Perfidia," The Ventures were one of the most successful instrumental bands in rock history. Their theme song for *Hawaii Five-O* rose to #4 on the charts in 1969. The CBS show itself first went on the air in 1968, the same year The Monkees went off the air on NBC.
GAME 28	**8.** What unusual musical instrument is featured prominently in Buddy Holly's song "Everyday"? **a.** Sitar **b.** Celeste **c.** Harpsichord **d.** Dulcimer	**GAME 28 Q7 ANSWER c** Other Lovin' Spoonful hits include "You Didn't Have to Be So Nice," "Daydream," "Younger Girl," and "Did You Ever Have to Make Up Your Mind?" The 1960s pop-rock band was accepted into the Rock and Roll Hall of Fame in 2000, at which time they enjoyed a resurgence of interest.
GAME 48	**8.** Who played guitar on Michael Jackson's 1983 megahit "Beat It"? **a.** Keith Richards **b.** Eddie Van Halen **c.** Eric Clapton **d.** Jimmy Page	**GAME 48 Q7 ANSWER a** Farrokh ("Freddie") was born on the island of Zanzibar off the coast of Africa in 1946, to parents of Indian Parsi descent. After moving to England in 1964, Bulsara was seduced by the hot sounds of rock and roll—a heat that changed him into a kind of "Mercury." His death from AIDS in 1991 shined a light on the disease.
GAME 68	**8.** Which of these songs about a woman is *not* by Steely Dan? **a.** "Aja" **b.** "Peg" **c.** "Valleri" **d.** "Josie"	**GAME 68 Q7 ANSWER a** Although FDR is the last historical voice heard in this 1989 political song hit by the African-American hard rock band Living Colour, it also includes word fragments spoken by John F. Kennedy and political activist Malcolm X. "Cult of Personality," which is from the band's 1988 debut album *Vivid*, earned a Grammy for Best Hard Rock Performance.

GAME 13

5. In "Lucy in the Sky With Diamonds," what did the rocking horse people eat?

a. Strawberry fields
b. Marshmallow pies
c. Lemon drop sunshine
d. Chocolate teardrops

GAME 13 Q4 ANSWER d
The Byrds had its first #1 hit in June 1965 with an electric version of Bob Dylan's song "Mr. Tambourine Man." They then went on to have hits with "All I Really Want to Do" and "My Back Pages" (also written by Dylan). Byrds' guitarist Roger McGuinn actually started the granny sunglasses look before John Lennon did in 1966.

GAME 33

5. Who had #1 hits on the 1970s Billboard charts with "Get Down Tonight" and "Shake Your Booty"?

a. Bay City Rollers
b. Steve Miller Band
c. Earth, Wind and Fire
d. KC & The Sunshine Band

GAME 33 Q4 ANSWER a
"When Doves Cry" was #1 for five weeks, helping *Purple Rain* become the #1 album of 1984. According to one source, the album—which was entirely written by Prince—sold over a million copies just on the day of its release. All told, it sold over 13 million copies in the US.

GAME 53

5. Which 1964 hit is the signature tune of The Shangri-Las?

a. "Leader of the Pack"
b. "Be My Baby"
c. "He's So Fine"
d. "Maybe"

GAME 53 Q4 ANSWER b
Formed in 1971, the short-lived New York Dolls played in a style that predated the chaos of '70s punk and dressed in a way that influenced hair metal bands of the '80s. As Buster Poindexter, Johansen had a hit in 1987 with "Hot Hot Hot." He later played the Ghost of Christmas Past in the 1988 Bill Murray comedy *Scrooged*.

GAME 73

5. For what song did Christina Aguilera win a 2004 Grammy?

a. "Peaceful"
b. "Wonderful"
c. "Beautiful"
d. "Enchanted"

GAME 73 Q4 ANSWER a
"We Belong Together" was released as a single from *The Emancipation of Mimi*. The song rose to the #1 position on several US charts, remaining there for weeks. After the poor commercial performance of the singles from 2001's *Glitter* and 2002's *Charmbracelet*, "We Belong Together" was hailed as Carey's comeback song.

---

9. What musical act hit it big in 2003 with the single "Seven Nation Army"?

a. The Hives
b. The Vines
c. The Strokes
d. The White Stripes

GAME 8 Q8 ANSWER c
Keith Carradine's song "I'm Easy" won the Academy Award for Best Original Song in Robert Altman's *Nashville* (1975). Irene Cara scored two big #1 hits with her theme songs for the films *Fame* (1980) and *Flashdance* (1983), and Patrick Swayze reached #3 in 1987 with his *Dirty Dancing* hit, "She's Like the Wind."

9. Which group had a big hit with the song "Gloria"?

a. Yardbirds
b. Troggs
c. Spencer Davis Group
d. Them

GAME 28 Q8 ANSWER b
The celeste part on this delicate song was played by Vi Petty—wife to Buddy Holly's manager Norman Petty. "Everyday" also has drummer Jerry Allison simply slapping his knee rather than playing his drums, giving the song a gentle feel. Following in Les Paul's footsteps, Holly also experimented with double-tracking guitar parts.

9. Written by Carole King and Gerry Goffin, what was Little Eva's one hit song?

a. "The Loco-Motion"
b. "Sugar, Sugar"
c. "Chapel of Love"
d. "Baby, I'm Yours"

GAME 48 Q8 ANSWER b
Eddie Van Halen played on the song as a favor to Jackson. At the time, Van Halen's lead singer David Lee Roth criticized Eddie for doing the track. But Roth soon quit the band (or was fired) in 1985 and released his debut solo album, *Crazy From the Heat*. Roth reunited briefly with Van Halen for two new songs in 1996.

9. The Dave Clark Five (DC5) had a Top 10 hit song in 1964 with:

a. "Purple Haze"
b. "California Girls"
c. "Glad All Over"
d. "Going to the Chapel"

GAME 68 Q8 ANSWER c
"Valleri" was a hit song for The Monkees in 1968. "Aja," "Peg," and "Josie" are all songs from Steely Dan's chart-topping 1977 album, *Aja*. This album won a Grammy in 1978 for Best Engineered Non-Classical Recording. Other Steely Dan songs about women have included "Rose Darling," "Janie Runaway," and "Rikki Don't Lose That Number."

4. Which group recorded the 1960s hits "Mr. Tambourine Man" and "Turn, Turn, Turn"?

a. Diamonds
b. Flying Burrito Brothers
c. Beach Boys
d. Byrds

GAME 13 Q3 ANSWER a
Both "Aquarius" and "Let the Sunshine In" are songs from the rock musical *Hair*. When put together by producer Bones Howe and performed by soul-singing sensation The Fifth Dimension, the single went straight to #1 and stayed there for six weeks. The song went on to win the 1969 Grammy for Best Record of the Year.

4. Which performer had the #1 Billboard single of 1984?

a. Prince
b. Madonna
c. Phil Collins
d. Olivia Newton-John

GAME 33 Q3 ANSWER c
"You Light Up My Life" sold 4 million copies when it was released in 1977. Later, Boone said that the popularity of the song was an annoyance because no one ever wanted her to sing anything else. Nevertheless, Boone has since recorded several albums and has also appeared on stage in a number of musicals, including *The King and I*.

4. Buster Poindexter is the alter ego of which former New York Dolls vocalist?

a. Syl Sylvain
b. David Johansen
c. Brian Setzer
d. Johnny Thunders

GAME 53 Q3 ANSWER a
Known by many as "the Godfather of Punk," Lou Reed also sang on popular Velvet Underground songs like "Heroin," "Venus in Furs," and "White Light/White Heat." After going solo in 1972, he had a hit with "Take a Walk on the Wild Side." His 1975 double-album, *Metal Machine Music,* features nothing but electric guitar feedback.

4. What 2005 hit single began Mariah Carey's comeback?

a. "We Belong Together"
b. "It's Like That"
c. "Shake It Off"
d. "Get Your Number"

GAME 73 Q3 ANSWER c
Nickolas Ashford and Valerie Simpson's "I'm Every Woman" was first recorded by Chaka Khan in 1978. A hit, it became Khan's signature song. Then in 1992, Houston covered the song in the soundtrack of *The Bodyguard,* and it rose to #4 on the charts. Interestingly, Houston—along with mother Cissy—had sung backup on the original Khan version.

10. Which band had a hit album in 2003 with *Welcome Interstate Managers*?

a. Train

b. Fountains of Wayne

c. Our Lady Peace

d. Finger Eleven

GAME 8 Q9 ANSWER d
The White Stripes' album *Elephant* won the 2003 Grammy for Best Alternative Music Album. In 2004, the group's front-man, Jack White, produced a new album for country legend Loretta Lynn called *Van Lear Rose*. This blending of country and rock 'n roll styles is something my fellow Monkee Mike Nesmith pioneered back in the '60s.

10. Who wrote the Chubby Checker hit "The Twist"?

a. Johnny Carter

b. Doc Pomus

c. Chubby Checker

d. Hank Ballard

GAME 28 Q9 ANSWER d
The 1966 hit was written by Van Morrison, who formed Them in 1964, becoming the group's lead singer. After a 1966 US tour, Morrison left the band, intending to quit the music business. Instead, he launched a successful solo career, almost immediately producing one of his biggest hits, "Brown Eyed Girl."

10. Which of the following songs is by '70s progressive rock group Yes?

a. "Heart of the Sunrise"

b. "21st Century Schizoid Man"

c. "For Absent Friends"

d. "Cogs in Cogs"

GAME 48 Q9 ANSWER a
As a teen, Eva Narcissus Boyd babysat for Goffin and King's children, and often danced around their house. The song-writers were inspired by Boyd to write a dance song. In 1962, Boyd recorded the song as "Little Eva," and it soon became a #1 hit. In 1988, a new version of the song reached the Top 10 for Australian singer Kylie Minogue.

10. Robert Plant was lead singer of what "other" group?

a. Night Ranger

b. The Honeydrippers

c. The Stray Cats

d. Great White

GAME 68 Q9 ANSWER c
This British group had seventeen Top 40 hits between 1964 and 1967. Reaching #6 in the US, "Glad All Over" hit #1 in the UK, knocking off The Beatles' "I Want to Hold Your Hand." In 1977, heavy metal group KISS paid homage to the DC5 by recording a new version of the 1964 hit "Anyway You Want It" for the album *Alive II*.

3. Which "trippy" 1960s song was a hit for The Fifth Dimension?

a. "Aquarius/Let the Sunshine In"
b. "Purple Haze"
c. "Good Vibrations"
d. "California Dreamin'"

GAME 13 Q2 ANSWER c
This song by one-hit wonder Strawberry Alarm Clock was resurrected by comic actor Mike Myers in his second Austin Powers film. "Green Tambourine" by The Lemon Pipers and "Everyday People" by Sly & the Family Stone were #1 hits in 1968, while "In the Year 2525" by Zager and Evans hit #1 in 1969.

3. In 1977, who became the first female solo artist to stay at #1 on Billboard for ten weeks?

a. Diana Ross
b. Olivia Newton-John
c. Debby Boone
d. Donna Summer

GAME 33 Q2 ANSWER d
Jamaican-born Carl Douglas reportedly wrote "Kung Fu Fighting" in only ten minutes to fill the B-side of the single "I Want to Give You My Everything." Eventually, the song was elevated to A-side status and was released in 1974, during the "chopsocky" film craze. The song quickly rose to the top of the US and UK charts.

3. Who played guitar in The Velvet Underground?

a. Lou Reed
b. Zal Yanovsky
c. Johnny Ramone
d. Carlos Santana

GAME 53 Q2 ANSWER a
Founded in 1973, Television became a mainstay at Manhattan's famous club CBGB. In the midst of the growing punk scene, Elektra Records signed the group and released its acclaimed debut album, *Marquee Moon*, in 1977. Television's unique sound combined the dissonance of The Velvet Underground and the rawness of The Ramones.

3. What song was a hit for Chaka Khan in the '70s, and for Whitney Houston in the '90s?

a. "Saving All My Love for You"
b. "I Wanna Dance With Somebody"
c. "I'm Every Woman"
d. "You Give Good Love"

GAME 73 Q2 ANSWER c
In 1964, "Downtown"—which was released in four languages—became a huge hit in the UK, France, the Netherlands, Germany, Italy, Australia, India, and Rhodesia. It then rose to #1 in the US. The 1964 Grammy was given to Clark for Best Rock & Roll Record, and in 2003, her recording was inducted into the Grammy Hall of Fame.

GAME 8

11. *Turn on the Bright Lights* was the 2002 debut album of which quartet?

a. Prodigy
b. Soundgarden
c. Interpol
d. The Strokes

GAME 28

11. Who played bass guitar for Motley Crue?

a. Tommy Lee
b. Vince Neil
c. Mick Mars
d. Nikki Sixx

GAME 48

11. Which band backed up British invasion singer Billy J. Kramer?

a. The Mindbenders
b. The Pacemakers
c. The Dakotas
d. The Beaters

GAME 68

11. Which lead singer and rock band is a mismatch?

a. Boy George/Culture Club
b. Rod Stewart/Yardbirds
c. Phil Collins/Genesis
d. Lionel Richie/Commodores

GAME 8 Q10 ANSWER b
This energetic New York quartet released its first album *Fountains of Wayne* in 1996 and quickly became one of the best-known practitioners of "power pop," a rock genre that leans heavily on the sounds of "British Invasion" hitmakers of the '60s. The group found major mainstream success from the song (and video) "Stacy's Mom."

GAME 28 Q10 ANSWER d
Hank Ballard was a member of the doo-wop group The Midnighters, whose songs "Finger-Poppin' Tune" and "Let's Go, Let's Go, Let's Go" were both in the Top 40 along with their own version of "The Twist" in 1960. Chubby Checker's classic version of "The Twist" set a record by hitting #1 twice: first in 1960, and again in 1962.

GAME 48 Q10 ANSWER a
This song is on the 1971 album *Fragile*. In his directorial debut, actor Vincent Gallo featured the song in the film *Buffalo '66* (2000). The 1969 song "21st Century Schizoid Man" is by King Crimson; "For Absent Friends" is a 1971 song by Genesis (when Peter Gabriel was lead singer); and "Cogs in Cogs" is a 1974 song by Gentle Giant.

GAME 68 Q10 ANSWER b
Led Zeppelin broke up in 1980, and Robert Plant began a solo career. In 1984, after two successful solo albums, he started The Honeydrippers—a short-lived all-star band featuring Zeppelin guitarist Jimmy Page, along with guitarist Jeff Beck and Phil Collins of Genesis on drums. Its cover of the '50s hit "Sea of Love" was a Top 10 hit.

2. Which 1967 #1 hit was featured in the 1999 Austin Powers' spoof, *The Spy Who Shagged Me*?

a. "Green Tambourine"
b. "In the Year 2525"
c. "Incense and Peppermints"
d. "Everyday People"

GAME 13 Q1 ANSWER c
Donovan Philips Leitch was a Scottish singer who was called the "British Bob Dylan" back in 1965. Donovan was close with The Beatles—McCartney even recorded some uncredited backing vocals on "Mellow Yellow," featuring a brass section arranged by John Paul Jones of Led Zeppelin. The song went to #2 on the US charts in 1966.

2. What was the first sport to have a song about it reach #1 on the Billboard charts?

a. Basketball
b. Golf
c. Sky Diving
d. Kung Fu

GAME 33 Q1 ANSWER b
"It's Too Late" appeared on King's 1971 album *Tapestry*, which ranked #1 for fifteen weeks and remained on the charts for six years. All of the songs on the album were written or co-written by King, and many—such as "Will You Love Me Tomorrow?"—had already been hits with other artists.

2. The rock group Television gained the attention of major record labels with which underground hit?

a. "Little Johnny Jewel"
b. "Foxhole"
c. "West End Blues"
d. "Prove It"

GAME 53 Q1 ANSWER b
Born in Israel in 1949, the fire-breathing KISS bassist once considered becoming a rabbi. Rock 'n roll, however, was more to his taste. An aggressive performer known for flicking his tongue and spitting fake blood at audiences, Simmons has also dated pop divas Cher and Diana Ross.

2. Which song won Petula Clark a Grammy in 1964?

a. "Don't Sleep in the Subway"
b. "My Love"
c. "Downtown"
d. "Color My World"

GAME 73 Q1 ANSWER b
Bette Midler began her career as an extra in the 1966 film *Hawaii*, but quickly landed a part in the Broadway production of *Fiddler on the Roof*. Within a few years, she had built the larger-than-life persona of "The Divine Miss M." In *Diva Las Vegas*, Midler mixed bawdy comedy with performances of hit tunes like "The Rose" and "Friends."

12. Which band had hits with "Yellow" and "Trouble" in 2001?

a. Dave Matthews Band
b. Limp Bizkit
c. Coldplay
d. Linkin Park

Founded in 1998 in New York City, Interpol takes the influences of '70s groups like Television and Talking Heads along with '80s New Wave-rs like the Psychedelic Furs and Joy Division, and mixes them in with their own brand of proto-punk soundscapes and angst-ridden lyrics.

---

12. How many #1 hits has Bruce Springsteen recorded to date?

a. 1
b. 0
c. 3
d. 5

Nikki Sixx was born Frank Carlton Serafino Ferrano in 1958, and formed Motley Crue in 1981. The group's most successful album—1989's *Dr. Feelgood*—was produced shortly after Sixx and his bandmates completed rehab as a result of Sixx's drug overdose. The album remained on the charts for over a hundred weeks.

---

12. Which group had a hit in 1991 with the song "Right Here, Right Now"?

a. Pearl Jam
b. Van Halen
c. Jesus Jones
d. Nirvana

This Liverpool native was managed by Brian Epstein, who also managed The Beatles. In the 1984 documentary *The Compleat Beatles,* Kramer recalled that the Beatles' haircuts were longer than anything else he'd ever seen. Most of Kramer's mid-'60s hits were actually Lennon/McCartney songs, including "Bad to Me" and "I'll Be On My Way."

---

12. In 1969, "Time of the Season" was the last hit for which British Invasion band?

a. The Dave Clark Five
b. The Yardbirds
c. The Zombies
d. The Kinks

Keith Relf was the lead singer for The Yardbirds from 1963 to 1968. When guitarist Jeff Beck left The Yardbirds in 1966, he hired Ron Wood on bass and Rod Stewart on vocals for his short-lived Jeff Beck Group. In 1969, Rod and Ron joined The Small Faces. By 1971, Rod Stewart was a solo act; by 1976, Ron Wood was a Rolling Stone.

GAME 13	**1.** Who recorded the '60s hits "Sunshine Superman" and "Mellow Yellow"? **a.** Bobbie Gentry **b.** Janis Joplin **c.** Donovan **d.** Bobby Darin	The answer to this question is on: **page 208,** **top frame,** **right side.**
GAME 33	**1.** Which song was a #1 Billboard single for Carole King? **a.** "Born to Be Wild" **b.** "It's Too Late" **c.** "Smells Like Teen Spirit" **d.** "Sweet Dreams"	The answer to this question is on: **page 208,** **second frame,** **right side.**
GAME 53	**1.** What is the given name of KISS frontman Gene Simmons? **a.** Robert Zimmerman **b.** Chaim Witz **c.** Adam Yauch **d.** Stanley Eisen	The answer to this question is on: **page 208,** **third frame,** **right side.**
GAME 73	**1.** Which entertainer won a 1996–1997 Emmy for her HBO special *Diva Las Vegas*? **a.** Whitney Houston **b.** Bette Midler **c.** Barbra Streisand **d.** Celine Dion	The answer to this question is on: **page 208,** **bottom frame,** **right side.**

GAME 9

The '80s

*Turn to page 213
for the first question.*

Turn to page 213
for the first question.

With over 10 million records sold, Coldplay is one of the most popular British groups since . . . well, *you know who.* Their first album, *Parachutes,* won a 2002 Grammy for Best Alternative Music Album. Their song "Clocks" won the 2004 Grammy for Record of the Year. Lead singer Chris Martin married actress Gwyneth Paltrow in 2003.

GAME 29

The MTV Generation

*Turn to page 213
for the first question.*

Turn to page 213
for the first question.

Amazingly, none of the songs that Springsteen wrote and recorded himself ever made it to the top spot in the charts. However, a Bruce Springsteen song *did* make #1 in 1977, when Manfred Mann's Earth Band went to the top of the charts with their version of "Blinded by the Light."

GAME 49

Rock Meets Classical

*Turn to page 213
for the first question.*

Turn to page 213
for the first question.

This Jesus Jones' song from the album *Doubt* went to #5 in the US pop charts. The song was later used as a jingle in Kmart commercials. Van Halen had a radio and video hit a year later with the song "Right Now." And in 1993, Van Halen released a live concert album and DVD called *Live: Right Here, Right Now.*

GAME 69

Women of Rock

*Turn to page 213
for the first question.*

Turn to page 213
for the first question.

"Time of the Season" is the last track on the last Zombies' album, *Odessey and Oracle.* Although this highly ambitious album was recorded in 1967, it wasn't released until April 1968, *after* the group had broken up. Due to poor promotion and bad timing, "Time of the Season" didn't become a chart hit for The Zombies until 1969.

GAME 13
Flower Power Songs

*Turn to page 210
for the first question.*

Turn to page 210
for the first question.

GAME 12 Q12 ANSWER b
This half-studio, half-live 1968 double album begins with Cream's signature hit "White Room," which reached #6 on the US pop charts. It also has an incredible live performance of the Robert Johnson blues classic "Crossroads," featuring Eric Clapton at the top of his game. If you want to hear Cream at its best, this album is it!

GAME 33
Billboard #1s

*Turn to page 210
for the first question.*

Turn to page 210
for the first question.

GAME 32 Q12 ANSWER d
The Clovers formed in 1946 in Washington, DC. In 1951, they had two #1 hits: "Don't You Know I Love You" and "Fool Fool Fool." Though it didn't reach #1, "Love Potion #9" remains the group's most popular song. Along with several other doo-wop favorites, it was featured in the 1973 film *American Graffiti*.

GAME 53
New York Bands

*Turn to page 210
for the first question.*

Turn to page 210
for the first question.

GAME 52 Q12 ANSWER a
O'Day also wrote Helen Reddy's 1974 #1 hit, "Angie Baby," and "Rock and Roll Heaven," which rose to #3 for The Righteous Brothers that same year. The fact that O'Day used the word "angel" in the song title only helped its popularity—after all, *Charlie's Angels* was one of the top TV shows at that time.

GAME 73
Pop Divas

*Turn to page 210
for the first question.*

Turn to page 210
for the first question.

GAME 72 Q12 ANSWER c
Nena—a group comprised of singer Nena, drummer Rolf Brendel, guitarist Carlo Karges, keyboardist Uwe Fahrenkrog-Petersen, and bassist Jurgen Dehmel—formed in 1981. In 1983, the band released its self-titled album, which launched the #1 hit single "99 Luftballons." An English version of the song, "99 Red Balloons," was also recorded.

1. Which group had the 1980 hit "Tainted Love"?

a. Erasure
b. Soft Cell
c. Depeche Mode
d. Duran Duran

The answer to this question is on:

page 215, top frame, right side.

1. *MTV Unplugged in New York* is an album by:

a. The Black Crowes
b. R.E.M.
c. Nirvana
d. Tony Bennett

The answer to this question is on:

page 215, second frame, right side.

1. Which was the first Beatles' song to feature orchestral instruments?

a. "I Am the Walrus"
b. "She's Leaving Home"
c. "Eleanor Rigby"
d. "Yesterday"

The answer to this question is on:

page 215, third frame, right side.

1. Who won a Grammy for Best Female Pop Vocal Performance with "If It Makes You Happy"?

a. Tori Amos
b. Sheryl Crow
c. Jewel
d. Natalie Merchant

The answer to this question is on:

page 215, bottom frame, right side.

GAME 12

12. *Wheels of Fire* was a hit album for which group?

a. The Mamas and the Papas

b. Cream

c. The Beach Boys

d. Creedence Clearwater Revival

GAME 12 Q11 ANSWER a
This song is from Los Lobos' second major-label album, *By the Light of the Moon,* and shot to #1 in the summer of 1987. That same year, the group recorded some cover tunes, as well as the popular title track for *La Bamba,* starring Lou Diamond Phillips as Richie Valens.

GAME 32

12. Which of these songs was first recorded in 1959 by the doo-wop group The Clovers?

a. "Do You Wanna Dance"

b. "Blue Moon"

c. "See You in September"

d. "Love Potion #9"

GAME 32 Q11 ANSWER b
The Kinks first gained prominence in the mid-1960s, and at one point, rivalled The Rolling Stones as the second most popular British group, behind only The Beatles. The group's fourth single, "All Day and All of the Night" rose to #2 in the UK and #7 in the US.

GAME 52

12. Whose only charted song, "Undercover Angel," went all the way to #1 in 1977?

a. Alan O'Day

b. John Sebastian

c. Frank Zappa

d. Mungo Jerry

GAME 52 Q11 ANSWER a
He played a true-to-life role as a songwriter who is often watched by the Jimmy Stewart character in this 1954 classic. (Hitchcock's cameo takes place in the songwriter's apartment!) His first big hit song was "Witch Doctor" in 1958. Bagdasarian also wrote "Come On-a My House" for Rosemary Clooney and, of course, "The Chipmunk Song."

GAME 72

12. "99 Luftballons" was the only hit song for which German group?

a. Taco

b. Falco

c. Nena

d. Toto

GAME 72 Q11 ANSWER a
"Blowin' in the Wind," from Dylan's second album *The Freewheelin' Bob Dylan,* was the folk-singing group's biggest hit single, rising to #1 throughout the world. Other Peter, Paul and Mary hits included Pete Seeger and Lee Hays' "If I Had a Hammer," and "Leaving on a Jet Plane," which was written by the then-unknown John Denver.

---

2. According to its name, the 1980s pop band that sang "Oh, Sheila" was Ready for the:

a. World

b. Big Time

c. Crossfire

d. Next Round

GAME 9

GAME 9 Q1 ANSWER b
Soft Cell began in the late '70s when British DJs Dave Ball and Marc Almond started to collaborate on dance records. "Tainted Love" had already been a double hit for singer Gloria Jones—once in the '60s, and again in the '70s when Jones' husband, Marc Bolan, produced it. After Soft Cell's one big hit, it disbanded in 1984.

---

2. Which of the following was used as an MTV emblem during the music channel's early years?

a. An astronaut

b. A lion trainer

c. A cowboy

d. An acrobat

GAME 29 Q1 ANSWER c
This was the first Nirvana album released after the April 1994 death of singer-guitarist Kurt Cobain. Featuring an acoustic concert played at New York's Sony Music Studios on November 18, 1993, it won a 1996 Grammy Award for Best Alternative Music Album.

---

2. Carl Palmer, Greg Lake, and ____ formed a rock group influenced by classical music.

a. Eric Clapton

b. Peter Frampton

c. Bruce Dickinson

d. Keith Emerson

GAME 49 Q1 ANSWER d
This immortal Beatles' classic featured Paul McCartney on both lead vocal and acoustic guitar, along with a string quartet. Featured on the 1965 *Help!* soundtrack, this song was the first of three McCartney-sung Beatles' tunes that relied on classical orchestration. "Eleanor Rigby" (1966) and "She's Leaving Home" (1967) are the others.

---

2. What was Pat Benatar's 1979 debut album?

a. *In the Heat of the Night*

b. *Crimes of Passion*

c. *Precious Time*

d. *Get Nervous*

GAME 69 Q1 ANSWER b
"If It Makes You Happy" is featured on Crow's 1996 self-titled album, which itself won a 1997 Grammy for Best Rock Album. But Crow lost sales when Wal-Mart banned the album because of the song "Love Is a Good Thing," which describes children killing each other with guns purchased in Wal-Mart discount stores.

GAME 12

11. "Set Me Free (Rosa Lee)" is an original recording by:

a. Los Lobos

b. Santana

c. Ricky Martin

d. The Del Fuegos

GAME 12 Q10 ANSWER a

Powerslave (1984) is the fifth album by British metal pioneer Iron Maiden. Ten years earlier, *Rush* was the debut LP by Canadian rockers Geddy Lee on bass and lead vocals, Alex Lifeson on guitar, and John Rutley on drums. By the time Rush had recorded its second album, *Fly By Night* (1975), Rutley had been replaced by Neil Peart.

GAME 32

11. Which group's distinctive sound is heard on such hits as 1965's "All Day and All of the Night"?

a. The Who

b. The Kinks

c. Herman's Hermits

d. Jefferson Airplane

GAME 32 Q10 ANSWER c

Born as Eugene Dixon in 1937 in Chicago, Chandler first started performing in the early '50s as a member of The Gaytones. By 1957, he was lead singer for The Dukays. Drafted into the US Army and stationed in Germany along with Elvis, Chandler had a #1 hit with "Duke of Earl" in 1962—and he has played as "The Duke" ever since.

GAME 52

11. Ross Bagdasarian—aka David Seville of Alvin & The Chipmunks—is featured in which Alfred Hitchcock thriller?

a. *Rear Window*

b. *Vertigo*

c. *Dial "M" for Murder*

d. *The Man Who Knew Too Much*

GAME 52 Q10 ANSWER c

Prior to this #11 single from the 1987 album *Bad*, the "King of Pop" had seventeen singles that were all Top 10 hits. The five singles that came before "Another Part of Me"—"Dirty Diana," "Man in the Mirror," "The Way You Make Me Feel," "Bad," and "I Just Can't Stop Loving You" (with Siedah Garrett)—all hit the #1 spot.

GAME 72

11. With what Bob Dylan song did Peter, Paul and Mary hit the charts in 1963?

a. "Blowin' in the Wind"

b. "Times They Are a-Changin'"

c. "Masters of War"

d. "Chimes of Freedom"

GAME 72 Q10 ANSWER a

Sheila, Jeanette, and Wanda Hutchinson formed The Emotions in 1968, and released their debut album *So I Can Love You* the following year. In 1977, the sisters topped the charts with "Best of My Love," and two years later, they had another hit with "Boogie Wonderland," which was produced in collaboration with Earth, Wind & Fire.

---

3. Who co-wrote "We Are the World" with Lionel Richie?

a. George Michael

b. Daryl Hall

c. Sting

d. Michael Jackson

GAME 9 Q2 ANSWER a
This six-member funk group from Michigan went to #1 in 1985 with "Oh, Sheila." This was the time of Prince's reign over the charts with songs from his film *Purple Rain*, and this song's title also reminded the public of Prince's percussionist protégé, Sheila E. The group had its second best-known hit in 1986 with "Love You Down."

3. Which of the following people were *not* VJs when MTV first aired in 1981?

a. Nina Blackwood

b. Martha Quinn

c. Mark Goodman

d. Tracey Ullman

GAME 29 Q2 ANSWER a
The emblem depicted an astronaut standing on the moon next to a flag bearing the MTV logo. At one point, the MTV slogan was "MTV . . . Proud as a Moon Man"—a spoof of NBC's 1979–1981 slogan "Proud as a Peacock."

3. Which singer-songwriter wrote a children's opera titled *Romulus Hunt*?

a. Carly Simon

b. Lou Reed

c. Danny Elfman

d. Yoko Ono

GAME 49 Q2 ANSWER d
Formed in 1970, Emerson, Lake, & Palmer (ELP) featured synthesized rock arrangements of classical pieces like Mussorgsky's "Pictures at an Exhibition." The group had moderate hits with songs like "Lucky Man" and "Karn Evil 9 (1st Impression Part 2)." In 1981, Palmer joined the group Asia along with Yes guitarist Steve Howe.

3. In her song "Don't Let Me Get Me," who does Pink complain of being compared to?

a. Britney Spears

b. Christina Aguilera

c. Gwen Stefani

d. Madonna

GAME 69 Q2 ANSWER a
The operatically trained Benatar's debut album went platinum, and also launched the single "Heartbreaker," which rose to #23 on the charts. Later hit singles by this Brooklyn-born singer included 1980's "Hit Me With Your Best Shot," 1983's "Love Is a Battlefield," and 1984's "We Belong."

GAME 12	**10.** Which of the following is *not* a Rush album? **a.** *Powerslave* **b.** *Caress of Steel* **c.** *Rush* **d.** *Moving Pictures*	**GAME 12 Q9 ANSWER c** Taken from his 1980 hit album *Scary Monsters*, Bowie's "Ashes to Ashes" changed Major Tom from an astronaut into a rock-star casualty. It also was one of the first videos aired on MTV in 1982. Bowie connected with '80s teens when words from his song "Changes" were shown onscreen in the opening credits of *The Breakfast Club* (1985).
GAME 32	**10.** What singer was "The Duke of Earl"? **a.** Jerry Butler **b.** Curtis Mayfield **c.** Gene Chandler **d.** Fats Domino	**GAME 32 Q9 ANSWER a** The white doo-wop group first hit the charts in 1962 with "Sherry," and followed with many well-known hits, including "Dawn," "Rag Doll," "Ronnie," "Big Girls Don't Cry," "Walk Like a Man," and "Working My Way Back to You." The Four Seasons were inducted into the Rock and Roll Hall of Fame in 1990.
GAME 52	**10.** Which Michael Jackson single did *not* make it to the Top 10? **a.** "Bad" **b.** "Billie Jean" **c.** "Another Part of Me" **d.** "Beat It"	**GAME 52 Q9 ANSWER b** With its mix of rock rhythm and syncopated ranting, "Subterranean Homesick Blues" (the opening track on the classic 1965 album *Bringing It All Back Home*) was, in many ways, the first rap song. An early video of the song, featuring Dylan dropping cue cards, was imitated by INXS in its 1987 video of "Need You Tonight/Mediate."
GAME 72	**10.** What '70s singing group consisted of the Hutchinson sisters? **a.** The Emotions **b.** Dawn **c.** The Dixie Cups **d.** Sister Sledge	**GAME 72 Q9 ANSWER c** Minogue began her career as an actor on the Australian soap opera *Neighbours*, but won a recording contract after singing "Loco-Motion" at a charity event. The artist's eighth album, *Fever,* reached #1 on the Australian charts, and launched the hit single "Can't Get You Out of My Head," which was a #1 hit throughout the world.

GAME 9

4. Which band's first #1 hit was "Keep on Loving You" in 1980?

a. Night Ranger
b. Starship
c. REO Speedwagon
d. Huey Lewis and the News

GAME 9 Q3 ANSWER d
Written in 1985 after the success of Band-Aid's "Do They Know It's Christmas?," this song by the USA for Africa project symbolized the efforts of American pop stars to help end world starvation. While Band-Aid featured Sting and George Michael, USA for Africa included voices as diverse as Cyndi Lauper, Ray Charles, and Bob Dylan.

GAME 29

4. Who was the original host of MTV's *Total Request Live*?

a. Rick James
b. Jimmy Kimmel
c. Jon Stewart
d. Carson Daly

GAME 29 Q3 ANSWER d
Besides Blackwood, Quinn, and Goodman, the early MTV VJs included Alan Hunter and J.J. Jackson. By 1987, this original gang of five—several of whom eventually became celebrities in their own right—had been replaced with younger VJs.

GAME 49

4. Which rock icon recorded the classical album *The Juliet Letters* with England's renowned Brodsky Quartet?

a. Elvis Costello
b. Sting
c. Elton John
d. Johnny Rotten

GAME 49 Q3 ANSWER a
Carly Simon wrote *Romulus Hunt,* which was commissioned by both The Kennedy Center and The Metropolitan Opera Guild, in 1993. The work is about divorce, something Simon and first husband James Taylor experienced in 1983. On Simon's 1995 three-disc boxed set *Clouds In My Coffee,* she sings "Voulez-Vous Danser"—an aria from this opera.

GAME 69

4. For which hit Santana song does Michelle Branch provide the vocals?

a. "Maria, Maria"
b. "Game of Love"
c. "Why Don't You and I"
d. "Smooth"

GAME 69 Q3 ANSWER a
The song is featured on Pink's 2001 album *M!ssundaztood,* which was a worldwide success. Largely written and produced by Pink and singer-songwriter Linda Perry, the album displayed the artist's new pop rock sound through smash hit singles such as "Get the Party Started," "Just Like a Pill," and "Family Portrait."

9. Which David Bowie song revisits the lone figure of Major Tom from "Space Oddity"?

a. "The Man Who Sold the World"

b. "Changes"

c. "Ashes to Ashes"

d. "Golden Years"

GAME 12 Q8 ANSWER d
Although it was only the B-side to the A-side single "At the Zoo," this tune is just one of the great Simon & Garfunkel songs that also became hits for other artists at the time. In 1967, Harpers Bizarre had its one Top 20 hit with this song, while The Cyrkle had a Paul Simon-penned hit with "Red Rubber Ball" in 1966.

9. Which of these girls was *not* the subject of a hit song by Frankie Valli and The Four Seasons?

a. Georgia

b. Dawn

c. Ronnie

d. Marianne

GAME 32 Q8 ANSWER b
Film buffs will recognize these album titles as being names of Marx Brothers films as well. At one point, plans were made to release the 1975 and 1976 albums together as a package, but the plan never came to fruition. *A Night at the Opera* is considered by many to be Queen's greatest effort.

9. Bob Dylan's "Subterranean _____ Blues" opened the door to a new songwriting style.

a. Submarine

b. Homesick

c. Pipeline

d. Waterway

GAME 52 Q8 ANSWER d
To speak the words "Please enjoy" on his song "Hell Yes," Beck had been searching for an impersonator of a Japanese sushi waitress. Christina Ricci, who just happened to be visiting the studio while Beck was recording the song, got the gig. She spoke the phrase exactly as Beck had wanted it.

9. What Australian singer hit it big with the 2002 CD *Fever*?

a. Sherrie Austin

b. Natalie Imbruglia

c. Kylie Minogue

d. Kasey Chambers

GAME 72 Q8 ANSWER d
In the early and mid-1960s, Presley had focused on his movie career and had not appeared on stage in front of a live audience. His comeback show, simply entitled "Elvis," allowed the singer to perform his classic rock-and-roll and pop hits, and also to introduce new material. The result was NBC's top-rated telecast of the year.

5. Which group did *not* have a #1 hit in the 1980s?

a. The Police

b. Men at Work

c. The Rolling Stones

d. Eurythmics

GAME 9 Q4 ANSWER c

Named after a top-of-the-line fire engine truck, REO Speedwagon was first formed in 1967. The group didn't really hit big until its 1980 album *Hi Infidelity*. Its live-concert videos were among the first shown on MTV in the early '80s. The group's two big #1 hit power ballads are "Keep on Loving You" and "Can't Fight This Feeling."

---

5. What song features the lyrics "I want my MTV"?

a. "Losing My Religion"

b. "Wild Thing"

c. "Money for Nothing"

d. "Thriller"

GAME 29 Q4 ANSWER d

Daly began his career as a DJ, first in San Diego and then in San Francisco. In 1997, he became a VJ for MTV, and a year later, MTV made him the host of *Total Request Live*. Daly was an overnight sensation, and continued hosting the show until 2003.

---

5. Which hard rock band adds a symphonic sound on its 1999 release, *S&M*?

a. Aerosmith

b. Marilyn Manson

c. Metallica

d. Van Halen

GAME 49 Q4 ANSWER a

Following a period of inspired punk, New Wave, and straight-ahead pop collaborations with none other than Sir Paul McCartney in the late '80s, Elvis Costello recorded *The Juliet Letters*—a concept album inspired by letters written to Shakespeare's Juliet—in 1993. He wrote his first full-fledged orchestral work, *Il Sogno*, in 2004.

---

5. Which of the following artists did *not* perform with Beyoncé Knowles as a member of Destiny's Child?

a. Michelle Williams

b. Tionne Watkins

c. LaTavia Roberson

d. LeToya Luckett

GAME 69 Q4 ANSWER b

"Game of Love," featured on Santana's 2002 album *Shaman*, won a Grammy Award for Best Pop Collaboration. The two artists teamed up again in 2005 for the song "I'm Feeling You," released on Santana's *All That I Am*. On her own albums, such as *The Spirit Room*, Branch writes or co-writes all of her songs.

---

8. The Simon & Garfunkel song "Feelin' Groovy" is properly known as "The _____ Song."

a. 42nd Street

b. 2nd Green Park

c. Broadway Delight

d. 59th Street Bridge

GAME 12 Q7 ANSWER d
Hailing from Cleveland, Ohio and led by Harvey Fuqua, The Moonglows were first called The Moonlighters, but pioneer rock-and-roll DJ Alan Freed suggested the name change. The group's first hit was the 1954 song "Sincerely." Marvin Gaye didn't join the Moonglows until 1957.

---

8. What group has albums entitled *A Night at the Opera* and *A Day at the Races*?

a. Dixie Dregs

b. Queen

c. Mothers Of Invention

d. Rush

GAME 32 Q7 ANSWER c
Blending New Wave and electronic pop rock, Missing Persons was formed in 1980 by drummer Terry Bozzio, vocalist Dale Bozzio, and guitarist Warren Cuccurullo. Bassist Patrick O'Hearn and keyboardist Chuck Wild were later added. Due to Bozzio's distinctive voice and unusual makeup, the band was a favorite on MTV in the early '80s.

---

8. Which actress has a spoken-word cameo in Beck's song "Hell Yes"?

a. Scarlett Johansson

b. Radha Mitchell

c. Amanda Peet

d. Christina Ricci

GAME 52 Q7 ANSWER b
U2 shot the video on the roof of a liquor store on 7th and Main in downtown LA. The video paid homage to the famous "rooftop" concert The Beatles gave from the Apple Records building in London (as seen in the film *Let It Be*). And just as they had for The Beatles, the police stopped U2's performance.

---

8. Which of these songs did Elvis Presley perform in his 1968 comeback special?

a. "Viva Las Vegas"

b. "Treat Me Nice"

c. "Mystery Train"

d. "Memories"

GAME 72 Q7 ANSWER a
As the album name implies, *Boy* focuses on themes of youth and adolescence. It made sense, then, when the original album cover showed a young boy—the brother of one of Bono's friends. In the US, however, to avoid accusations of child pornography, the album photo was replaced with a distorted picture of the band.

GAME 9

6. Which band had a hit in the 1980s with "I Ran"?

a. Spandau Ballet
b. A Flock of Seagulls
c. The Cars
d. Whitesnake

GAME 9 Q5 ANSWER c
The year 1983 featured #1 hits by The Police with "Every Breath You Take," the Australian group Men at Work with "Down Under," and the techno-pop duo Eurythmics with "Sweet Dreams (Are Made of This)." The Rolling Stones had a #1 in 1978 with "Miss You" from the *Some Girls* album. In 1981, "Start Me Up" from *Tattoo You* went to #2.

GAME 29

6. Who was the first woman to win best video at the MTV Video Music Awards?

a. Bonnie Raitt
b. Sinead O'Connor
c. Tracy Chapman
d. Mariah Carey

GAME 29 Q5 ANSWER c
The Dire Straits song first appeared on the band's 1985 album *Brothers in Arms*, and later became an international hit when it was released as a single. In August 1987, the "Money for Nothing" video was the first to be aired on MTV Europe when the network began.

GAME 49

6. What rock group's 2001 album *Symphonic Live* was recorded at a concert in Amsterdam, Holland?

a. Slayer
b. Yes
c. Joy Division
d. Foo Fighters

GAME 49 Q5 ANSWER c
Recorded live with the San Francisco Symphony in April 1999, Metallica gave the orchestral treatment to such band classics as "Enter Sandman," "Master and Puppets," and "For Whom the Bell Tolls." Metallica won a Best Rock Instrumental Performance Grammy in 2000 for *S&M's* rock-and-orchestra version of "The Calls of Ktulu."

GAME 69

6. Who featured her idol Joni Mitchell on the album *Fat City*?

a. Vanessa Carlton
b. Fiona Apple
c. Liz Phair
d. Shawn Colvin

GAME 69 Q5 ANSWER b
Tionne "T-Boz" Watkins is a member of TLC along with Rozonda "Chilli" Thomas and the late Lisa "Left-Eye" Lopes. A varying number of artists have made up Destiny's Child at different times. Besides Knowles, Williams, Roberson, and Luckett, the R&B group has also included singer-actress Kelly Rowland.

7. Marvin Gaye was a member of which famed doo-wop group?

a. The Platters
b. The Skyliners
c. The Cleftones
d. The Moonglows

GAME 12 Q6 ANSWER a
Reaching only #28 on the US pop charts, this Wings single came out in 1972 along with "Hi, Hi, Hi" which went to #10 in the US, and the pro-Irish "Give Ireland Back to the Irish," which went to #21. That same year, John Lennon and Yoko Ono wrote the two Irish political songs "Luck of the Irish" and "Sunday Bloody Sunday."

---

7. "Destination Unknown" and "Words" were the biggest hits for what LA-based act?

a. L.A. Guns
b. Kim Wilde
c. Missing Persons
d. The Knack

GAME 32 Q6 ANSWER b
Thirty-five years before it was used to such great effect in the 1990 movie *Ghost,* this haunting tune was featured in a 1955 low-budget prison movie appropriately named *Unchained.* Hirsch also starred for many years as an end for the Los Angeles Rams, and was dubbed "Crazy Legs" for his trademark shifty moves.

---

7. In which US city did U2 film the video for "Where the Streets Have No Name"?

a. New York City
b. Los Angeles
c. Miami
d. Washington, DC

GAME 52 Q6 ANSWER c
The *Donny & Marie* talk show aired from 1998 to 2000 and received twelve Emmy nominations. One of its highlights was the reunion of the Osmond family on the 1999 holiday show. Previously, Donny and Marie had their own TV variety show from 1976 to 1979. Each show ended with the duo singing "May Tomorrow Be a Perfect Day."

---

7. What was the title of U2's debut album, released in the US in 1981?

a. *Boy*
b. *The Joshua Tree*
c. *The Unforgettable Fire*
d. *War*

GAME 72 Q6 ANSWER d
A studio album by the Dave Matthews Band, *Everyday* was released in 2001, with Santana playing on the track "Mother Father." The album was a great commercial success, quickly zooming to #1 on the charts. Nevertheless, both the band and the fans were disappointed by the album's slick electronic sound.

---

7. Which best-selling artist of the 1980s had the hit "No One Is to Blame"?

a. Peter Gabriel

b. Robert Palmer

c. Bryan Adams

d. Howard Jones

GAME 9 Q6 ANSWER b
Like many New Wave groups of the '80s, A Flock of Seagulls really had only one hit single. "I Ran" reached #9 on the pop charts in 1982, while its other song "DNA" won a Grammy that same year for Best Rock Instrumental. The group disbanded in 1986, but reteamed in 2005 on TV's *Oops, I Did It Again* reality TV show.

7. In 1984, which group won Best Video of the Year at the first ever MTV Video Music Awards?

a. Men At Work

b. Dire Straits

c. The Cars

d. The Eurythmics

GAME 29 Q6 ANSWER b
In 1990, O'Connor won three MTV Music Awards: Best Video of the Year, Best Female Video of the Year, and Best Postmodern Video of the Year. All of the awards were for the Prince song "Nothing Compares 2 U." O'Connor's biggest hit single, this tune had originally appeared on her 1990 album *I Do Not Want What I Haven't Got.*

7. British rock group Procol Harum recorded a 1971 hit album with the _____ Symphony Orchestra.

a. Edmonton

b. Quebec City

c. Calgary

d. Regina

GAME 49 Q6 ANSWER b
As with many progressive rock bands of the '70s, Yes was heavily influenced by classical music. The group's 1971 album *Fragile* featured a Rick Wakeman keyboard track called "Cans and Brahms," based on the music of Johannes Brahms. Yes also opened many concerts in the '70s with the orchestral recording of Stravinsky's "Firebird Suite."

7. Which 2005 Gwen Stefani song chronicles the relationship between two former lovers?

a. "The Real Thing"

b. "Cool"

c. "Crash"

d. "The Danger Zone"

GAME 69 Q6 ANSWER d
Shawn Colvin credits Mitchell with being her primary musical influence. Colvin's initial performances, in fact, closely reflected Mitchell's inflections and unique guitar tunings. Besides featuring Mitchell on her 1992 album, Colvin also appeared in a 2001 tribute to her idol that was broadcast on the cable network TNT.

GAME 12	**6.** In 1972, Paul McCartney and Wings released a single based on which nursery rhyme? **a.** "Mary Had a Little Lamb" **b.** "Old King Cole" **c.** "Itsy Bitsy Spider" **d.** "Jack and Jill"	**GAME 12 Q5 ANSWER c** "She Loves You" and "Please Please Me" rounded out the top five spots. It was the only time in rock and roll history that a group achieved such a feat. The Beatles' #1 hit "Yesterday" was released in the US as a single in September 1965. It stayed at #1 for a month and featured a string quartet.
GAME 32	**6.** "Unchained Melody" was originally taken from the soundtrack of a movie starring which athlete? **a.** Jim Brown **b.** Elroy Hirsch **c.** Alex Karras **d.** Woody Strode	**GAME 32 Q5 ANSWER c** Following his father's suicide, Spector moved with his family from the Bronx, New York, to Los Angeles in 1953. The Teddy Bears had a #1 hit in 1958 with "To Know Him Is to Love Him" (the song title came from Spector's father's tombstone). Early in their career, The Beatles often played this song as "To Know *Her* Is to Love *Her*."
GAME 52	**6.** In 1998, singing siblings Donny and Marie Osmond embarked on a new joint venture as: **a.** Game show hosts **b.** Sitcom stars **c.** Talk show hosts **d.** Variety show hosts	**GAME 52 Q5 ANSWER b** Formed in 1956 by Joe Cook, this doo-wop quartet from Philadelphia cracked the Top 30 a year later with this catchy little tune. Featuring Joe Cook's falsetto singing style, the "Peanuts" sound influenced many doo-wop singers who were to follow—most famously, Frankie Valli of The Four Seasons.
GAME 72	**6.** Which guitar legend makes an appearance on the album *Everyday*? **a.** Eric Clapton **b.** Jimmy Page **c.** Eddie Van Halen **d.** Carlos Santana	**GAME 72 Q5 ANSWER b** Besides Dylan, The Traveling Wilburys included George Harrison, Tom Petty, Jeff Lynne, and Roy Orbison. Initially formed just to record a B-side track for Harrison's single "When We Was Fab," the group eventually produced two albums together—one in 1988 and one in 1990—using various pseudonyms.

8. Which synthesizer act had the popular 1980s hit "Just Can't Get Enough"?

a. Human League
b. Duran Duran
c. Culture Club
d. Depeche Mode

GAME 9 Q7 ANSWER d
A popular figure in '80s synth-pop, Howard Jones was another songwriter who first found mainstream success through MTV. He enjoyed moderate success with songs and videos for "What Is Love" and "Things Can Only Get Better," but it was "No One Is to Blame" from his *Action Replay* album that reached #4 on the pop charts in 1986.

8. "Video Killed the Radio Star" was the first MTV video. Who performed it?

a. Tom Petty
b. Gary Numan
c. Fleetwood Mac
d. The Buggles

GAME 29 Q7 ANSWER c
The title of the award-winning video was "You Might Think," which first appeared on *Heartbeat City*, a 1984 album that launched four Top 20 singles. The Cars' hits dominated the charts for nine years—until the band's breakup in February 1988. Their last album was 1987's *Door to Door*.

8. Who performs a series of operatic arias on his 1998 album *My Secret Passion*?

a. Michael Bolton
b. Seal
c. Julio Iglesias
d. Luther Vandross

GAME 49 Q7 ANSWER a
Although known for its 1967 hit "A White Shade of Pale," Procol Harum was the first group to record a successful album with an orchestra. *Procol Harum Live With the Edmonton Symphony Orchestra* went gold in 1972, and has sold well over 1 million copies to date. This album also spawned a hit version of the song "Conquistador."

8. Scandal lead singer Patty Smyth married which sports star in 1997?

a. David Justice
b. Lance Armstrong
c. John McEnroe
d. Andre Agassi

GAME 69 Q7 ANSWER b
Both a single and a track on Stefani's 2004 debut solo album *Love. Angel. Music. Baby.*, "Cool" has received praise from critics and is considered a worldwide hit. The song is thought to have been inspired by Stefani's relationship with bassist Tony Kanal of her former group No Doubt.

5. Which of these Beatles' hits was *not* among the top five singles in April of 1964?

a. "Can't Buy Me Love"

b. "Twist and Shout"

c. "Yesterday"

d. "I Want to Hold Your Hand"

GAME 12 Q4 ANSWER a
In a year that spawned five #1 hits by The Beatles, The Rolling Stones first reached the top of the US charts with "Satisfaction" in July 1965. Around that time, Bob Dylan reached the #2 slot with his trailblazing song "Like a Rolling Stone." The second Rolling Stones' single to go to #1 in 1965 was "Get Off of My Cloud."

5. Legendary rock music producer Phil Spector was originally a member of which group?

a. The Crystals

b. The Halos

c. The Teddy Bears

d. The Ronettes

GAME 32 Q4 ANSWER a
The John Fogerty-led group landed in the #2 spot seven times before breaking up in 1972. In 1969, their #2 hits were "Proud Mary," "Bad Moon Rising," and "Green River." By 1970, they had more hits with "Long As I Can See the Light," "Lookin' Out My Back Door," "Travelin' Band," and "Who'll Stop the Rain"—all of which reached #2.

5. What song was made famous by Little Joe & the Thrillers?

a. "Lollipop"

b. "Peanuts"

c. "Popsicles and Icicles"

d. "Peanut Butter"

GAME 52 Q4 ANSWER b
Killed in a tragic car crash in 1970 in New Mexico, Earl Grant was one of the most successful easy-listening organists of the '60s, selling well over 500,000 copies of his *Ebb Tide* album in 1961. One of his most memorable songs was the prophetic "The End" (not to be confused with The Doors' 1967 song of the same name).

5. Beginning in 1988, Bob Dylan recorded two albums as a member of which group?

a. Utopia

b. The Traveling Wilburys

c. Procol Harum

d. Blind Faith

GAME 72 Q4 ANSWER c
Michael Jackson began his musical career at the age of five as lead singer of The Jackson 5, and was only fourteen years of age when his #1 hit "Ben" was charted under The Jackson 5 franchise. The song was the theme of a 1972 film of the same name, and was the first of thirteen #1 pop hits for the singer.

9. Whose landmark albums include *Dirty Deeds Done Dirt Cheap* and *Back in Black*?

a. INXS

b. Midnight Oil

c. KISS

d. AC/DC

GAME 9 Q8 ANSWER d
Considered prophets of techno-pop, Depeche Mode, which started out as a quartet from England, first went platinum with its 1991 album *Music for the Masses*. The group's biggest song to date is the 1990 hit "Enjoy the Silence," which reached #8 on the US charts. As of 2005, Depeche Mode has sold over 70 million albums.

9. Which city was the setting for the first season of MTV's show *The Real World*?

a. London

b. Seattle

c. New York City

d. Venice, California

GAME 29 Q8 ANSWER d
The 1980s New Wave song "Video Killed the Radio Star" celebrates the golden days of radio, telling the story of a singer whose career is ended by television. Written by Trevor Horn, Geoff Downes, and Bruce Woolley, the song rose to #1 on the UK charts in 1979. Two years later, the video aired on MTV.

9. *Fantasies and Delusions* is the title of a classical album by which veteran rocker?

a. David Bowie

b. Billy Joel

c. Elton John

d. Neil Sedaka

GAME 49 Q8 ANSWER a
Michael Bolton started in the music biz in 1975 with the heavy metal group Blackjack. Although known best for his easy listening hits, Bolton has also written many songs for artists such as Kenny Rogers, Cher, and Patti LaBelle. *My Secret Passion* features Bolton performing a duet with world-renowned soprano Renee Fleming.

9. Singer-songwriter Aimee Mann had the hit song "Voices Carry" with which band?

a. Bananarama

b. 'Til Tuesday

c. Quarterflash

d. The Motels

GAME 69 Q8 ANSWER c
Not to be confused with punk poet Patti Smith, Smyth led Scandal to the 1984 Top 10 with the song "The Warrior." Her first marriage was to Richard Hell, founding member of '70s punk group The Voltoids. By the late '80s, the two were divorced, and in 1997, Smyth married tennis pro John McEnroe.

GAME 12

4. Which of the following was *not* a #1 hit in the 1970s?

a. "(I Can't Get No) Satisfaction"

b. "You Light Up My Life"

c. "Hotel California"

d. "Car Wash"

GAME 12 Q3 ANSWER a
Falco, born Johann Holzel, first had a dance-club hit in 1982 with "Der Kommissar." In the US, however, *After the Fire* cracked the Top 10 with its cover of that song. With "Rock Me, Amadeus," Falco went to #1 himself. It was later satirized as "Rock Me, Dr. Zaius" during a *Planet of the Apes* spoof on an episode of *The Simpsons*.

GAME 32

4. Which group holds the record for the most #2 hits without ever making it to #1?

a. Creedence Clearwater Revival

b. The Carpenters

c. Blood, Sweat, & Tears

d. Chicago

GAME 32 Q3 ANSWER b
When first formed, the progressive rock group Asia also included guitarist Steve Howe, keyboardist Geoff Downes, and bassist John Wetton. The group's debut album, *Asia*, enjoyed considerable commercial success, spending nine weeks at the top of the US album chart.

GAME 52

4. Which of these artists did *not* perish in a plane crash?

a. Patsy Cline

b. Earl Grant

c. Jim Croce

d. Ronnie Van Zandt

GAME 52 Q3 ANSWER a
"Love Me Tender," introduced in the 1956 film of the same name, featured lyrics by Ken Darby. In 1960, after Elvis finished a stint in the Army, Frank Sinatra produced a "Welcome Home Elvis" TV special. On that show, Presley and Sinatra shared a duet, with Sinatra singing "Love Me Tender" and Elvis singing "Witchcraft."

GAME 72

4. What was Michael Jackson's first #1 solo hit?

a. "Billie Jean"

b. "Bad"

c. "Ben"

d. "Barefootin'"

GAME 72 Q3 ANSWER b
"Come On Eileen" was the UK's biggest-selling single in 1982. Written by Kevin Rowland, Big Jim Paterson, and Billy Adams, it originally appeared on the 1982 album *Too-Rye-Ay*. In honor of flight commander Eileen Collins, the song was even used as the Space Shuttle Discovery's wake-up call in August 2005.

GAME 9

10. Which US city emerged briefly as a "new wave" music mecca in the 1980s?

a. Boise, Idaho
b. Salt Lake City, Utah
c. Athens, Georgia
d. Erie, Pennsylvania

GAME 9 Q9 ANSWER d
AC/DC's recording history is a bit tangled. Although it recorded *Dirty Deeds Done Dirt Cheap* with lead singer Bon Scott in 1976, the album wasn't released until 1981 (a year after Scott died). AC/DC had already released the 1980 *Back in Black* album with new singer Brian Johnson by the time *Dirty Deeds* came out.

GAME 29

10. Which band's initial success in the US came on MTV, not on radio stations?

a. Queen
b. Abba
c. The Village People
d. Duran Duran

GAME 29 Q9 ANSWER c
In 1992, *The Real World* spawned an entirely new television genre with its documentary/soap opera formula. Seven young people from all over the country moved to a New York City apartment, and viewers watched them pursue their dreams. One of the people featured on the show, Eric Nies, went on to host MTV's *The Grind*.

GAME 49

10. Which soul singer has added versions of operatic arias to her repertoire?

a. Aretha Franklin
b. Patti LaBelle
c. Jill Scott
d. Alicia Keys

GAME 49 Q9 ANSWER b
Although he composed all the pieces on this album, Billy Joel had classical pianist Richard Joo play them. Joel's classical music has been favorably compared to that of Chopin and Schumann. The album cover looks exactly like those famous Schirmer's classical piano books that are used to instruct so many young piano players.

GAME 69

10. From which country does singer Natalie Imbruglia hail?

a. England
b. Australia
c. United States
d. Italy

GAME 69 Q9 ANSWER b
In 1985, "Voices Carry" became a Top 10 hit and won the MTV Video Music Award for Best New Artist. By the time 'Til Tuesday broke up in 1988, Mann's songwriting had matured considerably. She married musician Michael Penn (Sean's brother) in 1997, and her song "Save Me" from the 1999 film *Magnolia* was nominated for an Oscar.

Answers are in right-hand boxes on page 233.

3. Whose hit was the 1986 novelty song "Rock Me Amadeus"?

a. Falco

b. Trio

c. Taco

d. Adam Ant

"Good Vibrations" was the midway point for Brian Wilson—between the ecstasy of the 1966 *Pet Sounds* album and the agony of the eventually abandoned 1967 *Smile* project (which was finally finished in 2004). Recorded at four separate studios over a seven-month period, the song blew everyone away . . . and went to #1, of course.

---

3. Drummer Carl Palmer quit Emerson, Lake and Palmer to join ____ in 1981.

a. Toto

b. Asia

c. Journey

d. Air Supply

With twenty #1 hits, The Beatles still reign supreme with the most songs to reach the top of the charts. The fact that they wrote and recorded these twenty songs over a six-year period is amazing. Elvis Presley and Mariah Carey are tied in second place with seventeen #1 songs each.

---

3. On which song is Elvis Presley accompanied solely by an acoustic guitar?

a. "Love Me Tender"

b. "Suspicious Minds"

c. "Don't Be Cruel"

d. "Treat Me Nice"

"Lonesome Town" is a 1958 Ricky Nelson song. The Everly Brothers had their first big hit in 1957, when "Bye Bye Love" reached #2 on the pop charts. "Wake Up Little Susie" and "Cathy's Clown" were both #1 hits. The Beatles were fans of the duo, and Paul McCartney mentions "Phil and Don" in his 1976 hit "Let 'Em In."

---

3. The song "Come On Eileen" was a #1 hit for which of the following groups?

a. Bananarama

b. Dexys Midnight Runners

c. Bow Wow Wow

d. Katrina and the Waves

No stranger to television, Maroulis had competed on the dating show *Elimidate* and was an extra on both *Law and Order: SUV* and *Astro Boy* before appearing on *American Idol*. He auditioned for *Idol* at the suggestion of an ex-girlfriend, but was eliminated after performing the song "How You Remind Me."

GAME 9

11. What was the only song to top the charts for the 1980s band The Police?

a. Roxanne

b. Message in a Bottle

c. King of Pain

d. Every Breath You Take

GAME 9 Q10 ANSWER c

Athens was home to '80s alternative rock groups R.E.M and the B-52's. Both groups were considered "college radio" phenomenons, who built their followings slowly on the college campuses and off the mainstream radar. By 1989, each group cracked the nation's Top 10—the B-52's with "Love Shack" and "Roam," and R.E.M with "Stand."

GAME 29

11. What was the first rap group to have a gold album and a video featured on MTV?

a. Run-DMC

b. Sugarhill Gang

c. Beastie Boys

d. Cypress Hill

GAME 29 Q10 ANSWER d

The electronic rock band Duran Duran—whose members were hailed by *Rolling Stone* as the first video rock stars—was a leading band in the MTV-driven Second British Invasion of the US. The band's reputation was built through music videos, which showcased the group's glamorous sense of style.

GAME 49

11. Who composed the seventy-five-minute symphonic poem *Standing Stone*?

a. Paul McCartney

b. Peter Gabriel

c. Billy Joel

d. Kate Bush

GAME 49 Q10 ANSWER a

America first heard Aretha Franklin sing opera during the 1998 Grammys. At the last minute, she agreed to fill in for Luciano Pavarotti, who had fallen ill. Franklin stole the show with her performance of Puccini's immortal aria "Nessun Dorma."

GAME 69

11. Kat Bjelland was lead singer in which all-female rock group?

a. The Breeders

b. L7

c. The Sugarcubes

d. Babes in Toyland

GAME 69 Q10 ANSWER b

Before starting her music career, Imbruglia co-starred in the Aussie soap opera *Neighbours*. Since then, she has released several albums, with the third one—2005's *Counting Down the Days*—zooming to #1 on the UK charts in its first week of sales. In 2003, Imbruglia briefly returned to acting in the British film *Johnny English*.

GAME 12

2. Which 1966 song's production costs topped $50,000 (the most for a song up to that point)?

a. "River Deep—Mountain High"

b. "Livin' Thing"

c. "Good Vibrations"

d. "Tangled Up in Blue"

GAME 12 Q1 ANSWER b
Carly Simon has always remained playfully vague about the person who is the focus of this song. The list of mystery men has most often included Warren Beatty, Kris Kristofferson, Cat Stevens, and Mick Jagger (who sings backing vocals on the track). The song hit #1 in January 1973, one month after Simon married James Taylor.

GAME 32

2. Which group had the most #1 hits in the US?

a. The Bee Gees

b. The Beatles

c. The Platters

d. The Supremes

GAME 32 Q1 ANSWER a
The 1989 album *Pump* featured four Top 10 singles. Released in 1993, *Get a Grip* was even more successful, delivering five hits. In fact, with the album selling 12,000,000 copies—compared with *Pump's* 8,000,000 copies—*Get a Grip* marked the peak of Aerosmith's commercial success.

GAME 52

2. Which of the following songs was *not* an Everly Brothers hit?

a. "Cathy's Clown"

b. "Lonesome Town"

c. "Wake Up Little Susie"

d. "Bye Bye Love"

GAME 52 Q1 ANSWER a
This 1967 chart-topping hit by female singer-songwriter Bobbie Gentry mentions Presley's hometown of Tupelo, Mississippi. The beguiling song about the mysterious Billie Joe McAllister won Gentry three Grammys in 1968, including that of Best New Artist.

GAME 72

2. Which former *American Idol* competitor fronts a band called Pray for the Soul of Betty?

a. Scott Savol

b. Bo Bice

c. Anthony Federov

d. Constantine Maroulis

GAME 72 Q1 ANSWER c
Written by Ray Davies, "You Really Got Me" was the The Kinks' breakthrough hit, and helped establish them as one of the top bands in the British Invasion. An unusually raw and gritty piece for its time, the song was eventually described by a critic as being "the track which invented heavy metal."

GAME 9

12. Which music act shot to stardom in the 1980s with hits like "Careless Whisper" and "Everything She Wants"?

a. Wham!

b. Depeche Mode

c. Tears For Fears

d. Bon Jovi

GAME 9 Q11 ANSWER d
In the summer of 1983, "Every Breath You Take," from the group's last album *Synchronicity*, remained at #1 for eight consecutive weeks. The video for this song won an MTV Video Music Award for Best Cinematography. The group's videos for "Wrapped Around Your Finger" and "Synchronicity II" were MTV viewer favorites.

GAME 29

12. Rapper Xzibit is the host of which MTV series?

a. *Pimp My Ride*

b. *Damage Control*

c. *Viva La Bam*

d. *Trippin*

GAME 29 Q11 ANSWER a
This trio from Queens, New York, made history when their 1986 album *Raising Hell* became the highest-selling rap album, selling over 3 million copies and launching the hit single "Walk This Way," a rap-rock collaboration. Run-DMC retired in 2002, shortly after the murder of group member Jayson "Jam Master Jay" Mizell.

GAME 49

12. London's Royal Philharmonic Orchestra recorded a classical album of music written by:

a. Oasis

b. U2

c. Sting

d. Eric Clapton

GAME 49 Q11 ANSWER a
While 1991 saw Paul McCartney write an opera with *Liverpool Oratorio*, he went about writing an orchestral symphony with *Standing Stone* in 1997. This popular classical album debuted at #2 on the UK classical charts, and at #1 in the US. Paul first wrote orchestral music back in 1966 for the British film *The Family Way*.

GAME 69

12. What is the title of the 2004 album by The Donnas?

a. *Blue Ribbon*

b. *Gold Medal*

c. *Grammy*

d. *Pulitzer Prize*

GAME 69 Q11 ANSWER d
Babes in Toyland, a Minneapolis-based group, formed in 1988. It grabbed attention with Bjelland's "baby doll" image, which was in stark contrast to her powerful voice and lyrics. The band split and reformed throughout the '90s, and finally dissolved after a 2001 tour.

GAME 12	**1.** The subject of this Carly Simon song has always been a mystery: **a.** "Super Freak" **b.** "You're So Vain" **c.** "Mr. Big Stuff" **d.** "Honky Tonk Woman"	The answer to this question is on: **page 234, top frame, right side.**
GAME 32	**1.** Which band's hit albums include *Pump* and *Get a Grip*? **a.** Aerosmith **b.** Air Supply **c.** Metallica **d.** Sonic Youth	The answer to this question is on: **page 234, second frame, right side.**
GAME 52	**1.** Which #1 single mentions Elvis Presley's birthplace? **a.** "Ode to Billie Joe" **b.** "Me and Bobby McGee" **c.** "American Pie" **d.** "House of the Rising Sun"	The answer to this question is on: **page 234, third frame, right side.**
GAME 72	**1.** In 1964, what song topped the pop charts and became The Kinks' first hit song? **a.** "Sunny Afternoon" **b.** "Waterloo Sunset" **c.** "You Really Got Me" **d.** "Lola"	The answer to this question is on: **page 234, bottom frame, right side.**

"Monkee Meets Beatle!"

That was the headline in the British press when—according to the cosmic keepers of the archives de pop trivia—on or about February 7, 1967, I was about to spend the evening with Paul McCartney and his sheepdog at his mansion in Maida Vale. It was my first trip to England and the first time I had met any of my idols, The Beatles.

Ever since the day I was driving down Ventura Boulevard in the San Fernando Valley (yes, the same Ventura Boulevard made famous in the Tom Petty song) and heard "I Want to Hold Your Hand," I had wanted to meet The Beatles.

Now was my chance. Not only was I going to meet Paul, but I was going to meet him as a peer, of sorts—as a Monkee.

Paul was incredibly gracious and welcoming (if only he'd known of the autograph book in my back pocket!), and at the end of the evening, he invited me to a recording session at Abbey Road. The Beatles were working on a new album called "Sergeant" something.

On the day of the session, I dressed up in my finest fab Carnaby Street gear, complete with hippy beads, tie-dyed shirt, and paisley bell bottoms, and was picked up by a black Daimler limo. As we pulled up to the studios, I was awash with excitement—looking forward to what I assumed was going to be a psychedelic manic mod music love fest. Imagine my surprise when I walked into the studio and was greeted by the four guys, who were sitting alone, in folding chairs, under the glare of neon lights. It looked like the inside of my high school gym.

John asked if I wanted to hear what they were working on and I replied in fluent hippyese, "Yeah . . . cool, man."

Up in the booth, George Martin, wearing a three-piece suit, started a four-track tape recorder and I listened to the early tracks of "Good Morning Good Morning."

At four o'clock, a gentleman in a white apron delivered the obligatory tea service and we sat and chatted for a while. Then John, the eternal slave driver, said, "'right lads, down the mines." And the four lads returned to their folding chairs and went back to work. And that, my friends, is how they managed to produce such a magnificent body of work in such a relatively short period of time—by working. ■

The Wrecking Crew

Sometime in early 1965—about the same time I was auditioning for a new television show called *The Monkees*—I was in a recording studio working on my first single, a song I had written called "Don't Do It."

When I arrived at the studio, I was introduced to the musicians who had been booked on the session. One of them, the guitar player, I remember quite well. His name was Glen Campbell.

Glen, of course, would go on to have a very successful solo career, but for a number of years, he was a member of a very elite group of session musicians affectionately known as "The Wrecking Crew."

The disciplines and techniques of the recording studio are quite different from those of live performances, and in the early days of rock and roll, it was not uncommon for groups to use studio musicians for their recording sessions, even though the group members may have been accomplished musicians in their own right. Along with Glen and other notables like Leon Russell and Dr. John, The Wrecking Crew consisted of musicians like Tommy Tedesco, Hal Blaine, Earl Palmer, and Carol Kaye. These names may not mean much to the layman, but to anyone in the music business, they will forever be associated with some of the greatest recordings of all time.

From The Byrds' "Mister Tambourine Man" to The Beach Boys' "California Girls," from The Association to The Carpenters, from The Mamas and the Papas to The Monkees, these classically and jazz-trained artists made such a contribution to pop music, it is almost impossible to give them enough credit. But I'll try . . .

Here's to The Wrecking Crew! ■

GAME 10

The Beatles

*Turn to page 241
for the first question.*

GAME 9 Q12 ANSWER a
"Careless Whisper" is just one of three
#1 hits that George Michael and Andrew
Ridgeley had from their 1984 album,
Make It Big. (The others were "Wake Me
Up Before You Go-Go" and "Everything
She Wants.") The British duo put out just
one more album, *Music from the Edge of
Heaven,* before George Michael went
solo in 1986.

GAME 30

The Piano Man

*Turn to page 241
for the first question.*

GAME 29 Q12 ANSWER a
Alvin Nathaniel Joiner, commonly called
Xzibit, is well known for his big-budget
superstar-laced albums such as *Rest-
less* and *Man Vs. Machine.* On *Pimp My
Ride,* Xzibit takes beat-up, unfashionable
old cars and "pimps" them—that is, re-
stores and customizes them.

GAME 50

Guitar Gods
(& Goddesses)

*Turn to page 241
for the first question.*

GAME 49 Q12 ANSWER a
To date, other artists who have been giv-
en the "Royal Philharmonic" treatment
include Genesis, Pink Floyd, Madonna,
R.E.M., and Queen, among others. It may
be just a matter of time before the RPO
grants the wish of Spinal Tap lead singer
David St. Hubbins (Michael McKean) to
perform his solo songs at a Philharmonic concert . . .

GAME 70

"Fool"-in' Around

*Turn to page 241
for the first question.*

GAME 69 Q12 ANSWER b
The Donnas formed in 1993, when the
members were in eighth grade, to play
for their school's "Day on the Green."
Until the release of *Gold Medal,* each of
the members used a pseudonym—the
name "Donna" followed by the first initial
of the member's surname. The stage
names were finally dropped to present a
more mature image.

239

GAME 12
GRAB BAG

*Turn to page 236
for the first question.*

GAME 11 Q12 ANSWER c
Hailing from Akron, Ohio, Ripper Owens was a member of a local Judas Priest tribute band. In 1996, guitarists K.K. Downing and Glenn Tipton asked him to replace original singer Rob Halford and actually join the group. In 2004, Owens split amicably with the group after Halford rejoined Judas Priest for a world tour.

GAME 32
GRAB BAG

*Turn to page 236
for the first question.*

GAME 31 Q12 ANSWER a
Sting and wife Trudie Styler introduced singer Madonna and film director Guy Ritchie at a 1998 dinner party. Madonna and Ritchie were married on December 22, 2000 at Skibo Castle in Scotland. Son Rocco John Ritchie—whose godparents are Sting and Styler—was born on August 11, 2000.

GAME 52
GRAB BAG

*Turn to page 236
for the first question.*

GAME 51 Q12 ANSWER d
A seasoned arranger, producer, and multi-instrumentalist, John Paul Jones is often the unsung hero of Led Zeppelin. He played organ on "Your Time Is Gonna Come" from the band's first album in 1969, and later is seen playing keyboards on "No Quarter" in the 1976 concert film *The Song Remains the Same*.

GAME 72
GRAB BAG

*Turn to page 236
for the first question.*

GAME 71 Q12 ANSWER d
Released in 1983 along with a concert video, *Under a Blood Red Sky* helped establish U2's reputation as an extraordinary live band. The album consists of recordings from the band's War Tour, and except for Stephen Sondheim's "Send in the Clowns," all of the music is by U2, with lyrics by Bono.

GAME 10	**1.** Ringo Starr does *not* sing lead vocal on which of the following songs? **a.** "Hello Goodbye" **b.** "Act Naturally" **c.** "Matchbox" **d.** "I Wanna Be Your Man"	The answer to this question is on: **page 243, top frame, right side.**
GAME 30	**1.** Which Billy Joel tune did VH1 name as one of the century's 100 greatest songs? **a.** "Piano Man" **b.** "My Life" **c.** "Only the Good Die Young" **d.** "Uptown Girl"	The answer to this question is on: **page 243, second frame, right side.**
GAME 50	**1.** Which song did *Guitar World Magazine* name as featuring the greatest guitar solo of all time? **a.** "Stairway to Heaven" **b.** "Eruption" **c.** "Freebird" **d.** "Comfortably Numb"	The answer to this question is on: **page 243, third frame, right side.**
GAME 70	**1.** Which Soul Asylum album includes the track "April Fool"? **a.** *Grave Dancers Union* **b.** *Hang Time* **c.** *While You Were Out* **d.** *Say What You Will*	The answer to this question is on: **page 243, bottom frame, right side.**

12. The movie *Rock Star* was based on the life of which member of Judas Priest?

a. Scott Travis
b. K.K. Downing
c. Ripper Owens
d. Glenn Tipton

GAME 11 Q11 ANSWER d
Ellen Dow plays the granny role in a film that features funny cameos by Steve Buscemi, Eugene Levy, and '80s icon Billy Idol. Just as the movie *American Graffiti* brought back '50s music in the '70s, *The Wedding Singer* played a key role in resurrecting '80s hits by groups such as Kajagoogoo, Thompson Twins, and Musical Youth.

12. Which musician and his wife introduced Madonna to Guy Ritchie?

a. Sting
b. Bono
c. Tom Petty
d. Chris Martin

GAME 31 Q11 ANSWER a
In 1967, Carter and Cash had their first duet hit with "Jackson," which rose to #2 on the country charts and won a Grammy. In 1970, their recording of "If I Were a Carpenter" also rose to #2 and earned a Grammy. The story of Carter and Cash's relationship is explored in the 2005 movie *Walk the Line*.

12. Who played keyboards for Led Zeppelin?

a. Robert Plant
b. Jimmy Page
c. John Bonham
d. John Paul Jones

GAME 51 Q11 ANSWER a
A joy to all rock fans, *The School of Rock* is the story of a diehard rock guitarist (Jack Black) who pretends to be a substitute teacher at a local prep school. After entering his students into a "Battle of the Bands" contest, Black's character sings this classic Zeppelin anthem like some kind of victory chant.

12. Which group's *Under a Blood Red Sky* was a hugely successful live album?

a. The Cranberries
b. The Beatles
c. Clannad
d. U2

GAME 71 Q11 ANSWER b
This album—formally titled *Bruce Springsteen & the E Street Band Live/ 1975–85*—consists of forty tracks recorded during that period of time. Released in 1986, the album launched two singles, "War" and "Fire," and hit #1 on the US charts, selling 13 million copies in the US alone.

GAME 10	**2.** Beatles' road manager Mal Evans does *not* appear in which of the following films? **a.** *Let It Be* **b.** *Magical Mystery Tour* **c.** *Help!* **d.** *A Hard Day's Night*	**GAME 10 Q1 ANSWER a** Ringo, as *Sgt. Pepper's* "Billy Shears," also sang lead on "With a Little Help From My Friends." Although he sang "Matchbox" on The Beatles' *Something New* LP in 1964, it was John Lennon who used to sing it in Liverpool's Cavern Club before Beatlemania. The only Beatles' #1 hit with Ringo on vocals was "Yellow Submarine" in 1966.
GAME 30	**2.** Christie Brinkley was the inspiration for which Billy Joel pop hit? **a.** "Everybody's Girl" **b.** "The Lady in Red" **c.** "Cover Girl" **d.** "Uptown Girl"	**GAME 30 Q1 ANSWER a** Joel wrote the song after playing piano for six months at the Executive Lounge in Los Angeles, under the name Bill Martin. (Joel's real name is William Martin Joel.) "Piano Man" is the title track of a 1974 album that sold roughly 4 million copies.
GAME 50	**2.** Pete Townshend is the groundbreaking guitarist for which group? **a.** Deep Purple **b.** Led Zeppelin **c.** The Who **d.** Black Sabbath	**GAME 50 Q1 ANSWER a** This 1971 Led Zeppelin song features Jimmy Page's best playing to date. The other three choices also contain classic solos—"Eruption" marked Eddie Van Halen's 1978 debut; Lynyrd Skynyrd's "Freebird" (1973) featured three guitarists when played live; and David Gilmour was "Comfortably Numb" on Pink Floyd's *The Wall* (1979).
GAME 70	**2.** Which singer declared himself a "Card Carryin' Fool"? **a.** Dwight Yoakam **b.** Randy Travis **c.** Willie Nelson **d.** Clint Black	**GAME 70 Q1 ANSWER a** The 1992 album *Grave Dancers Union* was officially the sixth album of the Minneapolis-based group Soul Asylum, and was their most popular album, reaching #1 on the Heatseekers chart and #11 on the Billboard 200. The album launched five singles, the most successful of which was the Grammy Award-winning "Runaway Train."

11. Which 1990s movie has a hip-hop granny performing "Rapper's Delight"?

a. *The Big Lebowski*

b. *The Full Monty*

c. *As Good As It Gets*

d. *The Wedding Singer*

GAME 11 Q10 ANSWER b
Jack Black did a smart thing by taking all of his own enthusiasm for '70s classic rock groups like Led Zeppelin, Black Sabbath, Yes, and AC/DC, and pouring it into a classic film role. This 2003 film was directed by Richard Linklater, who showed a similar appreciation for '70s culture in his 1993 hit movie *Dazed and Confused*.

---

11. Which musical couple won a Grammy together in 1969, and another in 1970?

a. Johnny Cash and June Carter

b. The Captain and Tennille

c. Sonny and Cher

d. John Lennon and Yoko Ono

GAME 31 Q10 ANSWER b
Michael Jackson married Lisa Marie Presley on May 18, 1994, two weeks after Presley's divorce from first husband Danny Keough became final. The Presley-Jackson marriage lasted only eighteen months, and there has been speculation that Jackson wed Presley only for public relation purposes.

---

11. Which Led Zeppelin song does Jack Black sing in the 2004 comedy *The School of Rock*?

a. "The Immigrant Song"

b. "Heartbreaker"

c. "D'yer Maker"

d. "Rock 'n Roll"

GAME 51 Q10 ANSWER a
The back cover photo of the group on its 1969 debut album shows drummer John Bonham as the only band member with a mustache. By 1972, all four members had big beards and/or mustaches. By 1973, as seen in the concert film *The Song Remains the Same*, everyone was clean-shaven again—except, of course, for Bonham.

---

11. With which band did Bruce Springsteen release his live album *1975–85*?

a. Manfred Mann

b. The E Street Band

c. Traveling Wilburys

d. The Heartbreakers

GAME 71 Q10 ANSWER c
"Do You Feel Like We Do" was first released on the 1973 album *Frampton's Camel*. The album was not a success. The song, however, became a popular part of Frampton's shows. Although the original track was under 7 minutes, the version found on *Frampton Comes Alive* clocks in at an impressive 14 minutes, 15 seconds.

---

3. George Harrison sang but did not write which of the following songs?

a. "I'm Happy Just to Dance With You"

b. "Something"

c. "I Need You"

d. "Taxman"

GAME 10 Q2 ANSWER d
In *Help* (1965), The Beatles' real-life roadie Mal "Gentle Giant" Evans made his first movie appearance as a soft-spoken swimmer who asks John directions to the "White Cliffs of Dover." He appeared as a magician in *Magical Mystery Tour* (1967), and as himself clanging an anvil on "Maxwell's Silver Hammer" in *Let It Be* (1970).

---

3. What was the name of the first band Billy Joel joined?

a. The Hassles

b. The Hicksville Three

c. The Echoes

d. Attila

GAME 30 Q2 ANSWER d
Joel and Brinkley met at a hotel bar when Joel was vacationing on the island of St. Barts. "Uptown Girl" was written soon after he returned from vacation, and the song was a worldwide hit when it was released in 1983. Brinkley, who became Joel's bride in May 1985, is featured in the song's video.

---

3. Which guitarist has *Rolling Stone* magazine called the greatest of all time?

a. B.B. King

b. Jimmy Page

c. Stevie Ray Vaughan

d. Jimi Hendrix

GAME 50 Q2 ANSWER c
Townshend was arguably the first in rock to use feedback as a soloing tool. However, The Who did not put the first recorded feedback on a rock-and-roll record. That honor stands with The Beatles—on the group's 1965 #1 single, "I Feel Fine," John Lennon plucked a string, which started feeding back wildly before the opening riff.

---

3. Bonnie Raitt's 1986 recording of "Who But a Fool" is found on which album?

a. *Give It Up*

b. *Nick of Time*

c. *Nine Lives*

d. *Green Light*

GAME 70 Q2 ANSWER b
The song "Card Carryin' Fool" is found on Travis's 1989 album *No Holdin' Back*, and is also featured in the 1989 film *Pink Cadillac*. In addition to Travis's recordings appearing in several movie soundtracks, the artist has acted in a number of films, including 2001's *Texas Rangers* and 2003's *The Long Ride Home*.

---

10. In *The School of Rock*, why does Dewey Finn (played by Jack Black) get kicked out of his band?

a. Heavy drinking

b. Self-indulgent solos

c. Excessive salary demands

d. Obnoxious girlfriend

GAME 11 Q9 ANSWER a
Ringo Starr and "Bond girl" wife, Barbara Bach, also appeared in this film along with Paul and his first wife, Linda. This film boasts cameo performances by Tracey Ullman and the great British actor Sir Ralph Richardson. It also spawned a Top 10 hit, "No More Lonely Nights," featuring a guitar solo by Pink Floyd's David Gilmour.

10. At the 1994 MTV music video awards, with whom did Michael Jackson share an uncomfortable kiss?

a. Britney Spears

b. Lisa Marie Presley

c. Debbie Rowe

d. Diana Ross

GAME 31 Q9 ANSWER a
Singer-actress Cher gave birth to Chastity Bono during her marriage to performer Sonny Bono. After the Bonos' 1974 divorce, Cher married Gregg Allman, of the Allman Brothers Band, and had son Elijah Blue Allman. Cher and Gregg Allman were divorced in 1979.

10. Which member of Led Zeppelin always had facial hair during the group's history?

a. John Bonham

b. Robert Plant

c. Jimmy Page

d. John Paul Jones

GAME 51 Q9 ANSWER a
Just as the Beatles' 1968 double album has become known as *The White Album,* Led Zeppelin's fourth studio album has become known as *Led Zeppelin IV* even though there is no title on the album cover. Actually, the album's technical title includes four handwritten symbols that represent each member of the band.

10. Peter Frampton's 1976 hit album *Frampton Comes Alive* features which radio staple?

a. "Heat of the Moment"

b. "Bohemian Rhapsody"

c. "Do You Feel Like We Do"

d. "Don't Answer Me"

GAME 71 Q9 ANSWER d
Released in 1984, *Alchemy* was Dire Straights' first live album, and features the group's best-known songs to that point. The tracks, which were recorded at London's Hammersmith Odeon, are very different from the studio versions of the same songs, and include numerous improvisations.

4. Which Beatles' hit had the longest stay at #1 in the US?

a. "Yesterday"

b. "She Loves You"

c. "Hey Jude"

d. "A Hard Day's Night"

GAME 10 Q3 ANSWER a
John and Paul gave George this song to sing on *A Hard Day's Night*. The first Beatles' song both written *and* sung by George was "Don't Bother Me" from *With the Beatles*. Although "Something" was George's first #1 song with the Beatles, Frank Sinatra always introduced it in his concerts as a Lennon/McCartney tune.

4. Named after a town in Long Island, New York, what was the title of Joel's first solo album?

a. *Cold Spring Harbor*

b. *Amityville Horror*

c. *Massapequa*

d. *Huntington Station*

GAME 30 Q3 ANSWER c
Joel was fourteen years old when he joined The Echoes. He performed with The Hassles in the late 1960s, and then, along with Hassles drummer Jon Small, formed the prog-rock band Attila. After having an affair with Small's wife Elizabeth Weber, and later marrying her, Joel embarked on a solo career.

4. Guitar virtuoso Jennifer Batten toured the world in the '80s with which singer?

a. Ozzy Osbourne

b. Michael Jackson

c. George Michael

d. Bruce Springsteen

GAME 50 Q3 ANSWER d
A left-handed guitarist, Hendrix would play the guitar with his teeth, behind his back, and between his legs. He opened for The Monkees during our 1967 summer tour. After all these years, it's still an honor to have met and been associated with Jimi Hendrix—even if only for a few weeks!

4. The Top 30 hit "A Fool in Love" was the first single of which duo?

a. Simon & Garfunkel

b. Les Paul and Mary Ford

c. Sonny and Cher

d. Ike and Tina Turner

GAME 70 Q3 ANSWER c
Nine Lives was a difficult release for Raitt. A 1983 corporate sweep at Warner Brothers resulted in the company's shelving recordings that Raitt had made for an album called *Tongue & Groove*. Two years later, Warner decided to put the record out, and after Raitt had recut half of it, it was released as *Nine Lives*.

9. Which rock star starred in the movie *Give My Regards to Broad Street* (1984)?

a. Paul McCartney
b. Elton John
c. Billy Joel
d. David Bowie

GAME 11 Q8 ANSWER c
This 2002 film chronicles the troubled path of the group's hit album *Yankee Hotel Foxtrot*, and marks the directorial debut of award-winning photographer Sam Jones. The scenes of conflict between Wilco bandmates Jeff Tweedy and Jay Bennett are reminiscent of Metallica's "group in therapy" documentary *Some Kind of Monster* (2004).

9. Which singer's two children, Elijah and Chastity, have two different musical fathers?

a. Cher
b. Madonna
c. Celine Dion
d. Tina Turner

GAME 31 Q8 ANSWER c
Elvis and Priscilla's daughter, Lisa Marie Presley, was born February 1, 1968. The couple was separated in 1972, and divorced in 1973. Although the divorce provided for mutual custody of their daughter, unfortunately, Elvis died only a few years later, in 1977.

9. How many Led Zeppelin albums were simply given numbers as titles?

a. Four
b. Five
c. Six
d. Seven

GAME 51 Q8 ANSWER a
Led Zeppelin typified the best (and sometimes worst) tendencies of '70s rock concerts. The group was known for incredibly long solos by guitarist Jimmy Page and drummer John Bonham. "Dazed and Confused" was Page's showcase; it featured his skill at playing guitar with a violin bow, and often ran well over thirty minutes.

9. Who released the live album *Alchemy* in 1984?

a. John Cougar
b. Billy Joel
c. Culture Club
d. Dire Straits

GAME 71 Q8 ANSWER b
INXS's first live album, *Live Baby Live*, borrowed its name from lyrics found in "New Sensation," the album's first track. The songs on the album were recorded in a number of places, including Paris, New York, Chicago, London, Dublin, Glasgow, Spain, Switzerland, Sydney, Melbourne, Philadelphia, and Las Vegas.

5. In the song "Penny Lane," what does the fireman keep in his pocket?

a. Golden hour glass

b. Portrait of the queen

c. Shiny whistle

d. Toy fire engine

GAME 10 Q4 ANSWER c

"Hey Jude" stayed at #1 for nine weeks here in the US; but, at seven minutes, eleven seconds, it's not the longest Beatles' song. That would be "Revolution 9" from their self-titled 1968 album (aka *The White Album*). The song is eight minutes and twenty-four seconds, and features Yoko Ono's voice.

5. For which album was Joel united with producer Phil Ramone for the first time?

a. *52nd Street*

b. *The Stranger*

c. *Nylon Curtain*

d. *An Innocent Man*

GAME 30 Q4 ANSWER a

Cold Spring Harbor was released in 1971. Produced by Family Productions, the album's songs were recorded slightly too fast, causing Joel's voice to sound high and reedy. In 1983, when Joel was with Columbia Records, a corrected version of the album was released.

5. Which Ozzy Osbourne song does *not* feature guitar hero Randy Rhoads?

a. "Diary of a Madman"

b. "Crazy Train"

c. "Mr. Crowley"

d. "Bark at the Moon"

GAME 50 Q4 ANSWER b

Called one of the best players of the '80s by her fellow musicians, Batten beat out over 100 guitarists to be a part of Michael Jackson's band for his Bad Tour of 1987–1989. In the '90s, she toured with Jackson for his Dangerous Tour and HIStory Tour. In 1998, legendary guitarist Jeff Beck invited Batten to join his band.

5. In 1978, The Doobie Brothers sang about "What a Fool..."?

a. Can See

b. Believes

c. Perceives

d. Conceives

GAME 70 Q4 ANSWER d

Tina Turner—originally, Anna Mae Bullock—was discovered by rock-and-roll pioneer Ike Turner at the age of eighteen. The two eventually married, and in the '60s and '70s, they recorded a number of hits together. "A Fool in Love" was the first, but perhaps the best known is the duo's manic cover version of CCR's "Proud Mary" from 1971.

8. *I Am Trying to Break Your Heart* is a documentary film about which band?

a. Soul Asylum

b. Weezer

c. Wilco

d. Styx

GAME 11 Q7 ANSWER d
Director Mike Nichols used Simon & Garfunkel songs throughout this movie, including "The Sounds of Silence," "April Come She Will," and "Scarborough Fair/Canticle." "Mrs. Robinson" was *not* written for *The Graduate*. The version in the film features only an acoustic guitar, and the song's chorus has different lyrics.

8. Which famous couple became new parents nine months to the day after they wed?

a. John and Yoko

b. Sid and Nancy

c. Elvis and Priscilla

d. Paul and Linda

GAME 31 Q7 ANSWER a
Rossdale and Stefani met at a 1995 concert in which she was performing to promote the album *Tragic Kingdom*. After dating on and off for several years, Rossdale proposed marriage on New Year's Day 2002, and the couple was wed in September of that year.

8. On the live concert album *The Song Remains the Same*, which song takes up an entire side of the album?

a. "Dazed and Confused"

b. "Since I've Been Loving You"

c. "Kashmir"

d. "When the Levee Breaks"

GAME 51 Q7 ANSWER b
Released in 1969 and named simply *Led Zeppelin*, the group's first album seems preoccupied with time. Other songs on the album with "time" in the title are "Your Time Is Gonna Come" and "How Many More Times." The only other Zeppelin song with "time" in the title is "In My Time of Dying" from *Physical Graffiti*.

8. What title did Australian pop group INXS give to its 1991 concert album?

a. *Never Tear Us Apart*

b. *Live Baby Live*

c. *The One Thing*

d. *Shabooh Tunes*

GAME 71 Q7 ANSWER a
Featured on the 1978 album *Live at Budokan*, "I Want You to Want Me" was written by Cheap Trick's lead guitarist and primary songwriter, Rick Neilsen. The single became the group's biggest hit, reaching #7 on the charts. Since then, it has been covered by Dwight Yoakam and Lindsay Lohan, and featured in a 2002 Coca-Cola commercial.

6. Which Beatles album sold the most copies in the US?

a. *Meet the Beatles*

b. *The Beatles*

c. *Rubber Soul*

d. *Abbey Road*

GAME 10 Q5 ANSWER b

Part of a 1967 double A-side single with "Strawberry Fields Forever," "Penny Lane" is about a real street in Liverpool where Paul and John used to play as kids. After hearing it played on a BBC radio broadcast of a Bach Brandenberg concerto, Paul asked producer George Martin to get a piccolo trumpet player for the song.

---

6. A Billy Joel song describes "Scenes from an _____ Restaurant."

a. Open

b. Ethiopian

c. Italian

d. Honest

GAME 30 Q5 ANSWER b

The 1977 album *The Stranger* produced four Top 40 hits and was a worldwide smash. Sales exceeded Columbia's previous top album, *Bridge Over Troubled Water*, and *The Stranger* was certified multi-platinum. Due to this success, Ramone produced every Billy Joel studio release up until the 1989 album *Storm Front*.

---

6. Angus Young is the lead guitarist for which hard rock band?

a. Def Leppard

b. Nirvana

c. AC/DC

d. The Allman Brothers

GAME 50 Q5 ANSWER d

"Bark at the Moon," the title track from Osbourne's first studio album after Rhoads' 1982 death, featured guitarist Jake E. Lee. Except for possibly Eddie Van Halen, Randy Rhoads was the most popular rock guitarist of the '80s. His devotion to classical music and proper playing technique influenced rock guitar history.

---

6. Which of the following musicians did *not* record the song "A Fool for You"?

a. Willie Nelson

b. James Taylor

c. Ray Charles

d. Neil Diamond

GAME 70 Q5 ANSWER b

This upbeat #1 hit was written by the Doobie's vocalist/keyboardist Michael McDonald and Kenny Loggins. It went on to win the Grammy Award for Song of the Year in 1979. Before McDonald joined the group in 1975, The Doobie Brothers had a string of classic rock hits like "Listen to the Music," "China Grove," and "Black Water."

---

7. Simon & Garfunkel's "Mrs. Robinson" is on the soundtrack of which movie?

a. *Easy Rider*

b. *Alice's Restaurant*

c. *American Graffiti*

d. *The Graduate*

GAME 11 Q6 ANSWER c
In this directorial debut from Tom Hanks, a small-time group hits it big with a single that's the title of the movie. The song, written by the real group Fountains of Wayne, was picked for the film after winning a contest held by the studio. As a joke, the bass player character has no name and is listed only as "T.B. Player."

7. To which musician is Bush frontman Gavin Rossdale married?

a. Gwen Stefani

b. Amy Lee

c. Meg White

d. Lauryn Hill

GAME 31 Q6 ANSWER a
Spears wed childhood friend Alexander in January 2004. An annulment was promptly arranged, ending the two-day marriage. Spears married Federline in September 2004. Prior to the two marriages, Spears is said to have had an affair with her married backup dancer Columbus Short.

7. What is the first song on the first Led Zeppelin album?

a. "Whole Lotta Love"

b. "Good Times, Bad Times"

c. "Black Dog"

d. "The Immigrant Song"

GAME 51 Q6 ANSWER c
Saddened by the tragic loss of drummer John "Bonzo" Bonham on September 25, 1980, the group decided to end its career that year. The eight studio albums do not include the 1975 concert album *The Song Remains the Same* or *Coda,* a 1982 album of outtakes and B-sides that was released after Bonham's death.

7. Which group performed the live version of "I Want You to Want Me"?

a. Cheap Trick

b. Timbuk Three

c. Thompson Twins

d. The Knack

GAME 71 Q6 ANSWER a
Genesis's 1982 live album was recorded during the group's 1981 promotional tour for *Abacab.* The words "Three Sides" refer to the original release, which included only three sides of live material and a fourth side of studio tracks. The album rose to #2 in the UK and #10 in the US.

GAME 10

7. In 1969, a DJ played a Beatles' record backwards and said he heard the phrase:

a. Paul is dead

b. I am Jesus

c. Drugs are for you

d. Lust is all you need

GAME 10 Q6 ANSWER b
Also known as "The White Album," 1968's double album *The Beatles* was the biggest-selling rock album of the 1960s. Following the Fab Four's prolonged trip to Rishikesh, India to learn about Transcendental Meditation, *The Beatles* featured more than thirty songs and sold nearly 2 million copies in the US in the first week alone.

GAME 30

7. In the summer of 1987, Joel performed in which of the following places?

a. Paris

b. The Nassau Coliseum

c. Tuscany

d. The Soviet Union

GAME 30 Q6 ANSWER c
A number of Joel's songs were based on specific personal experiences. The restaurant referred to in this 1977 song is, supposedly, either Christiano's, a well-known restaurant in Syosset, Long Island; or a similar eatery found in New York City's Little Italy.

GAME 50

7. Classical metal guitar virtuoso Yngwie Malmsteen hails from which European country?

a. Sweden

b. Germany

c. Poland

d. Italy

GAME 50 Q6 ANSWER c
Young plays a Gibson SG, which he affectionately calls "The Heavenly Beast." His brother Malcolm also plays in AC/DC as rhythm guitarist. Angus Young's Gibson SG and wild stage antics were copied by Jack Black in the smash hit movie *The School of Rock*. That film features AC/DC's "Back in Black" and "It's a Long Way to the Top."

GAME 70

7. In 1973, The Eagles sang about a "_____ Fool."

a. Dancin'

b. Certain Kind of

c. Mama's

d. Sunday Morning

GAME 70 Q6 ANSWER a
"A Fool for You" was originally written and performed by Ray Charles in 1955, and released as a single by Atlantic Records. In later years, the ballad was covered by a number of other artists, including not only Taylor and Diamond, but also Harry Belafonte, Stevie Wonder, Otis Redding, Otis Rush, and John Hammond.

Answers are in right-hand boxes on page 255. 253

6. What's the name of the rock group in the Tom Hanks' film *That Thing You Do!* (1996)?

a. The Saturns
b. The Shelters
c. The Wonders
d. The Fishtails

GAME 11 Q5 ANSWER b
Performing between Janis Joplin and The Who, Sly & the Family Stone closed its set with this great soul classic. Creedence Clearwater Revival finished its set with "Suzy-Q," while the Jefferson Airplane closed with "White Rabbit." Jimi Hendrix ended the festival with his wild rendition of "The Star-Spangled Banner."

6. Which of these men has *not* been romantically linked with Britney Spears?

a. Tyler Hilton
b. Kevin Earl Federline
c. Jason Allen Alexander
d. Columbus Short

GAME 31 Q5 ANSWER b
Simpson and Lachey were married in 2002, and allowed their early days of marriage to be chronicled in the reality TV show *Newlyweds*. The couple officially announced their separation in November 2005, and in December of that year, Simpson filed for divorce, citing "irreconcilable differences."

6. How many studio albums had Led Zeppelin made before retiring in 1980?

a. Four
b. Six
c. Eight
d. Ten

GAME 51 Q5 ANSWER d
One of the great inside jokes for guitarists, the "Stairway to Heaven" riff remains crucial for many aspiring guitarists who want to measure up to their peers. When I first started playing guitar in the '60s, *the* song to learn was Chuck Berry's "Johnny B. Goode." In fact, I performed this song for my Monkees audition.

6. What double album did Genesis release a year after its hit *Abacab*?

a. *Three Sides Live*
b. *Live at Carnegie Hall*
c. *Live at Red Rocks*
d. *Totally Live*

GAME 71 Q5 ANSWER b
This album of Jimi Hendrix and his band The Experience was recorded in February 1969, during two sold-out concerts at London's Albert Hall. Although marketed as the group's final performance, it was not, as they performed last in June of that year. By August, Hendrix had formed a new band—Gypsy Sun and Rainbows—to play at Woodstock.

8. What is the occupation of the title character in the song "Lovely Rita"?

a. Fire engine driver

b. Meter maid

c. Used car dealer

d. Pub singer

GAME 10 Q7 ANSWER a
The "Paul Is Dead" conspiracy theory has become an industry unto itself. There are zillions of alleged clues and hints to this theory, but the bottom line is that Paul was supposedly in a fatal car wreck in 1966 and replaced by look-alike William Shears, who is named to the world on the *Sgt. Pepper's* album. Oh, really?

8. Which Billy Joel hit was the theme song for the sitcom *Bosom Buddies*?

a. "Honesty"

b. "My Life"

c. "Don't Ask Me Why"

d. "Rocket Man"

GAME 30 Q7 ANSWER d
Joel was the first rock act to play in the Soviet Union after the construction of the Berlin Wall. To offset the cost of the tour, a 1987 album was made of the concerts. Nevertheless, it has been estimated that Joel lost over $1 million of his own money on the trip.

8. Which guitar great had a Gibson electric guitar named after him in 1952?

a. Elvis Presley

b. Buddy Holly

c. Eddie Van Halen

d. Les Paul

GAME 50 Q7 ANSWER a
Pronounced "ING-vay," Malmsteen first came to the US in 1982. Influenced both by the 19th century classical violin solos of Paganini and the fiery music of Jimi Hendrix, Malmsteen set a new standard for speed and accuracy in rock guitar technique. His style of playing gave birth to the "Neoclassical" metal movement of the mid '80s.

8. What "fool" song is found on the 1993 Van Halen live album *Right Here, Right Now*?

a. "Fool By Your Side"

b. "Married Man's a Fool"

c. "Fools Gold"

d. "Won't Get Fooled Again"

GAME 70 Q7 ANSWER b
The Eagles' "Certain Kind of Fool" appears on the group's second album, *Desperado*, and tells the story of a poor boy who longs to be—and finally becomes—an outlaw who must run for the rest of his life. The entire album, in fact, focuses on outlaws of the Old West, showing the group's penchant for conceptual songwriting.

GAME 11

5. Which band performed the ever-popular "I Want to Take You Higher" at Woodstock?

a. Creedence Clearwater Revival

b. Sly & the Family Stone

c. Jefferson Airplane

d. Jimi Hendrix

GAME 11 Q4 ANSWER c

Three years after Chuck Berry won a Lifetime Achievement Grammy in 1984, Rolling Stones' guitarist and Berry fan Keith Richards gave him a sixtieth birthday concert, which is the subject of this film. Along with the concert, the film also documents a few heated rehearsal moments when Berry corrects Richards' guitar playing.

GAME 31

5. Jessica Simpson's husband, Nick Lachey, was a member of which boy band?

a. Backstreet Boys

b. 98 Degrees

c. *NSYNC

d. LFO

GAME 31 Q4 ANSWER c

Cobain and Love met at a concert in 1989. In 1992, Love discovered that she was pregnant with Cobain's child, and the couple married. Their daughter, Frances Bean Cobain, was born on August 18 of that year. The child's unusual middle name came from the fact that Cobain thought she looked like a bean on her first sonogram.

GAME 51

5. In the film *Wayne's World*, which song are guitarists *not* allowed to play at the music store?

a. "Heartbreaker"

b. "Whole Lotta Love"

c. "Black Dog"

d. "Stairway to Heaven"

GAME 51 Q4 ANSWER a

The question, which asks for the whereabouts of "that confounded bridge," is on "The Crunge," a song that evolved from a jam session that mirrored early James Brown records. Robert Plant's mention of a "bridge" is a joke reference to how Brown—the Godfather of Soul—would often ask his band to "take it to the bridge."

GAME 71

5. *The Last Experience Concert: His Final Performance* was an album by which artist?

a. Ricky Nelson

b. Jimi Hendrix

c. John Denver

d. Elvis Presley

GAME 71 Q4 ANSWER d

Babylon by Bus was released by Bob Marley & The Wailers in 1978. Recorded mostly at the Paris Pavillion in June 1978, this is just one of Marley's live albums, the others being 1975's *Live*, 1991's *Talkin' Blues* (recorded in 1973), and 2003's *Live at the Roxy* (recorded in 1976).

---

9. Which Beatles' album was the first to feature an Indian instrument called a sitar?

a. *Magical Mystery Tour*

b. *Sgt. Pepper's Lonely Hearts Club Band*

c. *Revolver*

d. *Rubber Soul*

GAME 10 Q8 ANSWER b
The only Beatles' song to feature a toilet paper and comb kazoo, "Lovely Rita" is the most straight-ahead pop song to come from the *Sgt. Pepper's* album. Sung by Paul, the song also features a charming piano solo performed by George Martin. Listen for John's voice blurting out the words "Leave it!" near the end of the song.

9. Which of the following Billy Joel recordings includes no piano or other instruments?

a. "Uptown Girl"

b. "The Longest Time"

c. "You May Be Right"

d. "New York State of Mind"

GAME 30 Q8 ANSWER b
"My Life" was first released on 1978's *52nd Street*, an album conceived as a day in Manhattan. When the song was recorded for *Bosom Buddies*, though, it was performed by the cast of the show rather than Billy Joel.

9. What rock guitarist's instrumental "Misirlou" was featured in Quentin Tarantino's 1994 film *Pulp Fiction*?

a. Duane Eddy

b. Dick Dale

c. B.B. King

d. Chuck Berry

GAME 50 Q8 ANSWER d
Les Paul is known for building the first solid body electric guitar prototype. He is also the pioneer of multi-track recording, a technique that he perfected in the early '50s on the songs he recorded with his singer wife Mary Ford. Their version of "How High the Moon" was a #1 hit single for nine weeks in 1951.

9. Randy Newman's "You Can't Fool the _____ Man" typifies his plainspoken delivery.

a. Fat

b. Old

c. Thin

d. Wise

GAME 70 Q8 ANSWER d
Right Here, Right Now was the first live album produced by Van Halen, and this cover of The Who's "Won't Get Fooled Again" was the sole single launched by the album. The meaning of this song by Pete Townshend has long been debated. A popular interpretation is that it expresses disenchantment with the "revolution" of the '60s.

4. The 1987 movie *Hail! Hail! Rock 'n Roll!* was a tribute to which artist?

a. Fats Domino
b. Elvis Presley
c. Chuck Berry
d. Chubby Checker

GAME 11 Q3 ANSWER a
This song was performed by John Cafferty and The Beaver Brown Band. Meanwhile, The Bangles' version of Simon & Garfunkel's "A Hazy Shade of Winter" from the 1987 film *Less Than Zero* went to #2, while Survivor's "Eye of the Tiger" was a #1 hit for *Rocky III* in 1982. In 1986, Kenny Loggins' "Danger Zone" from *Top Gun* reached #2.

4. What musician was married to Nirvana's Kurt Cobain?

a. Joan Jett
b. Liz Phair
c. Courtney Love
d. Robin Zander

GAME 31 Q3 ANSWER b
Locklear was married to Motley Crue drummer Tommy Lee from 1986 to 1993. After the couple's divorce, the actress wed Richie Sambora, the Bon Jovi guitarist, in 1994. Sambora and Locklear's daughter, Ava Elizabeth, was born in 1997.

4. On *Houses of the Holy*, which Led Zeppelin song ends with a spoken question?

a. "The Crunge"
b. "The Ocean"
c. "The Rain Song"
d. "No Quarter"

GAME 51 Q3 ANSWER b
Released three years after *Presence*, this album relied on keyboards and synthesizers more than any previous Led Zeppelin album. Although it featured a somewhat softer sound than Zeppelin fans were used to, the album spawned such popular radio hits as "In the Evening," "Fool in the Rain," and "All of My Love."

4. Who released a live album called *Babylon by Bus*?

a. Gil Scott-Heron
b. The Rolling Stones
c. Kiss
d. Bob Marley

GAME 71 Q3 ANSWER a
The Bootleg Series is a live album from Bob Dylan's 1966 "world tour" of Australia and western Europe. After years of being bootlegged, the recording was released in 1998, and rose to #31 on the US charts. Evident on the album are disruptions from the crowd—negative reactions to Dylan's new use of an electric guitar.

GAME 10

10. What landmark did The Beatles achieve for the first time in 2001?

a. Song copyright ownership

b. Hall of Fame induction

c. #1 single in the US

d. Year's #1 album in the US

GAME 10 Q9 ANSWER d
Released in December 1965, *Rubber Soul* featured George Harrison playing sitar on John Lennon's song "Norwegian Wood (This Bird Has Flown)." "Love You To" (1966) on *Revolver* and "Within You, Without You" (1967) on *Sgt. Pepper* were both written by Harrison, who sang each song to the accompaniment of traditional Indian musicians.

GAME 30

10. Which Billy Joel album celebrates his return to New York after a sojourn to California?

a. *Turnstiles*

b. *52nd Street*

c. *The Bridge*

d. *Streetlife Serenade*

GAME 30 Q9 ANSWER b
Released on the 1983 hit album *An Innocent Man*, "The Longest Time" was intended to sound like a doo-wop hit of the late '50s and '60s. The song required fourteen background vocal tracks, each of which was first sung by Joel and then pieced together in production.

GAME 50

10. Which actor appeared in Bonnie Raitt's video for her 1989 song "The Thing Called Love"?

a. Dennis Quaid

b. Al Pacino

c. Danny Aiello

d. Bruce Willis

GAME 50 Q9 ANSWER b
Dick Dale, long recognized as the "King of the Surf Guitar," helped establish the mood for this tough-talkin' Tarantino gem. Released in 1962, "Misirlou" showcases Dale's super-fast picking and distinctive reverb-drenched guitar tone. He is still considered the father of surf rock.

GAME 70

10. In a 1974 song, Ry Cooder admits that he's a fool for a:

a. Pretty Lady

b. Hound Dog

c. Cigarette

d. Fast Car

GAME 70 Q9 ANSWER a
The song first appeared on Newman's 1977 album *Little Criminals*, which, like most of Newman's work, focuses on themes very different from that of most pop music. There is, in fact, not one love song on the album. Instead, Newman tells musical stories about short people, fat people, old people—and, of course, little criminals.

---

3. Which song from the *Eddie and the Cruisers* soundtrack reached #7 in 1984?

a. "On the Dark Side"
b. "A Hazy Shade of Winter"
c. "Danger Zone"
d. "Eye of the Tiger"

GAME 11 Q2 ANSWER d
Released in 1984, *Stop Making Sense* is about The Talking Heads. Demme made this film before his super-successful 1986 romp *Something Wild*, starring Melanie Griffith and Jeff Daniels. That same year saw the directorial debut of Talking Heads' frontman David Byrne with his film *True Stories*, featuring John Goodman and Spalding Gray.

3. Before Tommy Lee got involved with Pamela Anderson, to whom was he married?

a. Angelina Jolie
b. Heather Locklear
c. Teri Hatcher
d. Melanie Griffith

GAME 31 Q2 ANSWER c
At the time he wrote the 1970 song "Layla," Eric Clapton was suffering unrequited love for friend George Harrison's wife Patti Boyd. The title of the love song was inspired by the Persian love story *The Story of Layla.* Clapton eventually married Boyd in 1979. They were divorced in 1988.

3. What was the final Led Zeppelin studio album before drummer John Bonham's death in 1980?

a. *Led Zeppelin*
b. *In Through the Out Door*
c. *Houses of the Holy*
d. *Led Zeppelin IV*

GAME 51 Q2 ANSWER d
This classic 1975 album was the first one released under the group's own record label—Swan Song. A cult favorite in the '70s, it features such vital Zeppelin tunes as "In My Time of Dying," "Trampled Under Foot," and "Kashmir," which was used as make-out music in the film *Fast Times at Ridgemont High* (1982).

3. Which artist released the 1998 album *The Bootleg Series: Volume 4*?

a. Bob Dylan
b. Elvis Presley
c. Paul Simon
d. Kurt Cobain

GAME 71 Q2 ANSWER b
At Fillmore East was recorded at the legendary rock venue of the same name in March 1971. The album is one of the best-selling in The Allman Brothers Band's catalogue, and is regarded by many as the best live album of all time. The group was the last act to play at the Fillmore East before it closed in June of that year.

GAME 10

11. Which Beatles' album mentions "love" the most times?

a. *Rubber Soul*

b. *A Hard Day's Night*

c. *Revolver*

d. *Sgt. Pepper's Lonely Hearts Club Band*

GAME 10 Q10 ANSWER d

Aptly titled *#1*, this album showcases the group's singles that went to #1 in either the UK or the US. Before this, their highest album position was for *Beatles '65*, which hit #2. Released only in the US, *Beatles '65* includes songs from British LPs *A Hard Day's Night* and *Beatles for Sale*, along with the #1 single "I Feel Fine."

GAME 30

11. In "Movin' Out," Billy Joel sings about a guy named:

a. Andy

b. Anthony

c. Arthur

d. Alex

GAME 30 Q10 ANSWER a

Released in 1976, *Turnstiles* begins with the song "Say Goodbye to Hollywood." It also contains three tracks about New York: "Summer, Highland Falls"; "Miami 2017 (Seen the Lights Go Out on Broadway)"; and the now classic "New York State of Mind," Joel's love song to New York.

GAME 50

11. Eric Clapton's aching guitar solo gives way to a piano finale on which Derek & the Dominos hit?

a. "Sunshine of Your Love"

b. "Layla"

c. "Lola"

d. "Maybellene"

GAME 50 Q10 ANSWER a

Having already appeared as Jerry Lee Lewis in the 1989 film *Great Balls of Fire!*, Dennis Quaid was happy to do a cameo in Raitt's music video. The daughter of Broadway star John Raitt, Bonnie Raitt remains one of the best blues guitarists in America. She is most famous for her expert style of bottleneck guitar playing.

GAME 70

11. Which Led Zeppelin album introduced the hit "Fool in the Rain"?

a. *In Through the Out Door*

b. *Physical Graffiti*

c. *Coda*

d. *Houses of the Holy*

GAME 70 Q10 ANSWER c

The multi-talented Cooder plays a wide variety of musical instruments, but is best known for his skilled work with a slide guitar. In addition to turning out a long list of his own albums, Cooder has worked as a studio musician and has scored many film soundtracks, including that for the 1984 movie *Paris, Texas*.

---

2. Director Jonathan Demme won critical acclaim for which concert movie?

a. *Gimme Shelter*
b. *The Last Waltz*
c. *Rust Never Sleeps*
d. *Stop Making Sense*

GAME 11 Q1 ANSWER c
The movie is based on the Steven Gaines biography *Heroes & Villains: The True Story of the Beach Boys*. Documentaries like *I Just Wasn't Made for These Times* (1995) and *Beautiful Dreamer* (2004) have also been made about the life and career of Brian Wilson—the songwriting genius behind much of the Beach Boys' music.

---

2. Which song is about a famous rocker's affair with the wife of another rocker?

a. "Michelle"
b. "Sara"
c. "Layla"
d. "Alison"

GAME 31 Q1 ANSWER a
Lennon and Ono were married on March 20, 1969, and spent their honeymoon in Amsterdam in a "Bed-In" for peace. The 1969 Beatles song "The Ballad of John and Yoko," written by Lennon, includes a line about Gibraltar. The song was released while the couple was involved in their second Bed-In.

---

2. Which Led Zeppelin studio album is its only double album?

a. *Presence*
b. *Led Zeppelin III*
c. *In Through the Out Door*
d. *Physical Graffiti*

GAME 51 Q1 ANSWER c
The song, "Moby Dick," quickly became drummer John Bonham's showcase during Zeppelin concerts. In the group's 1973 concert film *The Song Remains the Same*, you can see Bonham actually playing the drums with his hands rather than drumsticks. The only other Zeppelin track to feature a drum solo is "Rock 'n Roll."

---

2. Which band's live album *At Fillmore East* features its hit "Whipping Post"?

a. The Bee Gees
b. The Allman Brothers
c. The Doobie Brothers
d. The Righteous Brothers

GAME 71 Q1 ANSWER d
Directed by Jonathan Demme, 1984's *Stop Making Sense* was shot over three nights during the Talking Heads' Speaking in Tongues Tour. Highly acclaimed, the documentary is different from many other concert films in that it contains no audience shots until the end, and uses no colored lights to illuminate the band members.

---

12. Which Beatles' song knocked The Monkees' "Daydream Believer" off the top of the charts in December 1967?

a. "All You Need Is Love"

b. "Lady Madonna"

c. "Hello Goodbye"

d. "Penny Lane"

GAME 10 Q11 ANSWER b
Released at the height of Beatlemania in 1964, *A Hard Day's Night* mentions the word "love" seventy-two times! (It's also the one album that features all Lennon/McCartney songs.) Although *Sgt. Pepper* was released during the 1967 "Summer of Love," ironically, it features the word "love" or a variation of it only twenty times.

12. What is the only Billy Joel single to finish the year in the Top 10 on Billboard?

a. "Uptown Girl"

b. "We Didn't Start the Fire"

c. "You May Be Right"

d. "The River of Dreams"

GAME 30 Q11 ANSWER b
"Movin' Out (Anthony's Song)" originally appeared on the 1977 album *The Stranger*. The song also furnished the title for a popular Broadway musical featuring Joel's songs. *Movin' Out,* Twyla Tharpe's dialogue-free "rock ballet," ran from 2002 to 2005.

12. Which guitar god's work is featured on the classic "Eruption"?

a. Leo Kottke

b. Joe Satriani

c. Eddie Van Halen

d. Kirk Hammett

GAME 50 Q11 ANSWER b
The guitar that he played on the track earned a record-setting $497,500 at auction. Equally effective in "Layla" is the impressive slide guitar work played by Duane Allman during the song's piano finale. As many already know, "Layla" was Clapton's song about his hidden love for George Harrison's first wife, Patti Boyd.

12. Which "foolish" song is identified with The Beatles?

a. "The Fool on the Hill"

b. "Heaven Help the Fool"

c. "My Foolish Heart"

d. "Why Do Fools Fall in Love"

GAME 70 Q11 ANSWER a
A Top 40 hit in 1980, "Fool in the Rain" was a departure from the heavy metal bombast that characterized most of the group's earlier releases. John Bonham's inspired use of conga drums and a steel whistle gives "Fool in the Rain" the sound of a Brazilian carnival. *In Through the Out Door* also features prominent use of synthesizers.

GAME 11	**1.** The 1990 TV movie *Summer Dreams* is the story of which rock group? **a.** Jan and Dean **b.** Everly Brothers **c.** The Beach Boys **d.** Gary Lewis & the Playboys	The answer to this question is on: **page 262, top frame, right side.**
GAME 31	**1.** Where were John Lennon and Yoko Ono married? **a.** Gibraltar **b.** Madrid **c.** Barcelona **d.** Toledo	The answer to this question is on: **page 262, second frame, right side.**
GAME 51	**1.** Which of the following Led Zeppelin albums includes a song with an extended drum solo? **a.** *Led Zeppelin* **b.** *Physical Graffiti* **c.** *Led Zeppelin II* **d.** *Houses of the Holy*	The answer to this question is on: **page 262, third frame, right side.**
GAME 71	**1.** What documentary film became a Talking Heads live album? **a.** *The Wall* **b.** *Heavy Metal* **c.** *Tape Worm* **d.** *Stop Making Sense*	The answer to this question is on: **page 262, bottom frame, right side.**

GAME 11

Rock Movies

See page 264
for the first question.

See page 264
for the first question.

GAME 10 Q12 ANSWER c
All of these Beatles' songs went to #1 in the US. They were all also released first as singles, not as part of studio albums. "All You Need Is Love," "Penny Lane," and "Hello Goodbye" were added to *Magical Mystery Tour* after the fact, while "Lady Madonna" was included on the *Hey Jude* album, available only in the United States.

GAME 31

Rock Romances

See page 264
for the first question.

See page 264
for the first question.

GAME 30 Q12 ANSWER b
Joel's third #1 single, "We Didn't Start the Fire" helped the 1989 album *Storm Front* sell over 4 million copies. Using a stream-of-consciousness style, the song is essentially a chronological list of news-worthy events, names, and places, be-ginning in Joel's year of birth and ending in 1989.

GAME 51

Led Zeppelin

See page 264
for the first question.

See page 264
for the first question.

GAME 50 Q12 ANSWER c
The song was featured on Van Halen's self-titled 1978 debut album. Picking up where Jimi Hendrix left off with a 1969 rendition of "The Star-Spangled Ban-ner," Eddie Van Halen changed forever the sound and speed of rock guitar play-ing, and introduced the world to the technique of playing the guitar with *both* hands on the fretboard.

GAME 71

Live Albums

See page 264
for the first question.

See page 264
for the first question.

GAME 70 Q12 ANSWER a
Paul McCartney and John Lennon's "The Fool on the Hill" was released on the 1967 album *Magical Mystery Tour*. The song was inspired by an early morning walk taken by McCartney. As the singer watched the sunrise from a hill, a man suddenly appeared, briefly spoke about the beautiful view, and then abruptly dis-appeared.

ABOUT THE AUTHOR

Micky Dolenz was born in Los Angeles on March 8, 1945. His dad, George, had starred in a number of films, and played the title character in the mid-1950s television series *The Count of Monte Cristo*.

Micky first established himself as a performer at age ten when, under the stage name of Micky Braddock, he starred in his first TV series, *Circus Boy*, which aired from 1956 to 1958. In his teens, Micky guest-starred on a number of television shows. He also learned to play guitar and performed with a number of rock 'n roll bands, including one called The Missing Links.

In autumn 1965, Micky was one of 400 applicants who responded to a trade ad announcing auditions for a new TV show about a rock band. Micky auditioned for *The Monkees* TV show playing Chuck Berry's "Johnny B. Goode," and was chosen along with three other actors—Davy Jones, Michael Nesmith, and Peter Tork.

The Monkees' debut single, "Last Train to Clarksville," featuring Micky on lead vocals, hit the charts September 10, 1966 and rocketed to number one. Two days later, the television show debuted on NBC to great success. The TV ratings remained high for two seasons and Micky and the band starred in their own feature film, *Head*, a 1968 psychedelic romp co-written by a young Jack Nicholson. The movie is now considered a cult classic.

Ultimately, The Monkees achieved their greatest success as recording artists. Their first four albums—*The Monkees* (1966); *More of the Monkees* (1967); *Headquarters* (1967); and *Pisces, Aquarius, Capricorn & Jones, Ltd.* (1967)—reached number one on the charts and launched three number-one singles: "Last Train to Clarksville," "I'm a Believer" (with lead vocals by Micky), and

"Daydream Believer." The group's first five albums also went gold.

In 1977, Micky flew to London to star in Harry Nilsson's West End Musical, *The Point!* He planned to stay three months but remained for twelve years. During that time, Micky honed his behind-the-camera skills—which he first practiced by directing episodes of *The Monkees*—as producer-director for the BBC and London Weekend Television. He also directed a short feature film, *The Box*, written by Michael Palin and Terry Jones of Monty Python, and helmed numerous music videos.

In 1986, MTV broadcast episodes of *The Monkees* show and exposed a whole new generation to Monkeemania. Micky and Peter Tork recorded new tracks for Arista Records and the single, "That Was Then, This Is Now," became their first Top 20 record since 1968. Micky, Peter, and Davy Jones subsequently reunited for a 1986 summer tour that was so successful it sparked the reissue of all The Monkees' classic LPs as well as *Pool It!* on Rhino Records. At one point in 1987, there were seven Monkees' albums on Billboard's Top 200 LP's chart. In 1996, The Monkees again joined together, this time for a "30 Year Reunion" summer tour around America. The response was so great that they also toured the following year, this time finishing up in England.

When Micky returned to the United States, he went out on the road with the National Touring Company of *Grease*. Micky enjoyed musical theater so much that he accepted the lead role in a Canadian production of *A Funny Thing Happened on the Way to the Forum* in 1993, and in 2004, he starred in Elton John's Broadway musical *Aida*.

In 1993, Micky's autobiography *I'm a Believer: My Life of Monkees, Music, and Madness* was released. In addition to writing, Micky has divided his time between acting (*The Drew Carey Show, Days of our Lives,* and *General Hospital*); directing (*Boy Meets World* for ABC/Disney and *Pacific Blue* for USA Networks); and touring with his sister, singer Coco Dolenz. Currently, he lives with his wife, Donna, in California.

JOE FRANKLIN'S GREAT ENTERTAINMENT TRIVIA

Here's the book that will put your knowledge of movies, radio, music, and television, to the test. New York's famous talk- and variety-show host Joe Franklin, whose guest list over the years reads like a who's who of celebrity royalty, has drawn on his own unique knowledge and personal experiences to create the *Great Entertainment Trivia Game*. Not only is the book packed with challenging questions, it also provides lots of interesting information along with the answers.

Guaranteed fun, dozens of individual games, each with twelve questions, will both challenge and amuse. But unlike other books of this type, which reveal the answers below the questions or group them together with all of the other answers, this book cleverly formats the games in a way that allows the reader to see only one answer at the appropriate time. This way, the reader can play along. In addition to the questions, Franklin shares some of his favorite memories in fascinating insets that are peppered throughout the book.

From cover to cover, the *Great Entertainment Trivia Game* is pure entertainment. And who better to create such a book than Joe Franklin, with his decades-long involvement in the business that he so dearly loves—and that so dearly loves him.

$7.95 • 288 pages • 4 x 7-inch paperback • ISBN 0-7570-0038-X

RICK BARRY'S SUPER SPORTS TRIVIA

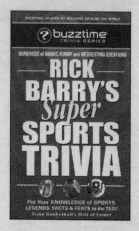

Irascible, opinionated, and absolutely brilliant, Rick Barry was named one of the fifty greatest players to have ever competed in professional basketball. A natural on the court, he possessed the physical ability, quick mind, and God-given talent to play among the best. Now, Basketball Hall of Famer Rick Barry challenges all those who pride themselves on their knowledge of sports with his unique book of trivia.

Drawing information from the history, legends, and lore of basketball, baseball, football, boxing, hockey, auto racing, and more, Barry has created a series of quizzes that are guaranteed to provide hours of entertainment and fun. But unlike other trivia books that simply supply the answers to the questions, this book includes interesting information along with each answer—you'll actually learn as you play! Furthermore, the answers are cleverly formatted in a way that allows the reader to play alone or with others. Each game is guaranteed fun—challenging, informative, and amusing.

Rick Barry's knowledge of sports results in a trivia book with a spin that's more challenging than a curveball. If you're ready for a game that is interesting, educational, and always fun to play, *Rick Barry's Super Sports Trivia Game* is the way to go.

$7.95 • 288 pages • 4 x 7-inch paperback • ISBN 0-7570-0134-3

About
Buzztime Trivia

If you are one of those people whose head is filled with obscure information, but you are never quite sure of what to do with all that knowledge, you're going to love Buzztime. Why? Because now you have a way to shine.

Buzztime is the company behind the world's largest interactive trivia game network. Go to any one of the nearly 4,000 Buzztime/NTN restaurants and sports bars located throughout North America, and you can compete against players at that location, or against the thousands of other trivia buffs across the United States and Canada. Since Buzztime is the largest repository of trivia facts, you know that the questions will always be fresh, current, and stimulating. These Buzztime/NTN locations are also great places to meet people and enjoy evenings of fun and entertainment. Interested? Simply log onto www.buzztime.com for a listing of local sites.

But there's more. You can also play Buzztime trivia games on the Internet, on your television, and even on your cell phone. That's right. If you're tired of standing in long lines, waiting around at airports, or sitting in office waiting rooms with nothing to do, you can simply pick up your cell phone and place a call to connect with Buzztime games.

Many cable and satellite television packages offer Buzz-time trivia as well. Check the Buzztime website to see if the games are offered by your local service provider. But if they aren't, don't worry—the Buzztime Home Trivia System will allow you to enjoy the Buzztime experience in the comfort of your own home. And since it is a multi-user game, you can play it with your family, friends, and neighbors.

Medical researchers have determined that if you don't exercise your brain, intellectual function weakens. Why take a chance on getting flabby brain cells when you can strengthen them with a daily dose of Buzztime? Your brain will thank you for it.

For more information about Buzztime trivia games,
visit
www.buzztime.com